RAISING FINANCE

RAISING FINANCE

The **Guardian** Guide for the Small Business

THIRD EDITION

Clive Woodcock

KOGAN PAGE

First published in Great Britain in 1982 by Kogan Page Limited, 120 Pentonville Road, London N1 9JN.
Second edition 1985
Third edition 1989

British Library Cataloguing in Publication Data
Woodcock, Clive
Raising finance. — 3rd ed.
1. Great Britain. Small firms. Capital sources. Management aspects
I. Title
658.1′522
ISBN 1-85091-515-6
ISBN 1-85091-516-4 Pbk

Printed and bound in Great Britain by Biddles Limited, Guildford

Contents

Introduction

For a surprisingly large number of small businessmen the motivating force for being in business is probably not just money but independence, and a variety of other factors. Yet the lack of money, whether real or apparent, certainly inhibits their ability to achieve the other objectives.

Finance enters into the situation no matter what the initial aims of the independent operator may be. The problem then is not just to find the money but to find it from the right sources at the right price and at the right time. While the larger or multinational companies have been favoured in the United Kingdom in recent years, small firms now appear to be having money thrown at them from all directions after decades of neglect.

But is it so easy? One still hears stories of potentially viable propositions which are unable to find support, and of existing companies with prospects for growth and expansion in high technology areas which cannot find the necessary funds to finance the expected increase in sales.

On the other hand, there are the financial institutions complaining that although they are trying hard to lend money they cannot find suitable customers. They have devised a number of imaginative schemes designed to meet all requirements of the entrepreneur yet still wonder why so many British ideas go overseas to be developed or lie still-born in laboratories.

Perhaps part of the problem is that, where there was once an information gap, with those who had money failing to inform those who needed it that they were willing to lend it, there is now a high degree of bewilderment. This is because all those with funds are shouting at once, leaving the small firm manager exasperated and confused. Unlike a large firm which would have a finance department, the independent operator has little time to spare from the everyday problems of ensuring the survival of his business. The result is that he often makes the mistake of applying for long-term finance from his clearing bank or asking for relatively small amounts from a merchant bank when what he really needs is a substantial injection of finance. Equally there are businessmen who think that money is easy to obtain, but they will always be disappointed. When the refusal comes, they often turn away in despair

thinking it is the end of the matter, or fall back on their own resources which results in the business developing more slowly than it should, or just lurching from crisis to crisis.

However, there is no lack of money for the independent operator who knows where and how to get his hands on it and use it to the best advantage in developing his business. It is the multiplicity of financial sources which the small business owner or manager finds intimidating, indeed mind-boggling in its complexity. Whether all the money available is being offered to the right people or aimed in the right direction at the right price, or whether lack of finance is really the major problem faced by small firms, are entirely different questions. The problem now is to make the best use of what is available. To do that the independent businessman needs a handy reference which will indicate clearly and briefly what finance can be used, for what purpose, and how much it is likely to cost. The aim of this book is to do that and to go one step further in making such technical details interesting and comprehensible by relating the stories of how a number of independent businessmen have started and developed their companies. They are straightforward accounts of how real businesses - including one co-operative - have met and have overcome the problems of finding the right finance for their particular situations.

Those described will not necessarily meet the requirements of other businessmen but will demonstrate how these particular firms, ranging from companies engaged in high technology areas (such as electronic testing equipment) to those making biscuits, have used Government, private, institutional and European sources of finance to develop their companies. It is to be hoped that the ways in which these companies have tackled their problems will generate ideas on how to use the various sources to meet different circumstances.

The author takes the view that it is as important for a firm to be able to organise its own financial affairs as to be able to borrow from a bank or other financial institution. It is possible that a company which considers it is in need of outside finance can find the funds from its own resources by proper management and financial controls. Setting up and applying such controls may take time, but the dividends are considerable as the cheapest source from which to obtain funds is always from one's own pocket. Some of the ways this can be achieved are indicated in this book.

If proper management and financial controls have been introduced, and it is clear that money is still needed for projects envisaged, any loan application to an external source is likely to be more reasonably based and have a greater chance of success. In this book the various alternatives which present themselves are outlined and the differences set out.

The choices range from short-, medium-, and long-term loans, money available from the European Economic Community (often at lower rates of interest than can be obtained within the United Kingdom), Government sources (where money can sometimes come in the form of grants), to factoring, leasing, and venture and development capital, right up to the stage of going public and floating shares on either the listed or unlisted securities markets.

The book looks at what the potential source of finance will want to know about the business, working out cash flow, how short-term finance can be obtained from the control of creditors, debtors, and stock, using and not using overdrafts, and the value of fixed-term loans of up to three years. Medium-term funds are those for between three and 10 years, often for refinancing overdrafts, buying or extending premises or for obtaining plant and machinery. Long-term finance is that which is repayable over a 10- to 20-year period, usually obtained from financial institutions other than banks, though that situation is changing for major capital spending projects.

Government sources of funds are examined at some length, but to cover all of them would need a book in itself, and so only the main schemes likely to be of interest are described, including regional aid, local authority assistance in the form, for example, of rent rebates, funds available under inner city partnership schemes, and special plans for firms using microprocessors.

The growth of the informal financial markets is described, taking in areas such as factoring and leasing, and considering whether they are worth the cost. These are matters which may be unfamiliar to many small-firm operators but can in certain circumstances offer benefits even if they cost more than, say, a straightforward bank loan.

Value for money is as important as the ability to borrow, and after describing a variety of export finance schemes, the book looks at a method by which the smaller firm can obtain high quality market research in overseas countries at a remarkably low cost. It also describes such instruments of export finance as irrevocable letters of credit and export factoring, as well as the assistance which organisations such as the British Overseas Trade Board can offer the smaller firm which wants to develop new markets.

The various special schemes now being established to fund high technology developments are also examined in detail, as is the provision of venture and development capital, where initiatives are often now backed by large firms or enterprise development organisations originally set up by local government authorities but now independent of them, such as those in the West Midlands and Greater Manchester.

Finally, management buy-outs are examined, and the question of how they are financed and whether interest will be maintained is considered as viable projects and managements become more difficult to find.

Most small businessmen are understandably reluctant to part with a share in the equity of their company to an outside shareholder, but sometimes it may be preferable to have a smaller share of a larger cake or to realise, in terms of hard cash, the benefits which have been built up over a period of years. Going public can be an expensive process, however, though the advent of the Unlisted Securities Market and the Third Market has eased the problem for the smaller company. The advantages and disadvantages of going to the stock market, at which point the company probably ceases to qualify for the description of small, are also analysed.

As the book is intended to be of practical reference value, the chapters follow a common structure. They start with a description and analysis of schemes offered by individual institutions, companies, and Government, are usually illustrated by a story of a company which has gone through the process, and conclude with a list of useful addresses from which full details can be obtained to suit particular circumstances.

The value of any form of finance depends, however, very much on the ability of the small firm manager to use it, on his or her understanding of what business is all about in general and on what management in particular entails. The picture of financial naivety and ineptitude on the part of small business managers – not to mention the almost complete lack of worthwhile help they receive from their advisers – revealed by the Robson Rhodes reports on the operation of the Loan Guarantee Scheme does not give any confidence that such ability is widespread, a situation which has changed only marginally over the years.

The small business owners spoken to by Robson Rhodes, who were commissioned by the Government to produce the report, were 'bereft of practical and forthright advice and assistance, not really knowing what is, or should be, available or from where. They are generally so tied down in the present that they find it difficult to visualise the future shape of their businesses with any conviction'. The study team was, however, heartened by the attitude, diligence and conscientiousness of the small firm managers they visited. 'They recognise that they were naive and optimistic before they set up in business but remain, in spite of some bitter experiences, enthusiastic and determined. They are still (in general) financially inept, although they have devised, mainly by trial and error, various rudimentary ways of monitoring their progress. Most of them are under-financed and are now feeling the effects of ill-conceived initial funding proposals.' Emphasis was laid in the report on distortions in the financial structure of companies, evidenced in one respect by the lack of equity – quite apart from the lack of any considered structure at all in many cases – and the failure of accountants to suggest to, let alone persuade, clients of their real needs.

Robson Rhodes found that many of the potential borrowers under the Loan Guarantee Scheme had little understanding of the way in which to set up a business, no research, planning, or proper gestation of their ideas, little or no knowledge of the finance required – either type or amount – and no experience of practical and usable assistance available to them. Borrowers were asked with hindsight what they wished they had known prior to starting. The most significant and constant theme was the consequences of under-financing; they appeared to seek the minimum required to run their businesses as they optimistically foresaw it. Once the borrower had set up in business he or she sought and received little outside help or assistance in spite of many borrowers frankly recognising their businesses' deficiencies – most particularly in the fields of finance, accountancy and business management.

The Loan Guarantee Scheme itself has also gone through some troughs since then, with the Government panicking at the level of losses. Its action in raising the premium payable by borrowers and reducing the level of guarantee to 70 per cent from 80 per cent (with the aim of concentrating the minds of the operating banks on keeping to the spirit of the scheme) very nearly killed the scheme stone dead. It was, indeed, moribund until the Government relented to some degree and reduced the premium to a more manageable level, as well as adding concessions for borrowers in inner cities, leading to a revival of interest.

It can be argued that the sample used by Robson Rhodes for the loan guarantee report is too small and too particular to give a valid picture, either of the shortcomings of small firms in general in their management or of the paucity of help from advisers. But wider research carried out seems to give credence to the view that the picture is more representative than many would like to think. For example, patterns of successful start-ups have been examined by academic researchers like Tom Milne and Marcus Thompson of Glasgow University, examining 89 business owners in Scotland, the North-east of England and the East Midlands. Financial management skills emerged from this study as a factor of prime importance. They found that the fulcrum of business development was financial management and concluded that a massive upgrading in the financial management abilities of managing directors was needed. 'There can be no doubt that were more of the founders able to add financial judgement to market judgement effectively there would be a much more positive development of manufacturing company foundations.'

Among the important elements in potentially successful firms they noted dedication to customers and an elusive but vital quality judgement of the market opportunity. 'It is the quality which seems to be possessed by the entrepreneurs who have carved a viable market niche out of very unlikely material.' Those entrepreneurs also seemed to have an exceptionally positive drive when it came to selling themselves, their firms, their projects, and their products. This focused strongly on the ability to convince financial backers so that it was possible to create financial packages appropriate to the start-up situation. Rapid development was also associated strongly with meticulous attention to management and commercial controls and general housekeeping.

These skills had to be added to dedication to work, long hours and the ability to persuade others to work long hours, at a kaleidoscope of tasks ranging from immediate response to operational emergencies through to cool appraisal of planning and development for the future – a process described by one of those interviewed as 'two years of hell on wheels'.

Weaknesses in financial management have been brought out in another study by Robert Arnold-McCulloch of Queen Margaret College, Edinburgh. He has found a reasonably high standard of record keeping – possibly arising from the operation of VAT and the need to keep records – and a high proportion of firms preparing sales or cash forecasts. Those forecasts, however, were essentially to satisfy lenders rather than for use as planning techniques within the businesses themselves. The picture of management accounting applications was disappointing largely because of the very limited use of management accounting. Pricing methods were 58 per cent cost based and 47 per cent market based among the firms he studied, all of which were in Scotland. Overhead recovery was 35 per cent production based, 28 per cent as a percentage of sales while there were a number of businesses who applied a job-cost approach to pricing and therefore recovered their overheads against each job.

Also within this group were some businesses whose pricing was virtually market based at start-up as they tested their markets. Once they gained a better idea of what customers were prepared to pay and had established themselves in their market, pricing became harder. In the financial accounting area budgetary control was increasingly used on a monthly basis for comparison with planned profit forecasts. Some businesses were using more effective credit control methods.

A retailer dealing with fabrics and materials for dressmaking was using more sophisticated control: with two years of trading experience she was forecasting sales and breaking down annual costs to weekly amounts for comparison with actual sales. She also related sales and costs to the business's break-even point. Mr Arnold-McCulloch found, however, that in general there was virtually no evidence of the use of break-even analysis techniques. On the other hand, he found the fact encouraging that improvements in recording and financial accounting control techniques were associated mainly with planning. They had been introduced by their owners against a background of increasing turnover and the operational complexity of their businesses. It was in management accounting that owners' views were at variance with those of the financial community at large, as owners clearly did not see the relevance of the techniques available.

Many similar attitudes were revealed in a number of areas of management through research by Dr Alan Hankinson of the Dorset Institute of Higher Education on the price-output decisions of small engineering companies in Dorset and Hampshire. Cost was found to be the essence of price calculation with little evidence of marginal or behavioural adjustments to price-fixing. Few firms were prepared to raise prices to the point which they themselves knew to be more profitable than any other. But the survey data revealed that while a significant raising of price by firms would contract demand, a marginal increase would not. Similarly, a marked lowering of price would extend demand but a nominal decrease would not.

Firms themselves admitted that prices could be raised and no sales lost, but in practice they did not do so and simply fixed prices by conventional cost-plus percentages. Dr Hankinson pointed out that one drawback in adopting cost-plus pricing is that the method relies on the assumption that firms actually knew what their costs of production were at given levels of output. It was by no means certain that firms in the sample did have such information to hand. The firms were unaware of the rapid erosion of profits by delayed price adjustments for increased costs of production and for inflation in particular. Some interviewees quoted current inflation at about 5 per cent and considered this to be manageable. But many engineering firms used materials which had risen by far greater amounts than 5 per cent, yet still believed that current inflation was 'self-correcting'. Only a small minority of firms considered the issues sufficiently to reach the conclusion that a more positive pricing approach was essential. An even more remarkable and disappointing feature was the significant number that believed that no action could be taken since activities were severely constrained by external market forces beyond their control. Hankinson found that the recession was held responsible to some extent for current pricing problems but in some instances substandard pricing approaches could have been more successfully tackled by resolute management rather than arbitrary economic recoveries.

These are the kinds of management weakness to which Brian Warnes, of Business Dynamics, refers when he says that there is no such thing as bad luck in business, only bad management. He believes that the overwhelming reason why many companies of all sizes do not seem to make the most of their opportunities is a basic lack of understanding, both inside and outside business, of how business works, a lack of what he frequently calls the 'barrow boy approach', encapsulated by the story he tells of the trader who says, 'I buy for £1, sell for £2 and live very well on the 10 per cent margin.'

Mr Warnes has set out his trenchant views on how businesses should be run in two excellent books, the *Genghis Khan Guide to Business* and the *Cash Flow Handbook*, both of which should be required reading for anyone in business or who advises businesses. He develops his theme for action on four main points. Business is about buying and selling production hours or buying for £1 and selling for £2 or £3 or £4 rather than about buying or selling products. Gross margin, not sales, constitutes the real income of a business. The third point, on which he asserts there is a widespread lack of understanding, is break-even points. He defines break-even point as the level of sales needed to cover all costs and suggests that management should focus its attention on narrowing the gap between break-even and actual sales rather than the conventional wisdom that increasing sales is the only way to cut losses.

He points out that companies often react to falling turnover by cutting prices, by increasing costs, and by trying to sell more, a response which as frequently as not merely hastens and precipitates the very end they are trying to avoid.

The fourth factor which is frequently overlooked is that of cash flow, a constantly mentioned phrase but one which is surprisingly little understood. It is cash flow, not profit, that is the lifeblood of a company, says Mr Warnes, adding that a company making a loss can sometimes have a stronger, more positive cash flow than one making a profit, absurd as it may seem. The bottom line is that unless the wages can be paid on Friday, every Friday, there will be no more Fridays on which to continue in business, however good the product potential and however good the skills of the management team. He instances the importance of understanding the differences between profits and cash flow and the ways in which traditional, perfectly acceptable accounting procedures can be misleading. He describes a company which wins a £100,000 contract which will take six months to complete. Costs for labour and materials would not show up as costs in the monthly profit and loss account until completion. Part of the overheads could similarly be transferred out to show a cosmetically favourable situation – but at the same time cash in the form of wages and payments to suppliers would be draining out of the company. The completed contract could then appear in the balance sheet as an asset at £115,000 under debtors. Although sales and profit may be included in the profit and loss account the situation could easily be upset by a small delay in payment by the customer, cutting off the cash flow abruptly – even though the company theoretically is profitable to the extent of £10,000 or so with a £115,000 asset as well.

He also recommends a technique of accurate sales pricing to enable management to be sure of the gross margin in their products, knowledge which should enable them to move in and out of the market and undercut competitors. He lays emphasis on management information and suggests that there are probably few companies which produce key data weekly, a couple of days after the end of the week. If data are produced less often than monthly the company cannot be regarded as well managed, he says.

But the purpose of this introduction is neither to praise the approach of a particular company nor to emphasise excessively the weaknesses of small business management. The point of highlighting these factors in what is basically a directory of sources of finance is that unless business operators are aware of and understand the essential elements of business, the less likelihood there is of potential sources of funding delivering up their bounty; equally unless they are understood there is likely to be little benefit to either investor or investee in obtaining the funding. Knowing where and how to obtain finance is of little value if the recipient does not know how to use it.

CHAPTER 1

Money to Start up a Business

Money for starting up a business can come from a wide variety of sources, depending on the intended scale of operations. Most businesses tend to start small, and the intention in this chapter is to assume that the start-up is from a basic level, the most common being the one- or two-man operation financed either entirely from personal resources or by a combination of personal finances and funds from a bank.

The micro-firm probably needs only £5,000, £10,000, £15,000 or perhaps even less to get off the ground but it is these sums which are hardest to find. It may be argued that many of the people who believe they only need a small sum to get started are sowing the seeds of their own failure by under-capitalisation at the outset. The observation has more than a grain of truth in it but even so there are many types of project which could well see their way to a viable future even on such minuscule amounts. There is undoubtedly a gap in the market but one for which it is difficult to offer constructive suggestions as a remedy.

One possible solution which has been suggested by a small firms' representative organisation, the Association of Independent Businesses, is loans through building societies based on additional mortgages secured on the increased value of a property. It is not as fanciful as it might first appear because the AIB has identified a number of building societies who are prepared to do just that and has established that business development loans, as it calls them, are legal and that the Treasury would not discourage this type of lending.

The societies which told the AIB that they were in principle prepared to lend money for investment – subject to availability of funds – included the Alliance, Yorkshire, Guardian, Chelsea, Principality, Newcastle, Sussex County, Norwich, Leeds Permanent, Cheltenham and Gloucester, Nationwide, and National Provincial.

The Association's survey showed that a number of societies already offer such loans and it sees the chance of friends or relatives of a business owner being able to borrow money from a building society and invest the funds in the business. With this equity the owner, or potential owner, of a small business is far more likely to persuade a bank manager to lend money under the Loan Guarantee Scheme to further his business interest, says the Association.

Whether the idea is taken up and developed remains to be seen but it is certainly an interesting proposal which deserves to be examined and extended. It should certainly be worth the while of any intending, or actual, business operator to approach a building society, especially one of those in the AIB's list, and see what response emerges.

The Clearing Banks

Although banks are frequently criticised (not always justifiably) for their lack of response to ideas for new businesses, clearing banks in fact provide more money to small businesses than any other source, through their 13,000 branches around the country, and are often the independent businessman's only point of contact with an external finance system. It is virtually impossible to go into business without personal resources of some kind as, not unreasonably, the banks expect a financial commitment from the potential businessman so that there is a sharing of the risks involved between him and the bank. Senior managers say, and there is really no reason to doubt them, that they no longer rigidly apply the general rule that commitments should be on a ratio of 1:1 of personal resources and bank advances. But it is still not difficult to find the branch manager who does not really approve of the more liberal trends in banking and does not consider that the time and effort on the part of the businessman and the laying of his whole livelihood on the line counts as a commitment or acceptance of risk. Anyone who is unfortunate enough to come up against this kind of manager should have no qualms about taking his ideas to a higher level, another branch, or eventually another bank. There are plenty of lenders today looking for viable propositions.

The Enterprise Allowance Scheme

An important source of finance for the starter with limited means is an imaginative scheme from the Government, the Enterprise Allowance Scheme. It is particularly designed for those who are unemployed, or about to be, enabling them to obtain an income from the state in the first year of trading, a situation in which they would otherwise lose the support of unemployment pay or supplementary benefit.

The scheme is clearly filling a need as demand has been such that the Government has regularly provided additional funds and increased the number of places available. In 1988 the scheme reached its fifth birthday, having given many thousands of people the chance to start their own business, a high proportion of which have survived after their year on the allowance came to an end. A recent study showed that 65 per cent of those who completed a year on the scheme were still in business three years after starting. The proportion of survivors is increasing as the previous survey showed that 61 per cent – compared with 65 per cent now – had survived. More than 350,000 people have taken advantage of the scheme and in 1988–1989 there were another 110,000 places available. EAS survivors are also job creators for others as the report showed that for each 100 businesses still trading at the three-year stage, 114 additional jobs – that is, over and above the job of the proprietor – had been created.

Details of the scheme can be obtained from Job Centres but basically it provides successful applicants with £40 a week for a year to offset the loss of benefit they might otherwise suffer. Applicants must either be receiveing unemployment benefit and have been out of work or under notice of redundancy for eight weeks. They must be over 18 and under retirement age and propose a business suitable for public support, a description which can be very wide indeed as there is no assessment of the viability of business ideas. This aspect has come in for criticism with suggestions that too often false hopes are raised and unsuitable people led into situations of inevitable failure.

Applicants must also be able to show that they have at least £1,000 available to invest in the business, a provision which has also been criticised and which fills some applicants with alarm. It is, however, not necessarily the insuperable obstacle it may seem and it is not actually necessary to be able to show £1,000 in notes - or coins. It could be in the form of assets or an overdraft at the bank for that amount.

There is also counselling advice available from the Small Firms Counselling Service run by the Department of Trade and Industry for new starters. As there is considerable demand for the scheme there can sometimes be delays in acceptance but the Training Commission, which is responsible for the scheme, generally manages to keep delay to a minimum.

The banks have also adopted a positive attitude towards the scheme, with several banks such as the Midland, the Co-operative and the National Westminster offering free business banking services to those taking part. Accounts, whether in credit or overdrawn, are operated free of charge for all normal banking services during the 52-week period of the scheme. Interest on any borrowing or other specific services is charged at normal commercial rates.

An independent assessment of the Enterprise Allowance Scheme, by Professor John Stanworth and Colin Gray of the Small Business Research Trust, has show that one of the reasons for failure is that EAS participants tend to start more businesses in the personal services and manufacturing sectors where failure rates are generally higher. Most businesses were inspired by participants' previous experience, mainly work but some leisure, though some more enterprising and more successful ones picked up their ideas through observing a local need for an already existing idea. More than half the participants sought no professional business advice at all, though more than half of those who survived did accept publicly available advice from private or Government sources. Despite the low take-up of advice or training, most participants expressed a need for training and counselling more specifically designed to meet their needs. Accounting and financial skills and marketing and selling skills were the most in demand.

Further information of the Enterprise Allowance Scheme can be obtained from Job Centres or by dialling 100 and asking for Freefone Enterprise.

Security

Although banks can and do sometimes lend without security if the proposition is sufficiently attractive, this is not common, and usually collateral or at least personal guarantees will be required. Those demands are a constant source of irritation to the small businessman and played an important part in the setting up of the Government-backed Loan Guarantee Scheme, designed to cover situations where the entrepreneur either could nor or would not be able to provide sufficient collateral or where the banks considered the risk went beyond their normal criteria. (The Loan Guarantee Scheme is described in detail later in this chapter, see pp 28–31.)

Investors in Industry plc (3i)

There are, however, other financial institutions which will provide start-up finance without the personal guarantees which can be so intimidating for the business venturer. The principal one of these is the Investors in Industry (3i), which is owned by the major clearing banks. 3i is interested in any sound proposition that needs funds from £5,000 up to £2 million.

A large proportion of their clients still receive relatively small amounts, less than £50,000, for instance; the lower limit of loans has been held at £5,000 because many firms want to have the services of an institution such as 3i in addition to an overdraft from their bank. The corporation does not have special schemes or plans but treats each application on its merits depending on the situation and the particular financial need. Its finance is tailored to fit individual requirements and can be obtained through 18 area offices throughout the UK, with three out of five investment decisions being made locally by area managers which speeds up the processing of applications.

3i, which for many years was known as the Industrial and Commercial Finance Corporation (ICFC), has over the years invested in well over 9,000 new and growing businesses which have received funds totalling well in excess of £3 billion to help them in their development. It is also heavily involved in the burgeoning management buy-out scene and has in fact been a major player from the outset, providing finance alongside investment by management teams. 3i is an experienced and cautious investor but even so it has found that one in three of the young companies with whom it deals fails in the early years. On the other hand, executives do point out that there is evidence to show that small companies can out-perform a group of the same size working on a similar project in a large company environment.

One of the advantages of obtaining funds from 3i is that it is not looking for a quick return on its investments or aiming at getting its investment out by forcing the enterprise to grow fast so that it can be floated on the stock markets or sold to a trade customer. 3i tends to stay with its clients through thick and thin and also does not have the interfering habits of some of its venture capitalist colleagues. It tends to operate a hands-off policy rather than hands-on, leaving the management to get on with the job of running the business. Its policy of staying with a business can also pay off, such as in the substantial price it received for its shareholding – taken early in the life of the airline – in British Caledonian when it was sold to British Airways. 3i in fact is probably one of the largest and most experienced sources of venture capital in the world, having been set up in 1945 by the Bank of England and the clearing banks – who still own it – to provide small and medium-sized businesses with long-term capital.

A Business Plan

The provision of a viable business plan is an essential step towards obtaining funds for establishing a business. On the other hand, if the idea itself is not viable then no amount of neatly prepared business plans will help.

Basically, a business plan should indicate the serious purpose of the promoter and should show that he has considered how the business should develop. Help and advice on preparing a plan can be obtained from a wide variety of sources and organisations, in addition to the many courses run by local authorities, polytechnics and further education colleges. These range from the Department of Trade and Industry's Small Firms Service and the local enterprise trusts which have sprung up all over the country in the last year or so (and are listed on pp 45–60), to the business advisory services run by some of the big clearing banks.

What the Bank Manager Wants to Know

The bank manager will want to be convinced that the proposer can offer sufficient security or guarantees to match the risks the bank takes. The alternative is to consider the project under the terms of the Government Loan Guarantee Scheme. As already stated, viability is a prime consideration and as bank managers are not usually particularly well informed as to the finer technical details or, for example, how to produce computer software or how to make biscuits, the case needs to be well prepared. He will want to be satisfied that the prospective businessman has a sound knowledge of the field he is proposing to enter, that he has done his market research properly, that he knows about the competition and has plans for meeting and overcoming it, and that the ideas have commercial potential; in other words, whether people will buy the products or services and whether the promoter has a technical understanding of his product. He needs to know how much money is required for investment in fixed assets, how much in working capital for stocks, customer credit, and so on, and how much revenue will be generated – a cash flow forecast in some detail for the first year and less detailed for the second and third years would be useful.

Cash Flow

It is perfectly possible to draw up a cash flow forecast oneself but the beginner may feel the need for some help from his accountant, though in any event he should understand what the cash flow statement represents, as the bank manager will be particularly interested in how the businessman proposes to manage his finances, especially during the times when his account is likely to be overdrawn.

There is nothing particularly mysterious about cash flow, which is the movement of money into and out of a business, although many people seem both mystified and intimidated by the notion; it is really a very simple concept. One way of coming to grips with it is to relate it to your own personal finances; everyone who is in employment usually has a good idea of how much he will earn over a 12-month period, even if that income depends on commission earned on sales rather than coming in 12 or 52 equal instalments. If the income depends on commission there will probably be considerable variations from month to month, but, even so, it is usually possible to predict the highs and lows, the good season and the bad season.

Income is the proceeds of selling your services to an employer, the same as a company selling its goods or services to its customers. The one difference is that payment from an employer tends to arrive rather more promptly than payments from a customer, unless the business involves purely cash over the counter.

On the other side of the coin, the individual has regular payments and overheads relating to everyday living, for example, food, electricity and gas bills and fares to and from work. Similarly, a company has to buy its raw materials to manufacture products such as biscuits or computer software as well as pay for the premises in which to carry on the business.

The payments which an individual has to make are not necessarily spread evenly through the year any more than are those which a company has to make. There is often a bunch of heavy payments just after Christmas or around summer holiday time. The amount received in income in the months in which those bills arrive is probably considerably less than what is needed to cover those bills. Yet over a 12-month period there should be a surplus of income over spending on those necessary bills.

To meet the problems of bunching of bills many people now make use of the facility which most banks call a budget account. They estimate, for example, how much they need to cover their bills (for electricity, gas, holidays, etc) and note the times at which those bills will have to be paid. An even payment is then made each month into the budget account and the individual can draw upon the account as and when the bills arrive without worry, even if this puts the budget account into debit. Equally the bank manager knows when the increased demand for cash is going to arrive and makes arrangements accordingly.

The exercise which the individual goes through in forecasting his income from selling his services to an employer (his 'sales'), and his 'expenditure' in the form of paying bills and identifying the pressure points at which demands will exceed available cash to pay at that moment, forms the basis of a rudimentary cash flow forecast. Having forecast the pattern of income and expenditure, he can make arrangements with his bank manager for facilities to cover the 'hot spots' when pressure will rise.

Translating this concept into business terms should not now present a difficulty. When producing a cash flow forecast (a basic chart showing how this can be done is given on p 27) the prospective businessman must remember that sales do not necessarily equal income, at least not immediately. Customers will require credit and will pay their bills with varying degrees of promptness, so the actual cash receipts for credit sales will arrive some time later; it has also to be remembered that increased sales do not automatically mean increased income and a corresponding decrease in the need for working capital. They usually mean the opposite, because bills for the raw materials with which to produce the goods will have to be paid before the money arrives from the customers who have bought the finished goods. This may seem a very obvious point but it is one which a proprietor starting up a business for the first time often fails to realise.

It is in fact the reason why a company can experience rapid growth in profitable sales and yet still go out of business because the cash is not available to pay immediate demands, such as those for wages or telephone bills. It is no good asking an employee or British Telecom to take a post-dated cheque for the end of the year when the surplus of income over expenditure will have emerged; they want the money when it is due – on the nail.

So, for the purpose of the cash flow forecast, enter in the cash receipts columns the amount of cash you expect to receive month by month; the amount of cash from credit sales in the months in which you expect it actually to arrive, not when the sale is made; the amount, if any, of value added tax (VAT) paid to you by customers on those sales and any other income or receipts.

Below that, enter in the cash payments columns the payments you will have to make for materials, either in cash or on credit. Remember it is the month or week in which you actually have to make the payment for a purchase on credit that matters. Also enter payments for wages, remembering that you will need to draw an income yourself, however small: overheads such as rent, lighting, heating, telephone; taxation in the form of Pay As You Earn (PAYE) and National Health Insurance payments; VAT payments to the Customs and Excise; capital spending on, say, plant and equipment; loan repayments; and any other payments which you think are likely to arise.

Total the various columns, deduct cash payments from cash receipts, and you will have the predicted net cash flow of your business over the year, showing the financial pattern over the period. From this you will be able to define your needs for funds during the period, and make appropriate arrangements. ments.

But the cash flow forecast is not just a tool for impressing the bank manager and squeezing money out of him, then to be forgotten. It is an important tool of cash management in a business, and cash management is probably one of the major keys to success and to survival in times of recession. Having drawn up a cash flow forecast you need another similar chart on which to enter what actually happens during the year as it occurs. It can be as detailed or as simple as your needs require. By comparing your forecast with what actually turns out you can obtain forewarnings of developing problems and take action to deal with them before they turn into disaster. You may, for example, find that your cash receipts from credit sales in a particular month are much lower than you anticipated in the forecast; investigation may show that a substantial customer has delayed payment of his bill for that month and gone over the credit period allowed. You are then in a position to chase him up promptly and put the situation right before it begins to have repercussions elsewhere in the cash position of the company. The importance of cash management cannot be stressed too strongly and time spent on it is well rewarded.

By producing a cash flow forecast you will have a map through the jungle of running a business and can check the accuracy of that map as you progress. In short, you should always know where you are in financial terms, because there is no one else to ask when you are running a business; if you do not know where you are, nobody else will.

What the bank manager will want to know, therefore, also has value for you in running your business and clarifying your whole approach to that business. At the start-up stage it is just as important to establish a realistic basis for assumptions of future trends as it will be when the business has been going for a few years. When you get down to the detail of working out the cost of postage when sending out 2,000 publicity leaflets, the cost of envelopes, the cost of printing, and the cost of putting those leaflets into the envelopes, and then predicting what those costs are likely to be next year and the year after, you will begin to realise just what running a business is about at the start-up level. If your forecasts have a realistic basis the bank manager is more likely to be impressed with your submission when deciding whether you are worth backing with his depositors' money.

Bank Lending

Every bank manager has a discretionary limit for lending without having to obtain approval from a higher level. These limits are supposed to be a closely

Cash Receivable from:	TOTAL	JAN	FEB	MAR	APRIL	MAY	JUNE	JULY	AUG	SEPT	OCT	NOV	DEC
Cash sales													
Credit sales													
Net VAT received													
Other income													
Asset sales													
Any other receipts													
TOTAL													
CASH PAID OUT													
Materials bought for cash													
Materials bought on credit													
Labour costs													
Overheads													
Tax payable													
Net VAT paid out													
Capital spending													
Loan repayments													
Any other payments													
TOTAL													
Net Cash Flow													
Starting balance													
Final balance													

Monthly cash flow forecast

guarded secret but are often well known in the locality among the business and professional community; it is far from unknown in banking circles to notice that a customer has pitched his request for finance just within that discretionary limit. This practice is both unnecessary and potentially damaging as the level of finance obtained may bear little relation to the actual needs of the business, and can be either too much for the firm to service or too little to satisfy its requirements. If the project has been considered realistically, then it should be worth waiting the extra few days for approval for finance which falls outside the discretionary limits of the branch manager.

It is always a good idea to make use of any connections you may have; that means approaching your own bank manager first, or at least one with which the accountant you choose has links, as there is always a greater readiness to lend to an established personal account customer whose integrity is known. If that fails, it is time to look for other potential sources of funds.

If the project is judged to be viable then the level of risk will be assessed and the higher the risk, the higher the likelihood of security being required. The loan can be secured against personal assets, such as a house, shares, or insurance policies, which is a system that can make the entrepreneur feel he is being asked for his body and soul.

Loan Guarantee Scheme

To overcome these problems, in 1981 the Government introduced what was undoubtedly the major initiative in small-firm financing in recent years, the Loan Guarantee Scheme, based on the belief that insufficient funds are available for some worthwhile projects; the funds were unavailable because there was no track record on which the proposer could be judged or could or would not provide guarantees or collateral which financial institutions judged to be adequate. Demand initially seemed to indicate that the scheme was going to be a success but the enthusiasm very quickly waned as some of the costs of the scheme began to emerge. The Government panicked and introduced restrictions which very nearly killed the scheme altogether, but there has since been a revival as the restrictions have been eased. The scheme has been extended to 1989 and there are signs that the Government may well continue with it as it is now being used as an instrument of policy in inner cities, for example.

The Government is currently undertaking a review of the scheme in order to reach a decision on its future, and it could well be that the result will be more favourable than the two earlier reports on the scheme produced by Robson Rhodes, the chartered accountants, which led to the Government's overreaction. Robson Rhodes suggested that appraisals of applications were not sufficiently comprehensive and that monitoring by the lending institutions after the loans were granted was inadequate. They were also critical of the borrowers' lack of understanding of the way a business should be set up and of their failure to appreciate the consequences of basic business decisions, such as pricing. On the other hand, they found that professional advisers failed to understand or promote the need for a proper business understanding and grasp of financial management.

In its peak year of 1982–1983, more than 6,000 loans were made under the scheme, with the Government then guaranteeing up to 80 per cent of approved bank loans up to £75,000 in exchange for a 3 per cent premium, paid in addition to the bank interest charge. The scale of losses caused the Government to cut its guarantee to 70 per cent and raise the premium to 5 per cent in 1984. This did not reduce the loss rate, however, and further restrictions were introduced later that year. One of the new requirements was that applicants had to provide, where possible, personal security, a requirement which cut right across the basis of the scheme. A major point of the scheme at the outset was that no personal security was required, though the Government expected banks to take as security any business assets which might be available, such as the premises from which a company operated. If, for example, the premises were personally owned by a director, then the bank could justifiably ask for the premises as security; it could, however, ask for personal guarantees from the directors or take a charge on personal assets not directly used in the business. For applicants other than corporate bodies, security was limited to assets used or available for use in a business, whether it was owned collaterally or directly. The situation became such that where an applicant had personal security which he or she was unwilling to pledge against a commercial loan the application was turned down, reversing the previous situation and sharply increasing the commitment of the borrower. Other curbs were more acceptable, including the need for a business plan giving details of management, products, markets, etc. Management accounts also had to be shown to the lending bank every three months. The result of these measures, however, was to reduce loan guarantees to 2,000 in 1984–1985 and to a mere 550 in 1985–1986 as banks were unwilling to market a scheme which they thought had no future – only one of the banks, the Co-operative, was actually in support of a Loan Guarantee Scheme in the first place – and which potential borrowers saw as too onerous and too expensive. The rate of loss, unfortunately, did not seem to show any reduction in spite of these measures and continued to run at a rate of around two out of five businesses, sharply higher than the generally accepted national average for failures among smaller firms of one in three.

But eventually the Government saw the advantages of what, at the very least, was a very cheap job creation scheme. The result was a move in 1986 to extend the life of the scheme by three years and to halve the premium to 2.5 per cent; if that is spread over the whole of the loan, including the guaranteed part, the cost of the premium comes down to 1.75 per cent. The original idea was that the premium income should cover the losses, but few apart from the Government believed that it would. Even so the scheme is a relatively low-cost creator of jobs and it has been estimated that each job supported or created by the scheme costs around £700, a figure which compares very favourably with the estimated cost of £5,000 to £7,000 for each person receiving unemployment benefit for a year.

This led to a revival of interest from borrowers, though it was on nothing like the scale of the early years, and the scheme seems to be enjoying a new lease of life. Since 1981 more than £600 million has been lent to around

18,000 small firms; in 1987–1988 1,234 loans to a value of £46.23 million were issued compared with 1,050 loans to a value of £40.37 million in 1986–1987. In an attempt to speed up decision-making the Government has simplified administrative procedures for loans up to £15,000 which enables banks to approve loan applications themselves without first referring them to the Department of Employment. Previously the scheme was seldom used for loans up to £15,000 because procedures were too complicated for relatively small loans.

The scheme now provides a 70 per cent guarantee on qualifying loans up to a maximum of £75,000 over periods of two to seven years, with monthly or quarterly repayments with capital repayment 'holiday' options of up to two years in some instances. Applicants can be sole traders, partners, co-operatives, or companies and can be engaged in manufacturing, construction or retailing and other services, but not banking, education and training, estate agents, postal or telecommunications services, or public houses. There is no precise definition of a small firm but, obviously, large or even medium-sized businesses are unlikely to be interested in relatively small loans of £75,000. Interest rates vary from bank to bank, ranging from as low as 1.75 per cent above base rate for National Westminster – which recently made its 5,000th loan under the scheme, bringing its total lending to £155 million since the start of the scheme, and accounting for about one-third of all scheme loans – to 2.5 per cent above base. In addition, borrowers usually have to pay an arrangement fee of 1 per cent, though there is usually a maximum charge, ranging from £100 to £500, as well as the Government premium. One other move the Government has made recently is to increase the amount of the guarantee to 85 per cent from 70 per cent for firms located in inner city task force areas, which should further boost the scheme, which is currently generating about 200 applications a month.

In addition to being a cheap job creation scheme the Loan Guarantee Scheme has undoubtedly enabled many firms which would never otherwise have got off the ground to do so, providing important benefits to the economy. The scheme has also had its outstanding successes, such as Sock Shop and Derwent Valley Foods, the Phileas Fogg snacks firm, leading to spectacular stock market flotations. With the benefit of hindsight and a few successes to show, the Loan Guarantee Scheme now looks as though it has a future.

Co-operative Bank/Local Authority Loan Guarantee Scheme

A bank which has developed a particularly novel product is the Co-operative, with its joint ventures with local authorities in what are called local authority loan guarantee schemes. These are not connected with the Government scheme described above, in which the bank is an active participant. The Co-op's distinct scheme seeks to enable businesses in economically hard hit areas of the country to raise finance which would not otherwise have been available.

It was the Local Authorities (Miscellaneous Provisions) Act 1982 which gave local authorities powers to give guarantees for industrial development. The bank saw the opportunity to develop this special loan scheme, designed to form an integral part of an overall financial and industrial aid package. The loans have a maximum limit of £50,000 and carry an interest of 3 per cent above base rate and the local authority guarantees a portion of the loan in the event of failure, though so far there have been none.

The package may also include local authority grants or the provision of low-cost premises, together with a mix of secured or unsecured facilities from the bank. Scheme loans are normally used for business start-up finance but they may also be used for the expansion of existing businesses where new jobs will result. The bank has made agreements with a number of local authorities, including Sheffield City Council, Merseyside County Council and the London Boroughs of Haringey, Waltham Forest, Hammersmith and Fulham, while a number of other councils around the country are engaged in detailed discussions on setting up similar schemes. It is an imaginative scheme which seems destined to grow and become a valuable part of the facilities open to small firms.

Funds for Young Entrepreneurs

Initiatives aimed at helping young people create their own jobs have increased rapidly in recent years, and alongside that development has come a growth in the sources of funds available to them. The amounts available are not huge but are growing significantly and are also in keeping with the fact that many projects planned by young people actually only require limited amounts of finance to get them off the ground. Normally, raising even these limited sums would present a problem owing to the young person's lack of both track record and many of the skills potential backers would be demanding. The sources of funds which have become available are not a soft touch by any means but their aim is to take a different approach from that normally taken by conventional sources. They aim really to provide pump priming finance which will enable the projects to start and develop to a point where other backers will provide funds needed for further development. But there is, too, a recognition that self-employment is an option which is open only to relatively few and is not in itself a complete answer to lack of jobs for young people.

The single largest private sector initiative in the United Kingdom to help young people set up and run their own businesses is the Prince's Youth Business Trust (PYBT), which was formed in 1986 by the merger of the Fairbridge Youth Enterprise Scheme and the Youth Business Initiative. It is established as a charitable trust and provides a comprehensive range of seedcorn finance, business advice and information, enterprise training, and marketing support. PYBT provides grants of up to £1,000 for disadvantaged young people to start a business and it also offers loans of up to £5,000 for both start-up and expansion. There are more loans available than grants. All business ideas must be viable propositions and the young people applying for support must be able to demonstrate a reasonable chance of success. When applying for loans they must be able to show that the business will generate sufficient profits to be able to make the regular loan repayments. As well as loans and grants, there are also small sums available for test marketing before the business is started and technical training where applicants for a grant or loan need to acquire more skills to be able to run their business. Marketing grants for existing grant and loan holders with growth potential who can use the marketing grant to lever additional professional marketing support are also available. PYBT is also planning to add second-stage financing for businesses looking for expansion finance or for first-time applicants with substantial growth potential. One factor which will help in this regard is the fact that the Department of Employment has agreed to match private sector donations to the Trust and in 1987–1988 the Department paid £1.5 million to the Trust. All the young people receiving financial support from the Trust are required to have continuing business counselling for at least one year. In the case of loans, business advice is usually provided through a recognised organisation, such as an enterprise agency. The facilities of the PYBT are open to young people between 18 and 25. Further information can be obtained from:

PYBT,
8 Jockeys Fields,
London WC1R 4TJ
Tel 01-430 0521

For slightly less young entrepreneurs, Sir Philip Harris, who built up the Harris Queensway stores group, has set up a Young Entrepreneurs Fund, which he backed with £1 million. The definition of young here is between 20 and 40 years old. The fund's purpose is to make investments in the range of £50,000 to £100,000 which will help those young people to build and develop successful businesses. A percentage of the fund is, however, being set aside for investment in smaller businesses and start-ups offering good growth and employment potential. Merchant bankers Hambros have also said that they will provide second- or third-stage finance when this is required and when their criteria are met. Any profits from the fund will be re-invested in other young entrepreneurs. Further information can be obtained from:

David Wells,
Young Entrepreneurs Fund,
Seymour Suite,
65–69 Walton Road,
East Molesey,
Surrey KT8 0DP.

The Enterprise Allowance Scheme described earlier under which unemployed people above the age of 18 can receive an allowance of £40 per week for one year is also a source of finance for young people. There have been criticisms that some young people are encouraged to join the scheme at too early a stage before they have done even basic market research, with the result that their year on the scheme ends just as the business gets off the ground and is in need of a boost to cash flow rather than a reduction. There are, however, a number of other schemes in local areas which can be useful to young people starting in business. For example, Birmingham Action Resource Centre Youth Enterprise Project linked with three ethnic business groups to operate a Loan Guarantee Scheme, with support from a local charity. The project itself does not provide funds but guarantees all or part of loans offered by commercial sources to the potential entrepreneur.

Another possible source of funds may be found among local charities in an area; they may be able to provide outright grants or soft, unsecured loans. The local enterprise agency will be a source of information on these. In some areas redundant local education charities – such as those intended for training young people in obsolete trades – may have funds which can be reallocated. In Leicester the Thomas White Foundation has been offering interest-free loans for up to nine young people in a business. In other areas local authorities are examining ways of reallocating similar funds.

The Scottish Development Agency also has a loan fund for young people under 25 and uses local enterprise agencies to run the scheme. In this way the funds and advice from the Enterprise Funds for Youth Scheme are available from one source. Local authorities may provide funds on their own account to support young people starting in business. Wandsworth Youth Development, for example, offers grants of up to £500 to young people, helping them to find appropriate advice, information and support, encouraging them to consider what they want to achieve during and beyond their project. This scheme is not purely for commercial projects; in fact it is aimed at encouraging the self-development of young people and can include drama groups and other community projects.

Some companies also provide funds in different forms; the insurance group, Legal and General, has for some time had a scheme which aims to help young people with soft loans of between £1,000 and £2,000. The Shell Enterprise Loan Fund, operated by a number of enterprise agencies, is aimed primarily, but not wholly, towards the young entrepreneur.

Another potential source of funds for the young venturer may be found in local competitions aimed at encouraging the development of small businesses, as these are often aimed at young people. A scheme which operates at both local and national levels and starts every September is Livewire; this is not a competition as such, indeed its prime objective is to encourage the idea of enterprise among young people and to link them with advisers who can help them to develop their ideas into viable propositions. There are, however, awards at both the national and local level for the most promising projects. Further information can be obtained from:

National Director,
Livewire UK,
60 Grainger Street,
Newcastle upon Tyne NE1 5JG
Tel 091-261 5584

Another organisation which operates from the same address is the youth oriented enterprise agency, Project North-east, which runs its own fund for young entrepreneurs, called the Northern Youth Venture Fund. Its investments are, of course, made for business projects located in the north-east of

England. Project North-east also operates an extensive business advice system for young people and was also responsible for the establishment, in Newcastle, of the country's first Youth Enterprise Centre, of which there are now several around the country, providing both accommodation and business advice for young starters. PNE's telephone number is 091-261 7856 and its address is the same as Livewire.

Other Sources of Funds for Start-up or Expansion

The Shell Enterprise Loan Scheme mentioned in the section on youth enterprise is also available to others and provides up to £5,000 for working capital or purchase of fixed assets in the UK. Recipients are also expected to provide funds from their own resources, and not to be solely reliant on the fund, and they must make use of counselling and training proposed by the participating enterprise agency. Loans are available only to clients of the six participating enterprise agencies, which are Bolton Business Ventures, London Enterprise Agency, Project North-east, Cardiff and Vale Enterprise, Falkirk Enterprise Action Trust, and the Action Resource Centre, Belfast.

The Royal British Legion also runs a small business advisory service and loan scheme which it uses to help unemployed ex-Service people. The loan scheme provides up to £2,500, interest free, for periods of up to five years Further information can be obtained from:

Ken Pugh,
Small Business Advisory Service and Loan Scheme,
Royal British Legion Village,
Maidstone,
Kent ME20 7NL
Tel 0622 76327

The Rank Xerox pension fund has made £1 million available, invested through the London Enterprise Agency and the Tyne and Wear Enterprise Trust in equal proportions, to build up a small business investment portfolio. The aim of the scheme is to support start-up and young companies with long-term growth projects, seeking their first external equity investment, and is aimed at manufacturing and service companies from any sector of the economy. The upper limit for first-stage investment is £50,000 and equity participation is in the range of 20–50 per cent with the majority being below 40 per cent. Tyne and Weat Enterprise Trust also operates a revolving loan fund for small sums for the Calor Gas company, a fund which is aimed at providing around £1,000 each to people who lack the £1,000 needed to qualify for the Enterprise Allowance Scheme. Barclays Bank and the City Action Team have each provided £50,000 towards a Tyne and Wear Enterprise Loan Fund, which is also administered by Tyne and Wear Enterprise Trust. This is aimed at new and young businesses employing fewer than 10 people and provides loans of up to £10,000 at preferential rates of interest, although a fee is charged.

The example of Tyne and Wear Enterprise Trust is by no means unusual, as an increasing role of enterprise agencies is that of operating loan or equity funds for relatively small amounts of money for a number of organisations who would normally find it uneconomic to do so. While enterprise agencies themselves do not actually lend money they do now have access to funds and can therefore be a valuable link for the new entrepreneur with no knowledge of where to start looking. The first call of any new or young business should be on the local enterprise agency, especially as another of their roles is that of linking local people with money to invest with local companies who are looking for development funds.

Local Investment Networking Company (LINC)

The Local Investment Networking Company was launched in 1987 with just the aforementioned purpose in mind, using a common register of investors, both of individual investors and venture capital companies, holding investors' meetings on a local basis and publishing a national bulletin of business opportunities. The idea was based on the London Enterprise Agency's 'marriage bureau' scheme pioneered as long ago as 1980. It is aimed particularly at those looking for funds of up to £50,000, which is where the major gap in the market exists. There are currently 11 enterprise agencies taking part in the scheme and it is expected that there will eventually be 15 to 18, giving the scheme a countrywide spread. The enterprise agencies involved are: London, Manchester, Aberdeen, Medway, Northamptonshire, Cleveland, Staffordshire, West Cornwall, Merseyside Education Training Enterprise, and a consortium of seven Tyne and Wear trusts. General information can be obtained from:

David Wood,
Manager, LINC,
London Enterprise Agency,
4 Snow Hill,
London EC1A 2BSA
Tel 01-236 3000

or from the participating agencies.

A financial introductory service has also been established in Cambridgeshire at which entrepreneurs and investors attend meetings and discuss investments. Further details can be obtained from either:

The Director,
Peterborough Enterprise Programme,
Broadway Court,
Broadway,
Peterborough PE1 1RP
Tel 0733 310159; or

The Director,
Cambridge Enterprise Agency,
71A Lensfield Road,
Cambridge CB2 1EN
Tel 0223 323533

Co-operatives

Raising funds to set up a co-operative has never been particularly easy but the

improved climate of opinion in the last few years towards this form of business organisation has led to a distinct and welcome expansion in the finance available, often from local authorities or the enterprise boards set up in some parts of the country. One indication of the change in the situation is the fact that more than 1,400 worker co-operatives were listed as trading in the last issue of the handbook published by the Co-operative Development Agency; the agency's director, George Jones, has predicted that the number of co-operatives is likely to grow by about 250 a year.

Many of those have obviously been and will be financed by the major high street banks, who will respond to a viable, well presented proposition for a co-operative enterprise as much as for a traditional private business, though there is, of course, the need sometimes to persuade individual managers.

It is, however, reasonable to expect a more sympathetic hearing from one of the small clearing banks, the Co-operative Bank, which is a subsidiary of the Co-operative Wholesale Society, the federal manufacturing, purchasing and services arm of the established consumer co-operative movement. Its sympathy with the aims of co-operatives is clear and it has made a point of providing start-up funds for new industrial and service co-operatives, matching pound for pound the money raised by members of the co-operative as their personal stake. The bank is also an active participant in the Government's Loan Guarantee Scheme and is often involved in local authority schemes.

However, it is not easy to obtain money from the bank for a co-operative enterprise simply because of its natural sympathy for such forms of business organisation. It also expects propositions to be viable, properly thought out and presented. On the other hand, there is now a very considerable amount of help and advice available for potential co-operative members in developing their business plan in a form which will satisfy the source of finance. In addition to the enterprise agencies which now exist all over the country there is also a network of local co-operative development agencies whose purpose is to nurture the co-operative alternative. Information about local CDAs can be obtained either from your local authority or from the national CDA.

The Enterprise Allowance Scheme (described in detail on pp 20–21) for unemployed people who want to start in business is also a method of financing a worker co-operative in its first year, as the individual members of the co-op are entitled to claim the allowance. If the proposed co-operative has more than 10 members, however, the allowance may not be paid; each individual who wants the allowance must be able to meet the eligibility conditions. Probably one of the best known sources of funds for co-operatives in the past has been Industrial Common Ownership Finance, an associate organisation of the Industrial Common Ownership Movement. ICOF – which is recognised as a relevant body under the Industrial Common Ownership Act, 1976 – the purpose of which was to further development of worker-controlled enterprises by supporting the work of ICOM – operates a revolving fund for co-operatives and common ownership enterprises.

The Act originally provided £250,000 for the revolving loan fund. Advances have been made for the start-up of new common ownership or co-operative enterprises, recovery of failed or nearly failed existing businesses which are re-established under worker ownership, and extension of existing co-operatives or co-operative businesses. Since it began in 1974 ICOF has lent well over £1 million to more than 100 worker co-operatives, helping to create more than 1,000 new jobs, including plant hire, restaurants, shops, printing, publishing, electronics, clothing, light engineering, building, carpet making, and many others.

ICOF cannot consider requests for less than £1,000 because of administration costs but there is technically no upper limit on the amount it can lend. In practice, however, the amounts involved are between £7,000 and £10,000, although as much as £35,000 has been lent. Capital repayments are usually spread over five years. The established revolving loan fund is somewhat limited as the funds are now out on loan and new loans can only be made as existing borrowers repay their loans; but ICOF expects to be able to lend £30,000 to £40,000 a year in this way. It is interesting to note that only 15 per cent of all ICOF loans have been lost, a rate which bears a very favourable comparison with conventional small business lending – and indeed with loans made under the Loan Guarantee Scheme where failures have run at about 30 per cent. Part of the reason for the good performance could well be attributed to the fact that there is a continuing link between ICOF and the borrowing co-op during the period over which the loan is repaid, the kind of monitoring which is often recommended for loan guarantee borrowers.

ICOF has increased the funds it has available for lending by setting up a subsidiary which raised £500,000 from the public at a low rate of interest. This will provide a separate fund for financing worker co-operatives but will be managed in the same way as the General Fund described earlier, with the same lending criteria.

To qualify for a loan an enterprise must be an incorporated company or registered co-operative society, must have a certificate under the Industrial Common Ownership Act, certifying that more than half of the people working in the enterprise are voting members of it; must be manufacturing a product rather than providing a service; and has to be able to satisfy ICOF that it has a reasonable prospect of success. As always where taxpayers' money is involved, there are a number of formalities to be cleared before a loan is granted, which can take about three months to complete, requiring a degree of determination and patience. ICOF finance would not be suitable for a very short-term project, or for a situation where funds were needed urgently to avert a closure.

The procedure to adopt if intending to apply to ICOF for funds is as follows:

1. Register the enterprise as a co-operative society (information on how to do this can be obtained from the Industrial Common Ownership Movement or the Co-operative Development Agency – addresses on p 45). The registration fee for those who register with ICOM model rules is lower than it would otherwise be, about half in fact, so there is a financial advantage in doing this. Blank forms and information are included in the booklet, 'How to form an Industrial Co-operative', published by ICOM at £5.

2. Complete form ICO 2 to apply for a certificate under the Industrial Common Ownership Act, obtainable from the Registrar of Friendly Societies at the address on p 45.

3. Obtain a letter of support from the trade union relevant to the project, which is a requirement under the regulations.

4. Complete an ICOF application form. ICOF will also need information that the first three stages have been completed, as well as a cash flow projection, details of security available, and information about the experience of the people who will be working in the co-operative. Blank forms and full details can be obtained from ICOF direct. The secretary of the ICOF trustees will usually visit the enterprise and discuss the application with those who are involved. While the loan is outstanding there is a continuing link between ICOF and the co-operative, merely in order to be helpful, as the aim is to encourage permanent trading enterprises.

Another way in which ICOF has increased the funds flowing to co-operatives is through the funds which it administers on behalf of local authorities, such as West Glamorgan, Northamptonshire, and the West Midlands. Its first local authority fund was the £500,000 it received from the West Midlands County Council and which it now operates on behalf of the West Midlands Enterprise Board, which took over responsibility on the abolition of the metropolitan authority. WMCC also set up its own co-operative finance organisation, West Midlands Co-operative Finance Ltd, which is now a subsidiary of the West Midlands Enterprise Board and has a £1.25 million fund for investment in co-operative enterprises, which it does with a high degree of success. In Scotland a venture capital fund for worker co-operatives has been established, called Co-operative Venture Capital (Scotland), which is open to new or existing co-operatives. Stringent rules ensure the commercial viability of each project. The fund is managed by chartered accountants Grant Thornton, with the secretariat being provided by:

Scottish Co-operatives Development
Committee,
Templeton Business Centre,
Templeton Street,
Bridgeton,
Glasgow G40 1DA
Tel 041-5543797

This kind of initiative has been followed by other local authorities creating co-operative loan funds in several parts of the country, often in conjunction with local co-operative development agencies. Many local authorities do in any case have the power to give financial assistance in the form of grant aid up to £1,000 to cover the research and administration costs involved in setting up a common ownership enterprise.

As already mentioned, local CDAs are an important link in the chain, carrying out feasibility studies on co-op ideas, drawing up business plans, and helping in applications for finance as well as bringing potential sources of finance into contact with potential borrowers and providing, too, the necessary 'after-care'.

Conclusion

Some of the principal sources of finance for starting up small businesses have been described in this chapter but these by no means constitute an exhaustive list. Further details of whether initiatives in one area are being followed in another can be discovered by contacting one or more of the following: your local authority; an appropriate local enterprise trust; the Government's Small Firms Service; your local Chamber of Commerce; a Chamber of Trade.

Funds for start-ups are also available from European sources, such as the European Investment Bank and the European Coal and Steel Community. These are channelled through the Department of Trade and Industry, BSC (Industry) (the job-creation arm of the British Steel Corporation), 3i, and some of the clearing banks. These sources are described in Chapter 6.

Company Story

A combination of redundancy and a six-month long strike at a firm which went out of business was the spark which led seven furniture workers (three men and four women) to set up in business on their own, a course which none of them previously had contemplated.

Phil Davies had been a shop steward at the Manchester factory of the furniture maker, Schreiber, a subsidiary of GEC, along with Bernard Heywood and Noel Robinson. The company reduced manning levels as part of a rationalisation programme and they were made redundant with no prospect of other jobs. Meanwhile, in 1981, their union had been supporting a strike over pay and conditions by women workers at a firm making headboards for beds in nearby Salford. After a strike lasting six months the Salford company closed down at about the same time as the Schreiber redundancies occurred.

Through their union activities during the dispute the three men from Schreiber had come to know the women strikers from the headboard-making firm. With four of the women, Elsie Broad, Marie Fennell, Jean Thornton, and Helen Weir, all skilled upholsterers, the idea of forming a co-operative was discussed and eventually pursued, as the woodworking skills of the three men complemented those of the upholsterers. Furthermore, because of the closure of the headboard firm, there seemed to be an opening in the market locally for high quality headboards and other items of bedroom furniture, such as ottomans and small chairs.

They began the process of organising the co-operative in August 1981, receiving help from Alan Chesney of the Salford Employment Trust, and it formally came into existence in January 1982.

The intervening period was spent setting up the loans needed to finance the operation and organising production facilities. They found premises in the church-owned Salford Central Mission building, which stands in the enterprise zone covering parts of Salford and the old Trafford Park industrial area, though the fact that it was an enterprise zone was not crucial to their choice of location. Being in an enterprise zone (see pp 111–12), however, means that they benefit from reduced rates or can even be exempted from them, which should relieve some of the pressure on cash flow, especially at a time when most businesses are suffering from the high level of rate demands. (Rates are exempted only on business premises; where a property in an enterprise zone is used for both residential and business purposes, relief is given only on the business part, and the overall rate demand is therefore reduced.)

The co-operative negotiated a loan of £7,500 from ICOF for five years, with an initial 'holiday' on repayments. Advice from Salford Employment Trust also enabled them to obtain £1,000 from the Industrial Training Research Unit which is part of the Manpower Services Commission. The money was used to buy a rip saw, which was an essential piece of equipment in the early stages. Altogether, they spent £8,000 on production equipment. Through the Greater Manchester Economic Development Corporation they negotiated £6,000-worth of assistance with rent for the premises over the first two years of the life of the co-operative. A grant of £1,000 towards setting-up costs, legal fees and so on was also obtained.

Another important part of the financial package was a loan of £15,000 from the Co-operative Bank under the Government's Loan Guarantee Scheme, at an interest rate of 1.5 per cent over base rate, and with a six-month capital repayment 'holiday'. The bank has taken a debenture on the assets of the co-operative as security.

A turnover of £125,000 was the target for the first year, in a market which the participants saw initially as a local one. Their first efforts to obtain orders consisted of walking into the major department stores in the Greater Manchester area and knocking on the buyers' doors. This produced results, one of the most encouraging being the interest shown by Lewis's, which gave them a pilot order worth £1,600 a fortnight; in addition, the store agreed to vary their usual payment terms and pay for goods within 14 days of delivery, again important for the cash flow situation in the early days of the co-operative.

Lewis's wanted to be able to draw on a full range of products and styles, and the co-operative was quickly able to provide this. 'We bent over backwards to supply this range and I think that impressed them,' said Phil Davies. It also provoked the seven to sit down and work out sales areas for the future and develop their marketing strategy. The co-operative, operating as Broadway Quality Furnishings, soon found that the woodworking side of the business could produce at a much greater rate than the upholstering side could cope with, giving an opportunity for diversification. This came in the form of wooden mouldings and skirting boards for use in quality building projects (such as banks) and the order was placed by a building contractor who could not find a local supplier.

All members of the co-operative take a full part in running the business, with regular weekly general meetings and daily meetings to plan production and sales efforts for the following day. Each individual has a special area of responsibility, such as sales, or purchasing of upholstery fabrics or timber which gives everyone a strong sense of involvement and commitment. To begin with, the amount of money taken out in wages was limited to cover needs only, but it is planned to raise this to the union minimum as soon as the finances of the company allow. 'We certainly do not intend to continue to exploit ourselves indefinitely. The business has to develop into a viable, going concern which can provide us with a proper income.'

The aim is not to make fortunes from the co-operative. It is intended to plough back surpluses to expand the capacity and output of the enterprise and to provide more jobs. Even so, there is no intention of compromising on quality simply to obtain orders at any price. This was a temptation put before them by potential buyers who wanted cheaply produced goods and was quickly rejected. It meant that initially orders were slow to build up, but eventually they came from sources which the members of the co-operative had hoped to supply.

Before setting up the Broadway Quality Furnishings co-operative all the participants were shop-floor workers, mostly in their early thirties, and with no previous experience of running a business. 'But so far running a business doesn't seem to have been as difficult as we expected,' said Phil Davies. This is probably because the co-operative started with the benefit of good advice, a sound financial base, a clear view of what it wanted to produce and the market for it, combined with a realistic, co-operative approach to those aims.

Useful Addresses

Loan Guarantee Scheme participating banks and financial institutions:

Allied Irish Banks,
64–66 Coleman Street,
London EC2R 5AL
Tel 01-588 0691

Bank Leumi (UK),
PO Box 2AF,
4–7 Woodstock Street,
London W1A 2AF
Tel 01-629 1205

Bank of Ireland,
36 Moorgate,
London EC2R 6DP
Tel 01-628 8811

Bank of Scotland,
The Mound,
Edinburgh EH1 1YZ
Tel 031-225 3431

Barclays Bank,
Small Business Group,
Corporate Division,
54 Lombard Street,
London EC3P 3AH
Tel 01-626 1567

British Linen Bank,
4 Melville Street,
Edinburgh EH3 7NZ
Tel 031-226 4071

Brown, Shipley & Co,
Founders Court,
Lothbury,
London EC2R 7HE
Tel 01-606 9833

Clydesdale Bank,
30 St Vincent Place,
Glasgow G1 2HL
Tel 041-248 7071

Co-operative Bank,
1 Balloon Street,
Manchester M60 4EP
Tel 061-832 3456

County Bank,
11 Old Broad Street,
London EC2N 1BB
Tel 01-638 6000

Coutts and Co,
440 The Strand,
London WC2R 0QS
Tel 01-379 6262

Hill Samuel & Co Ltd,
100 Wood Street,
London EC2P 2AJ
Tel 01-638 8011

Hong Kong and Shanghai Banking Corporation,
PO Box 199,
99 Bishopsgate,
London EC2P 2LA
Tel 01-638 2300

Investors in Industry (3i),
91 Waterloo Road,
London SE1 8XP
Tel 01-928 7822
3i has 18 area offices at:
Aberdeen, Birmingham, Brighton, Bristol, Cambridge, Cardiff, Edinburgh, Glasgow, Leeds, Leicester, Liverpool, London, Manchester, Newcastle, Nottingham, Reading, Sheffield, and Southampton.

Lloyds Bank,
71 Lombard Street,
London EC3P 3BS
Tel 01-626 1500

Midland Bank,
27–32 Poultry,
London EC2P 2BX
Tel 01-606 9911

National Westminster Bank,
41 Lothbury,
London EC2P 2BP
Tel 01-606 6060

Northern Bank,
PO Box 183,
Donegall Square West,
Belfast BT1 6JS
Tel 0232 45277

Norwich General Trust,
12 Surrey Street,
Norwich,
Norfolk NR1 3NJ
Tel 0603 22200

Royal Bank of Scotland,
42 St Andrew Square,
Edinburgh EH2 2YE
Tel 031-556 8555

TCB,
Century House,
Dyke Road,
Brighton BN1 3FX
Tel 0273 23511

Ulster Bank,
47 Donegall Place,
Belfast BT1 5AU
Tel 0232 20222

Yorkshire Bank,
20 Merrion Way,
Leeds LS2 8NZ
Tel 0532 441244

Other banks providing start-up finance but not participating in the Loan Guarantee Scheme:

Bank Hapoalim BM,
8–12 Brook Street,
London W1Y 1AA
Tel 01-449 0792

Banque Nationale de Paris,
8–13 King William Street,
London EC4P 4HS
Tel 01-626 5678

Canada Permanent Trust Company (UK),
1 Finsbury Square,
London EC2A 1AD
Tel 01-638 9046

Société Générale Bank,
Pinners Hall,
Austin Friars,
PO Box 61,
London EC2P 2DN
Tel 01-628 8661

TSB plc,
60 Lombard Street,
London EC3V 9EA
Tel 01-600 6000

General information, and specific information relating to finance in connection with co-operatives can be obtained from the following addresses:

Assistant Registrar of Friendly Societies,
19 Heriot Row,
Edinburgh
Tel 031-566 4371

Co-operative Development Agency,
21 Panton Street,
London SW1Y 4DR
Tel 01-839 2985

Industrial Common Ownership Finance,
12–14 Gold Street,
Northampton NN1 1RS
Tel 0604 37563

Industrial Common Ownership Movement,
Vassalli House,
20 Central Road,
Leeds LS1 6DE
Tel 0532 461737

Job Ownership,
42 Hanway Street,
London W1P 9DE
Tel 01-637 0780

Registrar of Friendly Societies,
17 North Audley Street,
London W1Y 2AP
Tel 01-629 7001

Specialist institutions

Knott Industrial Projects,
Small Business Centre,
Durham University Business School,
Mill Lane,
Durham DH1 3LB
Tel 0385 41919

Local Enterprise Trusts do not provide finance themselves but they often have access to funds and usually know what funds are available locally. This is a selected list of enterprise agencies; a full list of the 300 which now exist can be obtained from:

Business in the Community,
227a City Road,
London EC1V 1LX
Tel 01-253 3716

Alnwick Small Industries Group,
1 The Shambles,
Alnwick,
Northumberland NE66 1HU
Tel 0665 605075

Bedlington Station
South East Northumberland Trust Ltd (SENET),
20 School Road,
Bedlington Station,
Northumberland
Tel 0670 828686

Chester-le-Street and North Durham Enterprise Agency,
Mechanics Institute,
Newcastle Bank,
Chester-le-Street,
County Durham
Tel 0385 982648

Consett
Derwentside Industrial Development Agency,
Berry Edge Road,
Consett,
County Durham
Tel 0207 509124

Darlington & SW Durham Business Venture,
Imperial Centre,
Grange Road,
Darlington DL1 5NQ
Tel 0325 480891

Durham
Enterprise North,
Durham University Business School,
Mill Lane,
Durham DH1 3LB
Tel 0385 41919

Gateshead
1 Walker Terrace,
Gateshead NE8 1EB
Tel 091-477 6675

Hartlepool Enterprise Agency Ltd,
Suite 7,
Municipal Buildings,
Church Square,
Hartlepool TS24 7ER
Tel 0429 221216

Hartlepool New Development Support Ltd,
HANDS Enterprise Agency,
Old Municipal Buildings,
Upper Church Street,
Hartlepool TS24 7ET
Tel 0429 266522 (ext 374)

Cleveland Youth Business Centres,
6 North Street,
Middlesbrough,
Tel 0642 240656

Morpeth
Northumberland Business Centre,
Southgate,
Morpeth NE63 2EH
Tel 0670 511221

Newcastle
Tyne and Wear Enterprise Trust Ltd (Entrust),
Portman House,
Portland Road,
Newcastle upon Tyne NE2 1AQ
Tel 091-261 4838

Business Enterprise Centre,
Eldon Street,
South Shields NE33 5JE
Tel 091-454 3346

Project North East,
Marseilles Chambers,
45 Groat Market,
Newcastle upon Tyne NE1 1UG
Tel 0632 617856

81–83 High Street West,
Wallsend NE28 8JD
Tel 091-234 0895

Shildon & Sedgefield District Development Agency,
BREL Offices,
Byerley Road,
Shildon,
County Durham DL4 1PW
Tel 0388 777917

62 High Street West,
Sunderland SR1 3DP
Tel 0783 650601

North West Region

Accrington
Hyndburn Enterprise Trust,
19 Avenue Parade,
Accrington,
Lincolnshire BB5 6PN
Tel 0254 390000

Ashton-under-Lyne
Tameside Business Advice Service,
Charlestown Industrial Estate,
Turner Street,
Ashton-under-Lyne
Tel 061-339 8960

Barrow
Furness Business Initiative,
111 Duke Street,
Barrow-in-Furness
Tel 0229 22132

Birkenhead
In Business Ltd,
Small Business Centre,
Claughton Road,
Birkenhead L41 6EY
Tel 051-647 7574

Blackburn and District Enterprise Trust,
c/o Blackburn & District Chamber of Industry and Commerce,
14 Richmond Terrace,
Blackburn BB1 7BH
Tel 0254 664747

Blackpool & Fylde Business Agency Ltd,
20 Queen Street,
Blackpool,
Lancashire FY1 1PD
Tel 0253 294929

Bolton Business Ventures,
Bolton Centre,
46 Lower Bridgeman Street,
Bolton B12 1DG
Tel 0204 391400

Bootle
South Sefton Enterprise Agency Ltd,
Beaver Enterprise Workspace,
58–60 Strand Road,
Bootle,
Merseyside L20 4BG
Tel 051-933 0024

Bury Enterprise Centre,
12 Tithebarn Street,
Bury BL9 0JR
Tel 061-797 5864

Carlisle
Business Initiatives Carlisle,
Tower Buildings,
Scotch Street,
Carlisle CA3 8RB
Tel 0228 34120

Chester Enterprise Centre,
Off Hoole Bridge,
Chester CH2 3NQ
Tel 0244 311474

Clitheroe
Ribble Valley Enterprise Agency Ltd,
Bath House,
York Street,
Clitheroe,
Lancashire BB7 2DL
Tel 0200 22110

Crewe
South Cheshire Opportunity for Private Enterprise (SCOPE),
SCOPE House,
Weston Road,
Crewe CW1 1DD
Tel 0270 589568

Ellesmere Port
Entep Trust Ltd,
118 Whitby Road,
Ellesmere Port L65 0AA
Tel 051-356 3555

Kirkby
Knowsley Enterprise Agency,
Admin Buildings,
Room 33,
Admin Road,
Knowsley Industrial Park,
Kirkby,
Merseyside L33 7TX
Tel 051-548 3245

Lancaster
Business for Lancaster,
St Leonards House,
Room B32,
St Leonards Gate,
Lancaster
Tel 0524 66222

Leyland
South Ribble Business Venture Ltd,
176 Towngate,
Leyland,
Lancashire PR5 1TE
Tel 0772 422242

Liverpool
Business in Liverpool Ltd,
The Innovation Centre,
131 Mount Pleasant,
Liverpool L3 5TF
Tel 051-709 1231

Macclesfield Business Ventures,
Venture House,
Cross Street,
Macclesfield SK11 7PG
Tel 0625 615113

Manchester Business Venture,
c/o Manchester Chamber of Commerce & Industry,
56 Oxford Street,
Manchester M60 7HJ
Tel 061-236 0153

Nelson
Pendle Enterprise Trust Ltd,
19–23 Leeds Road,
Nelson,
Lancashire
Tel 0282 698001

Northwich
Vale Royal Small Firms Ltd,
Wallescote House,
Winnington Lane,
Northwich,
Cheshire CW8 4EG
Tel 0606 77711

Oldham
Business in Oldham,
Acorn Centre,
Barry Street,
Oldham OL1 3NE
Tel 061-665 1255

Ormskirk
The West Lancashire Enterprise Trust Ltd,
The Malthouse,
48 Southport Road,
Ormskirk,
Lancashire L39 1LX
Tel 0695 78626

Preston Business Venture,
43 Lune Street,
Preston PR1 2NN
Tel 0772 25723

Rawtenstall
Rossendale Enterprise Trust Ltd,
29 Kay Street,
Rawtenstall,
Rossendale BB4 7LS
Tel 0706 229838

Rochdale
Metropolitan Enterprise Trust Rochdale Area (Business Help),
c/o TBA Industrial Products Ltd,
PO Box 40,
Rochdale OL12 7EQ
Tel 0706 356250

Runcorn
Business Link,
62 Church Street,
Runcorn,
Cheshire WA7 1LD
Tel 0928 563037

Sale
Trafford Business Venture,
3rd Floor,
Six Acre House,
Town Square,
Sale,
Cheshire M33 1XZ
Tel 061-905 2950

Southport
Sefton Enterprise Trust,
54 West Street,
Southport PR8 1QS
Tel 0704 44173

St Helens
Community of St Helens Trust,
PO Box 36,
St Helens,
Merseyside
Tel 0744 692775

Warrington Business Promotion Bureau,
Barbauld House,
Barbauld Street,
Warrington WA1 2QY
Tel 0925 33309

Wigan New Enterprise Ltd,
45 Bridgeman Terrace,
Wigan WN1 1TT
Tel 0942 496591

Workington
Enterprise West Cumbria,
Thirlmere Building,
50 Lakes Road,
Derwent Howe Estate,
Workington,
Cumbria CA14 3YP
Tel 0900 65656

Yorkshire and Humberside Region

Barnsley Enterprise Centre,
1 Pontefract Road,
Barnsley
Tel 0226 298091

Bradford Enterprise Agency,
Commerce House,
Cheapside,
Bradford BD1 4JZ
Tel 0274 734359

Brigg
SoHBAC (South Humberside Business Advice Centre) Ltd,
7 Market Place,
Brigg,
South Humberside DN20 8HA
Tel 0652 57637

Doncaster
DonBAC (Doncaster Business Advice Centre),
50 Christ Church Road,
Doncaster DN1 2QN
Tel 0302 734665

Grimsby & Cleethorpes Area Enterprise Agency,
2nd Floor,
Norwich Union Chambers,
27 Osborne Street,
Grimsby DN31 1EY
Tel 0472 52109

Halifax
Calderdale Small Business Advice Centre,
OP53 Dean Clough Office Park,
Deanclough,
Halifax
Tel 0422 69487

Huddersfield
Kirklees & Wakefield Venture Trust,
Commerce House,
New North Road,
Huddersfield HD1 5PJ
Tel 0484 531352

Hull
Action Resource Centre,
Hull Business Advice Centre,
24 Anlaby Road,
Hull HU1 2PA
Tel 0482 27266

Leeds Business Venture,
2nd Floor,
26 Great George Street,
Leeds LS1 3DL
Tel 0532 446474

Rotherham Enterprise Agency Ltd,
2nd Floor,
All Saints Buildings,
21 Corporation Street,
Rotherham S60 1NX
Tel 0709 382121 (ext 3463)

Scarborough Filey & District Business Development Agency,
32 St Nicholas Street,
Scarborough YO11 2HF
Tel 0723 354454

Sheffield Business Venture,
317 Glossop Road,
Sheffield S10 2HP
Tel 0742 755721

Whitby Business Development Agency,
3 Bagdale,
Whitby YO21 3AE
Tel 0947 600827

York
Vale of York Small Business Association,
York Enterprise Centre,
1 Davygate,
York YO1 2QE
Tel 0904 641401

York Enterprise Ltd,
York Enterprise Centre,
1 Davygate,
York YO1 2QE
Tel 0904 646803

West Midlands Region

Birmingham Venture,
Chamber of Commerce House,
PO Box 360,
75 Harborne Road,
Birmingham B15 3DH
Tel 021-454 6171

3B's – Black Business in Birmingham,
c/o St Paul's Church,
St Paul's Square,
Birmingham B3 1QZ
Tel 021-236 9404

Burton Enterprise Agency,
Midland Railway Grain Warehouse,
Derby Street,
Burton-on-Trent DE4 2JJ
Tel 0283 37151

Coventry Business Centre,
Christchurch House,
Greyfriars Lane,
Coventry CV1 2GY
Tel 0203 552781

Dudley Business Venture,
Falcon House,
The Minories,
Dudley DY2 8PG
Tel 0384 231283

Hereford
Herefordshire Enterprise Agency Ltd,
Berrows House,
Bath Street,
Hereford HR1 2HE
Tel 0432 276898

Stoke on Trent
Business Initiative,
Commerce House,
Etruria,
Stoke on Trent
Tel 0782 279013

Wallsall Small Firms Advice Unit,
Jerome Chambers,
Bridge Street,
Walsall WS1 1EX
Tel 0922 646614

Warwickshire Enterprise Agency,
Northgate South,
Northgate Street,
Warwick CV34 4JH
Tel 0926 495685

Wellington
The Shropshire Enterprise Trust,
National Westminster Bank Chambers,
Church Street,
Wellington
Tel 0952 56624

West Bromwich
Sandwell Enterprise Ltd,
Sandwell Business Advice Centre,
Victoria Street,
West Bromwich,
Sandwell,
West Midlands B70 8ET
Tel 021-569 2231

Wolverhampton Enterprise Ltd,
Lich Chambers,
Exchange Street,
Wolverhampton WV1 1TS
Tel 0902 713737

Worcester
Worcestershire Enterprise Agency,
1st Floor,
Marmion House,
Copenhagen Street,
Worcester WR1 2HB
Tel 0905 424191

East Midlands Region

Chesterfield (ARC),
Business Advice Centre,
34 Beetwell Street,
Chesterfield S40 1SH
Tel 0246 208743

Corby Industrial Development Centre,
Douglas House,
37 Queens Square,
Corby NN17 1PL
Tel 0536 62571

Derby & Derbyshire Business Venture,
Saxon House,
Heritage Gate,
Friary Street,
Derby DE1 1NL
Tel 0332 360345

Grantham
Kesteven Enterprise Agency Ltd,
58 London Road,
Grantham,
Lincolnshire NG31 6ET
Tel 0476 68970

Kettering Business Venture Trust,
Douglas House,
27 Station Road,
Kettering,
Northants NN15 7HH
Tel 0536 513840

Leicestershire Business Venture,
Business Advice Centre,
30 New Walk,
Leicester LE1 6TF
Tel 0533 554464

Lincoln Enterprise Agency,
10 Park Street,
Lincoln LN1 1UF
Tel 0522 40775

Newark Enterprise Agency,
3 Middlegate,
Newark-on-Trent,
Nottinghamshire NG24 1AQ
Tel 0636 71881

Northamptonshire Enterprise Agency Ltd,
67 The Avenue,
Cliftonville,
Northampton NN1 5BT
Tel 0604 37401

Nottinghamshire Business Venture,
City House,
Maid Marion Way,
Nottingham NG1 6BH
Tel 0602 470914

Eastern Region

Basildon & District Local Enterprise Agency Ltd,
Keay House,
Room 101A,
88 Town Square,
Basildon SS14 1BN
Tel 0268 286977

Bedfordshire
Becenta (Bedfordshire & Chiltern Enterprise Agency),
Enterprise House,
7 Gordon Street,
Luton LU1 2QP
Tel 0582 452288

Braintree
BEES,
Enterprise Office,
Town Hall Centre,
Market Square,
Braintree CM7 6YG
Tel 0376 43140

Bury St Edmunds
Mid-Anglian Enterprise Agency Ltd,
79 Whiting Street,
Bury St Edmunds IP33 1NX
Tel 0284 60206

Cambridge
CEA (Cambridge Enterprise Agency Ltd),
71A Lensfield Road,
Cambridge CB2 1EN
Tel 0223 323553

Chelmsford
Essex Business Centre,
Church Street,
Chelmsford,
Essex
Tel 0245 350388

Clacton-on-Sea
Enterprise Tendring Ltd,
71B Station Road,
Clacton-on-Sea
Essex
Tel 0255 421225

Colchester Business Enterprise Agency,
Gate House,
High Street,
Colchester CO1 1UG
Tel 0206 48833

Grays
Thurrock Local Enterprise Agency Ltd,
79a High Street,
Grays,
Essex RM17 6NX
Tel 0375 374362

Great Yarmouth Business Advisory Service,
Queens Road,
Great Yarmouth NR30 3HT
Tel 0493 850204

Harlow Enterprise Agency,
19 The Rows,
The High,
Harlow CM20 1DD
Tel 0279 38077

Hatfield
The Welwyn & Hatfield Enterprise Agency,
5 Queensway House,
Town Centre,
Hatfield,
Hertfordshire AL10 0NR
Tel 07072 67635

Huntingdon
Huntingdonshire Enterprise Agency,
Castle Hill House,
High Street,
Huntingdon PE18 6TE
Tel 0480 50028

Ipswich Enterprise Agency (IPSENTA),
30a Lower Brooke Street,
Ipswich
Tel 0473 59832

Kings Lynn
West Norfolk Enterprise Agency Trust Ltd,
7 King Street,
Kings Lynn,
Norfolk PE30 1ET
Tel 0553 760431

Letchworth Garden City Business Centre,
Avenue One,
Business Park,
Letchworth Garden City,
Hertfordshire SG6 2HB
Tel 04626 78272

Loughton
Forest Enterprise Agency Trust (FEAT)
c/o Manager's Flat,
Swimming Pool,
Traps Hill,
Loughton,
Essex IG10 1SZ
Tel 01-508 7435

Lowestoft Enterprise Trust,
19 Grove Road,
Lowestoft NR32 1EB
Tel 0502 63286

Milton Keynes Business Venture,
Sentry House,
500 Avebury Boulevard,
Saxon Gate West,
Central Milton Keynes MK9 2LA
Tel 0908 660044

Norwich
NEAT (Norwich Enterprise Agency Trust),
112 Barrack Street,
Norwich NR3 1TX
Tel 0603 613023

Peterborough Enterprise Programme,
Broadway Court,
Broadway,
Peterborough PE1 1RP
Tel 0733 310159

St Albans Enterprise Agency Ltd (STANTA),
8a Chequer Street,
St Albans,
Hertfordshire AL1 3YZ
Tel 0727 40563

Southend Enterprise Agency Ltd,
Commerce House,
845 London Road,
Westcliff-on-Sea,
Essex SS0 9SZ
Tel 0702 78380

Stevenage Initiative,
Business and Technology Centre,
Bessemer Drive,
Stevenage,
Hertfordshire
Tel 0438 315733

Sudbury Enterprise Agency,
Guthrie House,
67 Cornard Road,
Sudbury,
Suffolk CO10 6XB
Tel 0787 73927

Watford Enterprise Agency Ltd,
Wenta Business Centre,
Colne Way,
Watford,
Hertfordshire WD2 4ND
Tel 0923 47373

Wisbech
Fens Business Enterprise Trust,
2 York Row,
Wisbech PE13 1EB
Tel 0945 587084

South Eastern Region

Aldershot
Blackwater Valley Enterprise Trust,
Old Town Hall,
Grosvenor Road,
Aldershot GU11 3DP
Tel 0252 319272

East Hampshire Enterprise Agency Ltd,
Agency Ltd,
c/o Bass Brewery (Alton) Ltd,
Manor Park,
Alton GU34 2PS
Tel 0420 87577

Ashford, Kent
Enterprise Ashford Ltd,
Enterprise Centre,
Old Railway Works,
Newtown Road,
Ashford,
Kent TN24 0PD
Tel 0233 30307

Aylesbury Vale Business Advice Scheme,
23A Walton Street,
Aylesbury HP20 1TZ
Tel 0296 89055

Banbury
North Oxfordshire Business Venture Ltd,
2nd Floor,
13 Horsefair,
Banbury OX16 9AH
Tel 0295 67900

Basingstoke & Andover Enterprise Centre,
9 New Street,
Basingstoke RG21 1DF
Tel 0256 54041

Brighton & Hove Business Agency Ltd,
23 Old Steine,
Brighton BN1 1EL
Tel 0273 688882

Canterbury
The Enterprise Agency of East Kent,
22 St Peter's Street,
Canterbury CT1 2BQ
Tel 0227 470234

Chatham
Medway Enterprise Agency Ltd,
Railway Street,
Chatham ME4 4RR
Tel 0634 400301

Dartford
North West Kent Enterprise Agency,
2 Hythe Street,
Dartford,
Kent DA1 1BT
Tel 0322 91451

Eastbourne and District Enterprise Agency Ltd,
c/o Birds Eye Walls Ltd,
Lottbridge Drive,
Eastbourne BN23 6PS
Tel 0323 644470

Fareham Enterprise,
75 High Street,
Fareham,
Hampshire
Tel 0329 282543

Folkestone
Shepway Business Advisory Panel Ltd,
24 Cheriton Gardens,
Folkestone,
Kent CT20 2AS
Tel 0303 59162

Gosport Enterprise,
Ferry Gardens,
South Street,
Gosport,
Hampshire
Tel 0705 586621

Gravesend
Gravesham Enterprise Agency,
22 Wrotham Road,
Gravesend DA11 0PA
Tel 0474 327118

Guildford
Surrey Business Enterprise Agency Ltd,
28 Commercial Road,
Guildford,
Surrey GU1 4SU
Tel 0483 506969

Hastings Business Ventures,
6 Havelock Road,
Hastings TN34 1BP
Tel 0424 433333

Isle of Wight Enterprise Agency Ltd,
6–7 Town Lane,
Newport PO30 1NR
Tel 0983 529120

Maidstone Enterprise Agency,
25A Pudding Lane,
Maidstone ME14 1PA
Tel 0622 675547

Oxford
Thames Business Advice Centre,
Osney Mead,
Oxford OX2 0ES
Tel 0865 249279

The Portsmouth Area Enterprise,
1st Floor,
27 Guildhall Walk,
Portsmouth
Tel 0705 833321

Sittingbourne
Swale Enterprise Agency,
Unit B4,
Smeed Dean Centre,
Eurolink,
Sittingbourne,
Kent ME10 3RN
Tel 0795 27623

Southampton Enterprise Agency,
Solent Business Centre,
Millbrook Road West,
Southampton SO1 0HW
Tel 0703 788088

Tonbridge
Great Weald Enterprise Agency,
34a High Street,
Tonbridge,
Kent TN9 1EJ
Tel 0732 360133

Worthing
West Sussex Area Enterprise Centre Ltd,
69A Chapel Road,
Worthing,
West Sussex BN11 1BU
Tel 0903 31499

South West Region

Barnstaple
North Devon Enterprise Group,
Bridge Chambers,
Barnstaple,
North Devon EX31 1HB
Tel 0271 76365

North Devon Manufacturers Association,
95 High Street,
Barnstaple,
Devon EX3 1HR

Bath Enterprise Ltd,
Green Park Station,
Green Park Road,
Bath BA1 1JB
Tel 0225 338383

Bath Control Centre,
Unit 1a Bath Riverside Business Park,
Lower Bristol Road,
Bath BA2 3DW
Tel 0225 337992/337967

Bridgwater
Small Industries Group Somerset,
68 Friarn Street,
Bridgwater,
Somerset TA6 3LJ
Tel 0278 424456

Bristol & Avon Enterprise Agency,
Cannons Road,
Bristol BS1 5UH
Tel 0272 272222

Kingswood (Bristol)
New Work Trust Co Ltd,
Avondale Workshops,
Woodland Way,
Kingswood,
Bristol BS15 1QH
Tel 0272 603871, 601106

Station Road Workshops,
Station Road,
Kingswood,
Bristol BS15 4PR
Tel 0272 575577

Paulton (Bristol)
Wansdyke Enterprise Agency Ltd,
High Street,
Paulton,
Bristol BS18 5NW
Tel 0761 415400

St Paul's (Bristol)
The Coach House Small Business Centre,
2 Upper York Street,
St Paul's,
Bristol BS2
Tel 0272 428022

Warmley (Bristol)
Small Firms Marketing Centre,
London Road,
Warmley,
Bristol BS15 5JH
Tel 0272 601109/677807

Yate (Bristol)
Northavon Business Centre,
Dean Road,
Yate,
Bristol
Tel 0454 324115

Camborne
West Cornwall Enterprise Trust Ltd,
Lloyds Bank Chambers,
Market Square,
Camborne TR14 8JT
Tel 0209 714914

Exeter
Business Enterprise Exeter,
39 Marsh Green Road,
Marsh Barton,
Exeter EX2 8PN
Tel 0392 56060

Frome Area Management,
Enterprise Agency,
South Parade,
Frome,
Somerset BA11 1EJ
Tel 0373 73101

Glastonbury
FACE (Facility for Art & Craft Enterprise),
Workface,
Market Place,
Glastonbury,
Somerset BA6 9HL
Tel 0458 33917

Gloucestershire Enterprise Agency (GEA),
90 Westgate Street,
Gloucester GL1 2NZ
Tel 0452 501411

Guernsey Enterprise Agency,
States Arcade,
Market Street,
St Peter Port,
Guernsey,
Channel Islands
Tel 0481 710043

Honiton
East Devon Small Industries Group,
115 Border Road,
Health Park,
Honiton EX14 8BT
Tel 0404 41806

Jersey Business Venture,
Chamber of Commerce Building,
19 Royal Square,
St Helier,
Jersey,
Channel Islands
Tel 0534 24536

Launceston
North & East Cornwall Trust (Enterprise TAMAR),
The National School,
St Thomas Road,
Launceston PL15 8BU
Tel 0566 5632

Newton Abbot
Teignbridge Enterprise Agency,
Greenhills,
Greenhill Way,
Kingsteignton,
Newton Abbot
Tel 0626 63189 or 4606

Plymouth
Enterprise Plymouth Ltd,
Somerset Place,
Stoke,
Plymouth PL3 4BB
Tel 0752 569211

Poole
Dorset Enterprise,
1 Britannia Road,
Parkstone,
Poole,
Dorset BH14 8AZ
Tel 0202 748333

St Austell
Restormel Local Enterprise Trust Ltd,
Lower Penarwyn,
St Blazey,
Par,
Nr St Austell
Tel 072 681 3079

Swanage
Purbeck Small Industries Group,
4 Streche Road,
Swanage,
Dorset BH19 1NF
Tel 0929 425627

Swindon Enterprise Trust,
54 Victoria Road,
Swindon
Tel 0793 487793

Tiverton
Mid Devon Enterprise Agency,
The Factory,
Leat Street,
Tiverton EX16 5LL
Tel 0884 255629

Totnes
South Hams Agency for Rural Enterprise,
4a Leechwell Street,
Totnes,
Devon TQ9 5SX
Tel 0803 864200

Trowbridge
West Wiltshire Enterprise,
Council Offices,
Bradley Road,
Trowbridge,
Wiltshire BA14 0RD
Tel 02214 63111 (ext 218)

Weston-Super-Mare
Woodspring Branch of BRAVE,
Argotill Estates,
Oldmixon Crescent,
(Off Winterstoke Road),
Weston-Super-Mare BS24 9BA
Tel 0934 418118

Yeovil
The Enterprise Agency,
South Somerset and West Dorset,
St Johns House,
Church Path,
Yeovil,
Somerset BA20 1HE
Tel 0935 79813

London

Battersea
Wandsworth Business Resource Service,
Park House,
140 Battersea Park Road,
London SW11 4NB
Tel 01-720 7053

Brentford
Enterprise Hounslow Ltd,
13 Boston Manor Road,
Brentford TW8 9DT
Tel 01-847 3269

Brixton
Lambeth Business Advisory Service,
Courtenay House,
9–15 New Park Road,
London SW2 4DU
Tel 01-674 9844

Bromley Enterprise Agency Trust,
7 Palace Grove,
Bromley BR1 3HA
Tel 01-290 6568

Camden Enterprise Ltd,
57 Pratt Street,
London NW1 0DP
Tel 01-482 2128

City
London Enterprise Agency (LENTA),
4 Snow Hill,
London EC1A 2DL
Tel 01-236 3000

Croydon Business Venture Ltd,
26 Barclay Road,
Croydon CR0 1JN
Tel 01-681 8339

Deptford Enterprise Agency,
146 Deptford High Street,
London SE8 3PQ
Tel 01-692 9204

East Ham
Newham Business Advice and Consultancy Service (BACS),
London Borough of Newham,
The Town Hall,
Barking Road,
London E6 2RP
Tel 01-552 5324

Edmonton
Enfield Enterprise Agency,
2–3 Knights Chambers,
32 South Mall,
Edmonton Green,
London N9 0TL
Tel 01-807 5333

Finsbury Park
North London Business Development Agency,
35–37 Blackstock Road,
London N4
Tel 01-359 7405/6/7

Hackney Business Venture,
219 Mare Street,
London E8 3DQ
Tel 01-986 0529

Hackney – Shoreditch
The London Fashion Centre Ltd,
46 Great Eastern Street,
London E2A 3LE
Tel 01-729 0962

Hammersmith & Fulham Business Resources Ltd,
PO Box 51,
Hammersmith Town Hall,
King Street,
London W6 9JU
Tel 01-741 7248

Harrow Enterprise Agency,
2 Courtfield Avenue,
Harrow HA1 2LW
Tel 01-427 6188

Islington – Holloway
Manor Gardens Enterprise Centre,
10–18 Manor Gardens,
London N7
01-272 8944

Morden
Merton Enterprise Agency Ltd,
12th Floor,
Crown House,
London Road,
Morden,
Surrey SM4 5DX
Tel 01-545 3067

Paddington
Westminster Enterprise Agency Ltd,
Beauchamp Lodge,
2 Warwick Crescent,
Harrow Road,
London W2 6NE
Tel 01-286 1740

Romford
North East Thames Business Advisory Centre,
Marshalls Chambers,
80A South Street,
Romford,
Essex RM1 1RP
Tel 0708 66438

Ruislip
Hillingdon Enterprise Agency Ltd,
170a High Street,
Ruislip,
Middlesex HA4 8LJ
Tel 08956 39789

Tower Hamlets Centre for Small Businesses Ltd,
99 Leman Street,
London E1 8EY
Tel 01-481 0512

Twickenham
Richmond upon Thames Enterprise Agency Ltd,
56–58 York Street,
Twickenham,
Middlesex TW1 3LT
Tel 01-891 3742

Walthamstow
Waltham Forest Enterprise Agency Ltd,
125A Hoe Street,
London E17 4RX
Tel 01-521 3316

Wembley
Brent Business Venture Ltd,
12 Park Lane (off High Road),
Wembley,
Middlesex HA9 7RP
Tel 01-903 7300/7329

Northern Ireland

Belfast
ARC – Northern Ireland,
3 Botanic Avenue,
Belfast BT7 1JG
Tel 0232 234504, 231730

Carrickfergus
Enterprise Carrickfergus Ltd,
75 Belfast Road,
Carrickfergus BT38 8PH
Tel 09603 69528

Larne Economic Development Company,
3–5 Prince's Gardens,
Larne BT40 1RQ
Tel 0574 70742

Newry & Mourne Co-operative Society Ltd,
5 Downshire Place,
Newry
Tel 0693 67011

Wales

Bargoed
Economic Development Partnership of the Rhymney Valley,
Enterprise Centre,
Bowen Industrial Estate,
Aberbargoed,
Bargoed,
Mid Glamorgan CF8 9EP
Tel 0443 821222

Bridgend
Ogwr Partnership Trust,
Enterprise House,
Tondu Training Centre,
Tondu,
Bridgend,
Mid Glamorgan
Tel 0656 724414

Cardiff & Vale Enterprise,
5 Mount Stuart Square,
Cardiff CF1 6EE
Tel 0222 494411

Deeside Enterprise Trust Ltd,
Park House,
Deeside Industrial Park,
Deeside,
Clwyd CH5 2NZ
Tel 0244 815262

Haverfordwest
Pembrokeshire Business Initiative,
Lombard Chambers,
14 High Street,
Haverfordwest,
Dyfed SA61 2LD
Tel 0437 67655

Holywell
Delyn Business Partnership Ltd,
Greenfield Business Park,
Bagillt Road,
Holywell,
Clwyd CH8 7HN
Tel 0352 711747

Llandrindod Wells
Powys Self Help Ltd,
The Old Town Hall,
Temple Street,
Llandrindod Wells,
Powys LD1 5DL
Tel 0597 4576

Llanelli Enterprise Company,
100 Trostre Road,
Llanelli,
Dyfed SA15 2EA
Tel 0554 772122

Merthyr/Aberdare Development
Enterprise (MADE),
Enterprise Centre,
Pentrebach,
Mid Glamorgan CF48 4DR
Tel 0443 692233

Mold
Clwydfro Enterprise Agency,
Shire Hall,
Mold,
Clwyd CH7 6NH
Tel 0352 2121

Neath
The Neath Development Partnership,
7 Water Street,
Neath,
West Glamorgan SA11 3EP
Tel 0639 5411

Newport Enterprise Agency,
Enterprise Way,
Newport,
Gwent NP9 2AQ
Tel 0633 54041

Swansea
West Glamorgan Enterprise Trust Ltd,
12A St Mary's Square,
Swansea,
West Glamorgan SA1 3LP
Tel 0792 475345

Scotland

Aberdeen Enterprise Trust,
Aberdeen Business Centre,
Willowbank House,
Willowbank Road,
Aberdeen AB1 2YG
Tel 0224 582599

Airdrie
Monklands Enterprise Trust,
Unit Z,
17 Upper Mill Street,
Industrial Estate,
Airdrie ML6 6JJ
Tel 02364 69255

Alloa & Clackmannan Enterprise Trust
(ACE),
70 Drysdale Street,
Alloa FK10 1JA
Tel 0259 217171

Arbroath Venture Trust,
115 High Street,
Arbroath DD11 1DP
Tel 0241 70563

Ardrossan-Saltcoats-Stevenston
Enterprise Trust (ASSET),
21 Green Street,
Saltcoats,
Ayrshire KA21 5HQ
Tel 0294 602515

Ayr Locality Enterprise Resource Trust (ALERT),
88 Green Street,
Ayr KA8 8BG
Tel 0292 264181

Bathgate Area Support for Enterprise (BASE),
19 North Bridge Street,
Bathgate EH48 4PJ
Tel 0506 634024

Cumbernauld & Kilsyth Enterprise Trust Ltd,
5 South Muirhead Road,
Cumbernauld G67 1AJ
Tel 0236 739394

Cumnock & Doon Enterprise Trust (CADET),
46 Townhead Street,
Cumnock,
Ayrshire KA18 1LD
Tel 0290 21159

Dalkeith
Midlothian Campaign Ltd,
Enterprise Trust,
115 High Street,
Dalkeith,
Midlothian EH22 1AX
Tel 031-660 5849

Dumbarton District Enterprise Trust,
2/2 Vale of Leven Industrial Estate,
Dumbarton G82 3PD
Tel 0389 50005

Dumfries
The Enterprise Trust for Nithsdale Annandale/Eskdale and the Stewartry,
Heathhall,
Dumfries DG1 1TZ
Tel 0387 56229

Dundee Industrial Association,
Blackness Trading Precinct,
West Henderson's Wynd,
Dundee DD1 5BY
Tel 0382 26001

East Kilbride Business Centre,
PO Box 1,
10th Floor,
Plaza Tower,
Town Centre,
East Kilbride G74 1LU
Tel 03552 38456

Edinburgh Venture Enterprise Trust (EVENT),
2 Canning Street Lane,
Edinburgh EH3 8ER
Tel 031-229 8928

Leith Enterprise Trust,
25 Maritime Street,
Leith,
Edinburgh EH6 5PW
Tel 031-553 5566

Elgin
Moray Enterprise Trust,
9 North Guildry Street,
Elgin IV30 9JR
Tel 0343 49644

Falkirk Enterprise Action Trust (FEAT),
Suite A,
Marchmont Avenue,
Polmont,
Falkirk FK2 0NZ
Tel 0324 716713

Fraserburgh Ltd,
51 Mid Street,
Fraserburgh AB4 5EP
Tel 0346 27764

Glasgow Opportunities (GO),
7 West George Street,
Glasgow G2 1EQ
Tel 041-221 0955

Glasgow
Greater Easterhouse Partnership,
16 Strandwick Street,
Easterhouse,
Glasgow G34 9BP
Tel 041-771 5591

Glenrothes Enterprise Trust,
North House,
North Street,
Glenrothes,
Fife KY7 5NA
Tel 0592 757903

Greenock
Inverclyde Enterprise Trust,
Inverclyde Initiative Office,
64–66 West Blackhall Street,
Greenock PA15 1XG
Tel 0475 86240

Kilbirnie
Garnock Valley Development Executive,
44 Main Street,
Kilbirnie,
Ayrshire KA25 7BY
Tel 0505 685455

Kilmarnock Venture Enterprise Trust,
30 The Foregate,
Kilmarnock KA1 1JH
Tel 0563 44602

Kirkintilloch
Strathkelvin Enterprise Trust,
10 Rochdale Place,
Kirkintilloch G66 1HZ
Tel 041-777 7171

Levenmouth Enterprise Trust,
Hawkslaw Development (Levan) Ltd,
Riverside Road,
Leven,
Fife KY8 4LT
Tel 0333 27905

Motherwell Enterprise Trust (MET),
28 Brandon Parade,
Motherwell,
Lanarkshire ML1 1UJ
Tel 0698 69333

Lanarkshire Industrial Field Executive (LIFE),
Old Town Hall,
1–11 High Road,
Motherwell ML1 3HU
Tel 0698 66622

Newton Stewart
Wigtown Rural Development Company,
Royal Bank Building,
44 Victoria Street,
Newton Stewart DG8 6BT
Tel 0671 3434

Paisley and Renfrew Enterprise Trust,
5 Sandyford Road,
Paisley PA3 4HW
Tel 041-889 0010

Pitlochry
Highland Perthshire Development Company Ltd,
First Floor,
Bank House,
82 Atholl Road,
Pitlochry,
Perthshire PH16 5BL
Tel 0796 2697

Stirling Enterprise Park (STEP),
John Player Building,
Stirling FK7 7RP
Tel 0786 63416

CHAPTER 2

Short-term Finance

The cheapest money you will ever be able to borrow is your own! So always ensure that there is no spare cash washing around in your own business, which could be used for your own advantage rather than that of your customers or suppliers, before going to a bank or other financial institution to take out a loan where you will be paying terms which may be onerous for using someone else's money.

Cash management is vital, and if a company takes advantage of all the incentives which a supplier may offer in terms of discounts for prompt payment, and ensures that its own customers meet the terms of credit which are offered, then it may be possible to avoid the need for much costly short-term finance. A company in control of its cash flow is in control of its life. This is the next best thing to an infallible rule.

Remember that once you have made a sale, and have delivered the goods or services contracted for, then the money received in payment is yours. If you delay taking steps to ensure that that money is put into your bank account at the time it is paid to you, then you are making an interest-free loan to the customer who is paying the money while paying interest yourself on the funds involved.

Cash Flow

There are perhaps four main elements in controlling cash: debtors, creditors, stock and costs. To consider the first three, it is possible to achieve rapid improvements in cash flow by ensuring that debtors pay more promptly, that full benefit of the credit terms offered by suppliers is taken, and that stocks of raw materials, work in progress, and finished goods, are cut to the minimum required to provide an efficient service.

There are a number of useful ratios that can be worked out that are of limited value on their own. But when used to compare previous performance in your own company with others in a similar line of business they can indicate trends which, if not dealt with quickly, could lead to problems.

For example, if the ratio of credit taken from suppliers gets shorter and the ratio of credit given to customers increases, there could be the problem of running out of cash between the time you pay your suppliers and the time your customers pay you, even though actual sales may be booming. These ratios need to be checked on a regular basis (eg monthly) for action to be taken in time. To work out the ratio of credit taken, you need to multiply the sums owed by 52, and then divide by the amount of yearly purchases:

$$\frac{\text{Creditors} \times 52}{\text{Yearly total of purchases}} = \text{Number of weeks credit taken}$$

To work out the ratio of credit given, multiply the sums owed by debtors by 52 and then divide by yearly sales.

$$\frac{\text{Debtors} \times 52}{\text{Yearly total of sales}} = \text{Number of weeks credit given}$$

These can be worked out in days or months as well, depending on the detail required.

To check on stock turnover, multiply the value of stock by 52 and divide by sales, after first deducting gross profit from that figure.

$$\frac{\text{Stock} \times 52}{\text{Sales minus gross profit}} = \text{Number of weeks taken to turn over stock}$$

There are any number of ratios which can be worked out to cast light on various aspects of the business, but if you are a small businessman who cannot hand over to a finance department the job of producing them, it will probably be sufficient for you to monitor your cash flow, together with the ratios described above. By using the equations over a period of time it will soon become obvious whether you are tending to leave your debts outstanding for too long, or whether your creditors are keeping you on a tight rein. It is then up to you to manipulate the trends so that they benefit you instead of your creditors.

Debtors

If a company can gather in its debts quickly it can either use the funds to reduce its own borrowings, and so cut down interest costs, or it can re-invest the cash in short-term interest bearing deposits to produce a quick return. The first step is to send out invoices as soon as goods are supplied, rather than waiting until the end of the month, as this delay gives the customer the chance to take extra days of credit over and above those stated in your terms of business. It is surprising how many companies are efficient in executing and delivering orders, and then fall down on the paperwork of invoicing and collecting debts due.

In general, invoices can be paid any time between 50 and 60 days after their date, even though the aim of most companies is that they should be paid within 30 days. Invoices should be simple to understand and should contain all the necessary information, such as quantities, order numbers, descriptions of goods. Otherwise the customer will have an excuse to delay payment by asking for clarification. A monthly statement to customers should show all invoices outstanding, even those not actually due at that point, so that the customer has a reminder of his due and future debts.

Decide on the period you are going to allow after the due date before sending out a polite reminder, say seven to 10 days. You will already have set up a system for signposting when an invoice reaches the due date without being paid, such as filing copies of invoices sent out 30 days ahead, and then checking the file day by day. It is essential to set up a routine and keep to it. If, during the days of grace allowed for postal delays and so on, a monthly statement has to be issued, do not forget to note on it that it contains items for which payment is overdue – just to jog the customer's memory.

Immediately the days of grace are up, first make a telephone call. Check that there are no queries on the invoice just in case a dispute over one item is holding up payment of the whole. During the call, establish a definite date by which you can expect payment.

It is always worth the time spent finding out the name of the right person to speak or write to. Immediately after making the first telephone call, send a written reminder, confirming matters discussed in the call and repeating the payment date. By this time, some 40 days will have elapsed since the invoice was sent to the customer and you will have to decide how much longer you are going to allow if the cheque still fails to arrive. If the cheque is not received by the new agreed date, you will either have to send a final reminder, together with a warning that collection will be passed to an agency, or put the matter directly into the hands of a collection agency. Firmness will always pay off, and if there are customers who take offence, you will probably be better off without them, anyway.

It is tempting to offer discounts to prompt payers, say, a reduction of 2 per cent on the price if payment is made within 14 days. This can raise more problems than it is worth, as some customers will take the discount even though they are not entitled to it and attempts to get that money back can result in loss of good will; you also have to consider the administrative cost of ensuring that only those entitled to discounts actually get them.

Finally, once a cheque has arrived, it is no use wasting all the effort involved in obtaining it by hanging on to it for a few days before paying it into the bank. *Always* pay cheques into the company's bank account as soon as possible after they arrive. Where large amounts of money are involved, it may be worth investigating whether there is any advantage in paying the additional cost of special cheque clearance.

Creditors

Having dealt efficiently with your own debtors, remember that you are a debtor to your own suppliers and that it is in your interest, short of indulging in sharp practice, to take advantage of what is available. There is no point in paying a bill before you have to; if creditors are paid immediately you receive their invoices, you are depriving yourself of the opportunity of making productive use of your money during the 30-day period for which they are prepared to give you credit. So bills should be paid only when they become due. If a supplier is offering a discount for early payment work out (or get your accountant to do so) the relative advantages of taking the discount and making use of the money yourself. Basically, whether a discount is worth taking depends on whether the effective interest rate is more than that which the company would have to pay on its own borrowings. Discounts are not necessarily all that they appear to be.

If a company finds itself, as it will at various times during the year, with more cash in hand than it needs for its immediate requirements, then opportunities for short-term investment should be examined in conjunction with the bank manager or accountant. Only investments which can be converted back into cash very quickly should be considered.

Stock Control

The third major factor which can influence needs for short-term finance is stock control, and this is one where an impact can be made relatively quickly. During the recent recession, most firms have needed to review in some detail the levels of stock they hold, an exercise which might result in maintaining lower stock levels even when business is flourishing again.

In the past there was a tendency to hold too much stock, because of the fear of being caught short when an unexpected boost in demand occurred. Recent levels of inflation and high interest rates have caused businessmen to think hard about this policy, because overstocking means too much cash tied up; stocks cost money to maintain because they need to be stored in expensive warehouses, they have to be insured against hazards such as fire and theft, and they are in danger of deteriorating or becoming obsolete as time passes. Furthermore, interest has to be paid on the money borrowed to buy or manufacture them. Looked at another way, potential interest is being lost on the money tied up in their cash value.

It is therefore necessary to review all stocks held (especially where particular kinds of stock represent a large proportion of the value of the whole stock) and decide whether changes can be made in the levels held. This can be done by increasing sales, if the opportunity to do so is there, or by cutting orders for replacement of new stock. If the stock turnover ratio described earlier has fallen it may be possible to reduce the levels of stocks held of either raw materials or finished goods; here, decisions will need to be made on whether, for instance, a higher risk of being caught short of stock is acceptable. If the goods sold are subject to seasonal variations in sales then it may be possible.

Examine the point at which you normally re-order stock and see if it is possible to go a little closer to the margin (ie, ordering a little less) before re-ordering, making sure there is enough to cover emergencies and reasonable delays in delivery.

When you re-order, make sure you relate orders to potential needs, and examine the relative values of discounts for bulk orders as compared with the need to tie up money in those stocks over a longer period. The need for re-ordering must also be considered in relation to sales, because if sales of a particular line of goods are declining there is no point in continuing to re-order the same quantity of raw materials as in the past; equally, if a line shows signs of moving, make sure that you are not deprived of the benefits by being caught short of the stock needed to make it.

Careful and realistic sales forecasts are of great importance in making decisions on stock levels, because once there is an assessment of what can be sold it can be worked back into needs for stock of finished goods, and ultimately to stock of raw materials for the production process.

Never imagine that these are exercises which only have to be carried out once; control means regular monitoring and reassessment in the light of constantly changing circumstances. Awareness of where the company is at and where it should be going is the key to flexibility of response to changes, survival and, it is to be hoped, success.

It is only when these exercises have been carried through that a businessman knows what kind of finance, if any, he needs from those whose business it is to lend money at a profit - at the expense of his profits.

Overdrafts

The most common form of short-term finance in use in business is the overdraft and it is also generally the least costly type of finance from sources outside a company, as interest is charged only on the outstanding debit balance of the bank account each day. Most companies, in fact, operate on a permanent overdraft, a major attraction being the flexibility of this facility. There is a tendency for many firms to use overdrafts for capital spending which should really be financed by medium- or long-term funds, and this increases companies' vulnerability; the wild swings in monetary policy which have been a feature of Government policy over a long period can cause havoc to the small, under-capitalised firm if it is using its overdraft in the wrong way.

Overdrafts are subject to varying interest rates, usually between 2 and 4 per cent above bank base rate, and are technically repayable on demand. They are usually agreed with the bank manager for a period of 12 months, a review of needs and what the overdraft is being used for being carried out at the time of renewal. They are intended for working capital and not generally for financing the purchase of plant and machinery.

The owner of a small manufacturing firm who wants to buy equipment and also finance the increase in stocks and debtors which will arise from the increased production may decide that he needs £60,000 to do this. In simple terms the cheapest way to finance the whole operation would be to draw on his overdraft facilities, but in fact this would not be the right course to take.

First, it is necessary to clarify what the funds are needed for. There is the financing of fixed assets, such as equipment, and the financing of the growth in current assets (the stocks and debtors). The buying of the equipment is better funded by a short- to medium-term loan of, say, five years, linking the assets to their ability to generate extra earnings for the firm, and remembering that the equipment bought may have an economic life of about seven years. Assuming that the equipment costs £30,000, this could be financed through one of the short-term loan schemes offered by banks and described later in this chapter.

The remaining £30,000 needed for working capital to cover the cost of buying stocks and bridging the gap between making a sale and the customer actually paying for the goods, is where the overdraft comes in. The company can draw on the facility when it is needed, and interest will be paid only on the money used, day to day. Separately, the assets themselves will be paid for under a formalised short-term loan repayment plan with a firm beginning and end, the amount which has to be found every month being known, and the company is less vulnerable to changes in Government monetary policy and its financial base has greater stability.

Remember, however, that having an overdraft is not a way of evading demands for security which may be made with other forms of finance. Such borrowing may, though not necessarily, have to be backed by some form of security, such as property deeds, a life assurance policy, shares, or a personal guarantee.

As already noted, an overdraft facility can be affected by the imposition of official credit control, so if a large part of the facility has been used to buy machinery it may not be possible to increase it in order to cope with the additional spending which arises from its improved production capacity. It is no good being able to produce more at a faster rate if you cannot afford the raw materials, wages or telephone bills while waiting for debtors to pay up. A full order book is no use without the cash to finance it. Once again it is a matter of proper cash management; if you organise your cash effectively you minimise the chances of problems arising.

There are two other useful forms of short-term finance: factoring and invoice discounting, both of which are described in detail in Chapter 7.

Bridging Loans

These are loan accounts for specific periods for which the source of repayment is known; there is usually no need for regular reductions; the full sum is usually repaid in its entirety when due. In business, bridging loans are most frequently used for covering the gap between an exchange of contracts and the date of completion in a property sale or purchase. The interest rate charged is usually slightly higher than on an overdraft, perhaps 3 to 5 per cent above base rate, and an arrangement fee may be charged by the lending institution.

Bills of Exchange

Bills of exchange are a source of short-term money which are mostly used in export and import trade but there is no reason why they cannot be used in domestic business as well.

A bill of exchange is in effect a form of post-dated cheque which can be sold at a discount for cash. This enables the businessman selling the goods to turn his sale into cash very quickly after sending the goods on their way, while there are benefits for the buyer in that he does not have to pay for the goods until they are delivered, or even until they have been marketed, depending on the payment date of the bill. This method can be useful even if the company providing the goods does not want to discount the bill (that is, sell it to a third party for slightly less than its face value for cash) because as long as the customer has accepted the bill he is tied down to the date of payment specified on it.

The consequences for the customer who fails to pay on the due date are laid out in the Bills of Exchange Act 1882, because a bill of exchange is a legal document. A bill can be used as security for an advance from a bank or other lending institution, too, making it a flexible instrument, provided you can persuade the customer to agree to it in the first place. Bill finance is competitive with overdrafts and can sometimes be cheaper; discount rates are fixed at the outset and are not subject to later movements in interest rates which enables a businessman to make a precise calculation of the cost of a sale. Bill finance also releases part of his overdraft for other uses. It is never wise to rely too much on bill finance (or overdrafts) for anything other than short- to medium-term requirements.

Bills cover periods ranging from 60 to 180 days and usually for somewhere in between, such as 90 days, so if you can get your customer to pay in 30 to 50 days, they are of limited value. Banks can give advice on drawing up a bill and there are specialists in the field, called discount houses.

There are two types of bills of exchange, *trade bills* and *bank bills*. A seller of goods draws up a trade bill, which is accepted by the buyer; it is payable on a specific date for the goods which have been bought. The trader's own bank or a discount house will accept the bill at a discount, the rate depending usually on the creditworthiness of the seller and buyer. A better or 'finer' rate of discount can be obtained if a credit insurance company guarantees the bill. Trade bills are not quite as negotiable as bank bills, and rates are not quite as good. Also, if for example, there are a large number of bills either issued by you or by your customer or in the particular types of goods involved circulating in the discount market, it may affect the speed at which you can turn new bills into cash.

The bank bill largely overcomes this problem but naturally costs a little more; on the other hand the cost of opening what is known as an *acceptance credit* with a bank is balanced by the greater saleability of the bill and the better rate available on it. Opening an acceptance credit involves arranging the payment or acceptance of bills of exchange with a bank. When a bill is presented, the bank on which it is drawn puts its name on the bill, promising to pay on the due date. The bank takes a commission for providing this acceptance facility. There are specialist *acceptance houses* which offer this facility too and the choice of a bank or an acceptance house needs to be discussed with the firm's financial adviser. An acceptance facility does not necessarily need to be for one transaction alone; it can be and usually is used for financing a range of different transactions. The name of the bank or accepting house on the bill acts as a guarantee that the bill will be paid when it is due, and means that it is more acceptable in the discount market when it is offered.

A list of accepting houses is given on pp 71–2 and the clearing banks offering these facilities include all the major high street banks. Foreign banks operating in the United Kingdom are usually more interested in the financing of foreign trade with their own countries, and a list of these is given on pp 165–8.

Short-term Loans

Short-term loans are generally considered to be those taken for periods of up to three years for specific purposes, such as buying vehicles, fixtures, costly tools, or even re-financing part of an overdraft. They are what the banks describe as 'hard core' overdrafts, where there is a need for more formal arrangements. Some of the special short-term schemes offered by banks are for slightly longer periods and can run up to five years. All the banks have been making considerable efforts in this area for smaller firms in recent years and now have schemes designed for most requirements.

The advantage for the borrower is that the asset bought is paid for over the period of its life, the loan is usually less costly than hire purchase or other forms of finance, and the regular plan of repayments means that the businessman can plan his cash flow more accurately. On the other hand, a rapidly growing company may find that the extra expense of hire purchase or leasing is worthwhile, enabling it to reserve the full bank facilities for working capital requirements. Just how the package should be drawn up is a matter for the individual firm in consultation with its advisers. Rates of interest on short-term loans can sometimes be fixed, but are probably more likely to vary according to base rate, usually being about 3 to 5 per cent above base rate compared with 2 to 4 per cent for an overdraft.

The Business Development Loan plan offered by National Westminster can be for a minimum of £2,000 and a maximum of £250,000 for a period of one to 20 years so it can in fact also be considered as a medium- or long-term loan. National Westminster is currently lending £1.8 billion to 150,000 small businesses in Business Development Loans, which makes it the biggest scheme open to the smaller firm, and also probably the oldest. The borrowing term is based on an appraisal of the profit flow and the expected life of the assets bought with the loan. Interest is added to the initial amount of the loan and the total amount is repaid in equal monthly instalments over the period of the loan. The bank also charges an arrangement fee which is paid at the start; at present this is 1 per cent for periods from one to five years and 1.5 per cent for longer-term loans. There is usually a difference of 1 per cent flat between the amount of interest paid on a secured loan and on one which is unsecured, the unsecured being more expensive. As a Business Development Loan is repaid on a regular reducing basis, this means that the effective rate of interest on a secured loan would be 15.9 per cent if the flat rate were 9 per cent and on an unsecured loan 17.5 per cent if the flat rate were 10 per cent, over a 10-year term. These rates can change from time to time and current rates can be obtained from bank branches. Interest rates on loans from six to 10 years are usually 0.5 per cent above the flat rates for one- to five-year loans. The borrower is normally required to have a life policy covering the amount of the loan.

Outside of this particular scheme, NatWest also provides two- to three-year loans to meet a specific purpose and individual arrangements can be made to suit cash flow patterns.

The interest rate depends on the nature and purpose of the borrowing and the assessment of the risk involved; it will be a percentage over base rate, fluctuating with changes in base rate. Again, an arrangement fee is usually payable. Interest is charged on the balance outstanding at any one time and is payable at quarterly intervals. Drawings on the loan account may have to be backed by documentary evidence, such as the provision of architects' certificates supporting stage payments to be made where a loan is taken to finance a building project.

Midland Bank has a particular package which it aims at new and young businesses called Credo, which because it requires recipients to undertake a course of management training enables the bank to offer loans at a rate of 0.5 per cent below their standard small business loan interest rate. Businesses taking part in the Credo plan also qualify for an interest-free overdraft of up to £1,000 for three months. A management fee is payable for setting up the overdraft but not the loan. The bank's standard small business loans are available in sums of up to £15,000 and the period is geared to the expected working life of the asset being bought but will be not less than six months and not more than 10 years. The rate of interest is fixed when the loan is agreed and remains the same throughout the period of the loan.

Barclays offers a fixed fee overdraft of up to £2,000 to new or existing small business customers with an anticipated annual turnover of up to £100,000. New small business customers can also apply for a business starter loan for working capital and/or asset purchases of up to £15,000 over one to five years at a fixed rate of interest, with a six-month capital and interest 'holiday' option. Lloyds Bank also has a special small business loan scheme for any business purpose in amounts of £1,000 to £15,000 at a fixed rate of interest for periods of up to five years. Among the smaller – but innovative – clearing banks the Co-operative has re-launched its business purchase loan scheme offering sums from £15,000 to £250,000 to a wide range of businesses, available for any business which can be valued as a going concern, ranging from hotels and restaurants to leisure centres and other enterprises. A customer can borrow up to 100 per cent of the bricks and mortar valuation of the property or 75 per cent of the current market value of the business, and the funds can be used for buying an existing business, buying a business property, or to expand or re-finance a business. There is also automatic access to a 'stand-by' overdraft facility of between £2,500 and £5,000, according to the size of the loan. Other banks have similar schemes of this kind.

Since it became a unified public company the TSB has been trying to say 'Yes' more often to the small business customer and has launched a fixed repayment loan scheme which offers amounts of £25,000 to £250,000 over periods of up to 20 years, though for most purposes the repayment period is up to 10 years. The bank says its terms allow the businessman to take advantage of interest rate changes in whichever direction they move. If rates fall, payments remain at the agreed level but the term of the loan shortens; but if rates rise the repayments stay the same but the term of the loan is extended, thus reducing the worry of fluctuating repayments as interest rates change. Other British banking institutions, and many of the foreign banks operating in the United Kingdom, are also prepared to offer short-term funds, usually for established companies.

Financial Services

A financial service which could be useful to many companies is described by its operators as 'cash regeneration'. The service operated by Resource Evaluation Ltd (REL) is aimed at quantifying quickly the sums of cash capable of being released from the outstanding balances on a firm's sales ledger. Preliminary Assessment of the Regeneration of Cash (PARC) means that companies supply a limited amount of financial data about their debtors to Resource Evaluation on a completely confidential basis. The consultants study the figures and report back the potential cash flow improvement. No charge is made for this initial assessment, but normal time-based fees are charged if and when consultants become involved in implementing changes needed.

The company says that its experience in more than 100 companies in the United Kingdom has shown that virtually all companies are able to reduce their debtors by 10 per cent and some by amounts of up to 50 per cent. REL gives as an example brokers who are losing millions of pounds of potential investment income by allowing clients to ignore terms of payment of premium income and letting them pay four to six months late. Studies by the company showed that the average broker could substantially improve net profitability (without trying to increase market shares) by collecting premium balances due from clients much more quickly.

The experience of REL, specialist financial consultants to Lloyds' brokers, showed that management attention was usually intensified only when balances became three or more months overdue.

The objective of the exercise is to get more of a company's good customers to pay within their terms of trade. Once again it comes down to effective cash management.

Useful Addresses

Branches of clearing banks are the first point of approach for overdrafts, bills of exchange, and short-term loans. Additionally, there are accepting houses for bills of exchange.

Members of the Accepting Houses Committee

They also offer a full range of merchant banking services.

Arbuthnot Latham & Co Ltd,
131 Finsbury Pavement,
Moorgate,
London EC2A 1AY
Tel 01-280 8400

Baring Brothers & Company,
8 Bishopsgate,
London EC2N 4AE
Tel 01-283 8833

Brown Shipley & Company,
Founders Court,
Lothbury,
London EC2R 7HE
Tel 01-606 9833

Charterhouse Japhet Ltd,
1 Paternoster Row,
London EC4M 7DH
Tel 01-248 4000

Robert Fleming & Company,
25 Copthall Avenue,
London EC2R 7DR
Tel 01-638 5858

Guinness Mahon & Company,
32 St Mary-at-Hill,
London EC3P 3AJ
Tel 01-623 9333

Hambros Bank Ltd,
41 Tower Hill,
London EC3N 4HA
Tel 01-480 5000

Hill Samuel & Company,
100 Wood Street,
London EC2P 2AJ
Tel 01-638 8011

Kleinwort Benson Ltd,
20 Fenchurch Street,
London EC3P 3DB
Tel 01-623 8000

Lazard Brothers & Company,
21 Moorfields,
London EC2P 2HT
Tel 01-588 2721

Samuel Montagu & Company,
10 Lower Thames Street,
London EC3R 6AE
Tel 01-260 9000

Morgan Grenfell & Company,
23 Great Winchester Street,
London EC2P 2AX
Tel 01-588 4545

Rea Brothers Ltd,
Aldermans House,
Aldermans Walk,
London EC2M 3XR
Tel 01-623 1155

N M Rothschild & Sons,
PO Box 185,
New Court,
St Swithin's Lane,
London EC4P 4DU
Tel 01-280 5000

J Henry Schroder Wagg & Company,
120 Cheapside,
London EC2V 6DS
Tel 01-382 6000

Singer and Friedlander Ltd,
21 New Street,
Bishopsgate,
London EC2M 4HR
Tel 01-623 3000

S G Warburg & Company,
33 King William Street,
London EC4R 9AS
Tel 01-280 2222

The following companies provide many merchant banking services but are not necessarily banks

Henry Ansbacher & Company,
Priory House,
1 Mitre Square,
London EC3A 5AN
Tel 01-283 2500

Barclays Merchant Bank,
PO Box 188,
15-16 Gracechurch Street,
London EC3V 0BA
Tel 01-623 4321

British Linen Bank,
4 Melville Street,
Edinburgh EH3 7NZ
Tel 031-226 4071

Cayzer Ltd,
2-4 St Mary Axe,
London EC3A 8BP
Tel 01-626 0931

Close Brothers Ltd,
36 Great St Helens,
London EC3A 6AP
Tel 01-283 2241

G R Dawes & Company
Neville House,
42-46 Hagley Road,
Edgbaston,
Birmingham B16 8PZ
Tel 021-454 5431

Energy, Finance and General Trust,
Dauntsey House,
Frederick's Place,
Old Jewry,
London EC2R 8HN
Tel 01-606 2167

E T Trust Ltd,
Bank House,
The Paddock,
Wilmslow Road,
Handforth,
Wilmslow,
Cheshire SK9 3HQ
Tel 0625 532535

Federated Trust Corporation,
1 Love Lane,
London EC2V 7JJ
Tel 01-806 3744

James Finlay Corporation,
Finlay House,
10-14 West Nile Street,
Glasgow G1 2PP
Tel 041-204 1321

Anthony Gibbs Holdings,
3 Frederick's Place,
Old Jewry,
London EC2R 8HD
Tel 01-588 4111

Gray Dawes Bank,
40 St Mary Axe,
London EC3A 8EU
Tel 01-283 6921

Grindlay Brandts,
23 Fenchurch Street,
London EC3P 3ED
Tel 01-626 0545

Gwent Enterprises,
PO Box 17,
24-26 Newport Road,
Cardiff CF1 1UN
Tel 0222 484484

Ionian Securities,
1 Crown Court,
Cheapside,
London EC2V 6HT
Tel 01-236 7411

Leopold Joseph & Sons,
31-45 Gresham Street,
London EC2V 7EA
Tel 01-588 2323

Manufacturers Hanover Trust,
7 Princes Street,
London EC2P 2LR
Tel 01-600 5666

Matheson & Company,
Matheson House,
142 Minories,
London EC3N 1QL
Tel 01-480 6633

J F Nash and Partners,
9 Station Road,
Kettering,
Northants NN15 7HY
Tel 0536 85921

Noble Grossart Ltd,
48 Queen Street,
Edinburgh EH2 3NR
Tel 031-226 7011

Orion Royal Bank,
1 London Wall,
London EC2Y 5JX
Tel 01-600 6222

Scandinavian Bank,
Scandinavian House,
2-6 Cannon Street,
London EC4M 6XX
Tel 01-236 6090

Standard Chartered Merchant Bank,
33-36 Gracechurch Street,
London EC3V 0AX
Tel 01-623 8711

Standard Industrial Trust,
Shelley House,
Noble Street,
London EC2V 7DL
Tel 01-628 5641

United Dominions Trust,
1 Lyonsdown Road,
New Barnet,
Hertfordshire EN5 1HU
Tel 01-440 8282

Banks and lending institutions which provide both short- and medium-term funds

AP Bank,
21 Great Winchester Street,
London EC2N 2HH
Tel 01-588 7575

Bremar Holdings,
Bremar House,
Sale Place,
London W2 1PT
Tel 01-262 5000

Commercial Bank of Wales,
114-116 St Mary Street,
Cardiff CF1 1XJ
Tel 0222 396131

Coutts Finance Company,
143 Cannon Street,
London EC4N 5BJ
Tel 01-623 9661

Robert Fraser & Partners,
28b Albemarle Street,
London W1X 3FA
Tel 01-499 7551

Grindlays Bank,
23 Fenchurch Street,
London EC3P 3ED
Tel 01-626 0545

C Hoare,
37 Fleet Street,
London EC4P 4DQ
Tel 01-353 4522

Investment Bank of Ireland,
1-3 Donegall Square South,
Belfast BT1 5LU
Tel 0232 46241

National Bank of New Zealand,
100 Pall Mall,
London SW1Y 5EL
Tel 01-930 7366

Northern Bank Development Corporation,
1-7 Bedford Street,
Belfast BT2 7LJ
Tel 0232 45277

P S Refson & Company,
13 Austin Friars,
London EC2N 2HE
Tel 01-638 3511

E S Schwab & Company,
128-140 Bishopsgate,
London EC2M 4HX
Tel 01-247 8506

Standard Chartered Bank,
10 Clements Lane,
London EC4N 7AB
Tel 01-623 7500

TCB,
Century House,
Dyke Road,
Brighton BN1 3FX
Tel 0273 23511

Ulster Investment Bank,
Bulloch House,
2 Linenhall Street,
Belfast BT2 8BA
Tel 0232 26222

Vernons Trust Corporation,
Vernons Building,
Mile End,
Liverpool L5 5AF
Tel 051-207 3181

Whiteway, Laidlaw & Company,
Ambassador House,
Brigstock Road,
Thornton Heath,
Surrey CR4 7JG
Tel 01-684 9831

Wintrust Securities Ltd,
Imperial House,
Dominion Street,
London EC2M 2SA
Tel 01-920 0331

Discount houses which provide short-term credit through bills of exchange

Alexanders Discount Company,
1 St Swithin's Lane,
London EC4N 8DN
Tel 01-626 5467

Cater Allen & Company,
1 King William Street,
London EC4N 7AU
Tel 01-623 2070

Clive Discount Company,
1 Royal Exchange Avenue,
London EC3V 3LU
Tel 01-283 1101

Gerald Quin, Cope & Company,
19-21 Moorgate,
London EC2R 6BX
Tel 01-628 2296

Gerrard and National,
32 Lombard Street,
London EC3V 9BE
Tel 01-623 9981

Gillett Brothers Discount Company,
65 Cornhill,
London EC3V 3PP
Tel 01-283 3022

Jessel, Toynbee & Company,
30 Cornhill,
London EC3V 3LH
Tel 01-623 2111

King and Shaxson,
52 Cornhill,
London EC3V 3PF
Tel 01-623 5433

Page and Gwyther,
1 Founders Court,
Lothbury,
London EC2R 7DB
Tel 01-606 5681

Seccombe, Marshall and Campion,
7 Birchin Lane,
London EC3V 9DE
Tel 01-283 5031

Smith St Aubyn & Company,
2 White Lion Court,
London EC3V 3PN
Tel 01-283 7261

Union Discount Company of London,
39 Cornhill,
London EC3V 3NU
Tel 01-623 1020

Credit Insurance Companies

Credit and Guarantee Insurance Company,
Colonial House,
Mincing Lane,
London EC3R 7PN
Tel 01-626 5846

Trade Indemnity,
12-34 Great Eastern Street,
London EC2A 3AX
Tel 01-739 4311

Financial Services

The Credit Protection Association,
CPA House,
350 King Street,
London W6 0RX
Tel 01-741 4401

Resource Evaluation Ltd,
133 Aldersgate Street,
London EC1A 4JA
Tel 01-606 1761

CHAPTER 3

Medium-term Finance

During the past decade there has been a tremendous growth in the provision of medium-term finance for business, as the traditional bank practice of lending for short periods only has been relaxed following two major reports published in the early 1970s on competition and credit control and on small firms. The range of choice for the smaller business is now wide, and is a recognition of the dominant desire of most small businessmen to raise their finance through loans, rather than part with any degree of control by selling a share stake in their companies to an outsider.

Medium-term Loans

About 40 per cent of the funds taken by manufacturing industry is now in medium-term loans, which are generally considered to be those taken for periods of three to ten years. They are usually, though not always, secured and have the advantage of not being repayable on demand as an overdraft would be, though if a borrower defaulted on the terms of the loan then the money would technically become repayable immediately. Perhaps one of the main advantages is the flexibility of the terms which can be arranged with the providers of medium-term finance.

It is possible, for example, to arrange for repayments to be scheduled in a variety of ways, even on a seasonal basis if the borrower's business is subject to seasonal variations in income, though the repayments will probably be yearly, half-yearly, quarterly, or monthly. Another variation can be the payment of interest only during the life of the loan, with capital being repaid only when the full term expires. Increasingly common is the repayment 'holiday' of one or two years before repayments start.

Interest rates are often linked to the London Inter-Bank Offered Rate (LIBOR), varying with the size and duration of the loan, or they can be fixed at the start, and will usually be in a range of 3 to 5 per cent above bank base rate. Some banks also charge an arrangement fee of around 1 per cent of the amount of the loan. Rates will usually tend to be a little higher than on shorter-term loans.

Medium-term loans are suitable for virtually every type of business and can be used for buying assets which have a significant life cycle, in which case there will be a link with the length of time over which the loan is taken. They can be used for re-financing overdraft facilities on a more disciplined basis, or buying or extending premises, or maybe for general working capital. In this way they give stability to the balance sheet by indicating that a company's finances are not wholly at the mercy of the credit policies being followed by the Government of the time. And because of the disciplined programme of repayments the loans allow the businessman to plan his cash flow with a degree of confidence. A repayment 'holiday' (or to give it its correct name, a *moratorium*) can be very useful here, for example, where the purchase of new premises or machinery will cause disruption to production or affect sales to the point where profits decline for a period during re-organisation. The repayments begin when the business has settled down again into its natural rhythm.

Medium-term loans are in fact often part of a package of other facilities, such as overdrafts or short-term finance, and are provided largely by the clearing banks, but also by other banks and financial institutions.

The more informal, less structured type of medium-term loan of, say, £25,000 to £50,000, will depend on the credit status, size and profitability of the company concerned, and can be influenced by the funds which the firm or its directors have on deposit at the bank. The local branch manager will arrange the loan and will expect to be provided with balance sheet details and cash flow and profit projections over the period of the loan. The bank will usually take a first charge on assets, such as the factory building, as security in case the project or company runs into difficulties.

The next step in medium-term credit will be the formal five- to seven-year variety, generally attached to major capital spending and often involving fairly substantial sums of money. The customer in this case, who will probably be the more mature small firm (on the verge of qualifying for the description of medium-sized), will have to provide much more detailed information in terms of potential profitablity and cash flow implications. Informal guarantees from the directors would not be sufficient security on their own, and a fixed charge or even a debenture over a substantial asset will be required. (A *debenture* is a secured, transferable loan stock; security is on specific fixed assets, such as a factory building, or on a floating charge on the assets of the business as a whole.) The holder of a debenture has top priority for payment if the firm fails, and so the issue of a debenture usually means that a more favourable interest rate can be negotiated. Debentures are not as commonly used at present as they were in the past.

The terms of the loan will be set out in a facility letter from the bank, laying down gearing restrictions (that is, limits on total borrowing) and requiring that after-tax profits cover the interest charges by a specified amount, such as two-and-a-half or three times; it will also require regular updating of current cash flow forecasts, and those which show the cash position over the whole term of the loan.

Midland Bank Business Development Loan

Most smaller business, however, will probably find themselves using, or being steered towards, the various special schemes set up by the banks in recent years. Midland Bank's business development loan is a flexible method of financing the purchase of higher value fixed assets. Starting at £15,000 these medium- to long-term loans offer a choice of repayment terms: you can choose either a fixed rate of interest agreed at the start or you can elect to link the rate of interest to base rate. There is an option to switch from one scheme to the other during the life of the loan. It should also be remembered that all banks offer standard term loans, usually available for larger sums, which are negotiated on an individual basis with the applicant, depending on requirements.

Like other banks, Midland has loan schemes for professional practices, such as solicitors and accountants, providing secured or unsecured term lending for amounts of £10,000 upwards for periods of up to 10 years to assist with working capital or other capital requirements, such as fitting and equipping an office. It also has a loan scheme for medical practitioners and dental surgeons for term finance of between £10,000 and £500,000 over periods of up to 20 years to assist with acquiring or extending surgery premises, or for buying a share in such premises.

Lloyds Bank Business Loan

Lloyds Bank offers general medium-term lending facilities to industry and commerce and the professions but in addition provides for the independent business a special scheme called the Business Loan, which incorporates a unique interest rate conversion option. The new scheme enables customers to borrow from £15,000 to £1 million for plant and machinery, premises and extensions, working capital, and for research and development. Repayments can be made on a flexible basis over a period related to the life of the asset. In appropriate cases loans may be for up to 30 years so the scheme is suitable for short-, medium- and long-term requirements. The bank has lent £1 billion to 50,000 businesses under this scheme.

An important feature of the Business Loan scheme is the innovatory interest rate conversion option. This allows long-term borrowers to switch every five years from fixed rate to a rate linked to base rate or vice versa. They can enjoy the benefits of a fixed interest rate, knowing exactly how much a loan is going to cost over a specific period, without being locked in at that rate for an unrealistically long term when interest rates might be falling. At each five-yearly review the bank will reconsider interest rates and these will be aligned to reflect prevailing market conditions. The basis of the rate agreement will then remain firm for the subsequent five-year period. In addition to the conversion option, repayments can be arranged on a monthly or quarterly basis, with the possibility of a two-year 'holiday' on capital repayment or stepped repayments in the early years. Particularly useful for a company undertaking a major expansion or re-equipment programme is the drawdown facility. For amounts of more than £20,000 borrowed over more than five years, the loan may be taken in slices over a maximum of two years, subject to a commitment fee.

Base rate linked loans are charged at between 3 and 5 per cent over Lloyds' base rate. Fixed rates depend on the prevailing rates at the time the loan is

taken. An arrangement fee of 1 per cent of the loan is levied, subject to a maximum of £500, and all loans in excess of 10 years require security.

Lloyds has also introduced new loans for medium-sized businesses which it calls its Premier range. The Deferred Loan enables a business to raise £100,000 to £5 million without payment of interest or capital for a period of from six months to three years, with floating or fixed interest rates. It also has Premier Revolving Loan Scheme and Premier Term Loan Scheme, each with a minimum amount of £100,000 but no maximum, for periods of up to five years and 15 years respectively.

National Westminster Bank Business Development Loan

National Westminster Bank's special scheme for the smaller business is called the Business Development Loan, and was briefly described in Chapter 2. The bank has arranged more than 150,000 Business Development Loans under the scheme which began in 1971, and more than £1.8 billion is now out on loan. The bank's recent experience has been that between 3,000 and 4,000 new loans are being granted each month for total sums of around £50 million. The Business Development Loan is similar to the Farm Development Loan available to the agricultural community. (Most other banks also have lending schemes for farmers.)

Both schemes provide for loans ranging from £2,000 to £250,000 over periods of one to 20 years. Rates on unsecured loans are usually 1 per cent flat higher than for secured loans, and loans for six to ten years are 0.5 per cent flat higher than those for one to five years.

The arrangement fee for six- to ten-year loans is 1.5 per cent of the amount borrowed and for one- to five-year loans it is 1 per cent. The rates quoted are fixed for the duration of the loan, and repayments are taken on a monthly basis, including the interest element. The borrower is expected to have a life policy covering the amount of the loan; borrowers can be either businesses or professional practices, including those buying into a practice, as well as farmers. Farm Development Loans are provided for buying farms, livestock, machinery and new buildings, modernisation of old buildings, and other projects likely to improve profitability, such as drainage, fencing, liming and fertilisation.

Where a customer requires a loan of, say, £100,000, but wants to negotiate a repayment programme which can be tailored to his anticipated cash flow needs, NatWest has an alternative Fixed Rate Medium Term Lending scheme which its managers can offer.

NatWest has relaunched its personal pension loanback scheme for professional and self-employed people which provides finance for up to 30 years. They can borrow up to 2.5 times their annual earned income or 80 per cent of the underlying policy's anticipated lump sum, whichever is the lower. Loans are for five to 30 years and can be used for buying a professional practice or a capital injection into a new or established business. Interest rates are generally 3–5 per cent above base rate with an arrangement fee of 0.5 per cent.

TSB Pension Loan for Self-employed

The TSB also has a pension-linked loan scheme to help the self-employed expand their businesses. The minimum loan is £15,000 with repayment periods ranging from 5 to 35 years, and can be used for expansion, buying a business or partnership, commercial premises or equipment.

Barclays Bank Business Loan

Barclays has developed, in addition to the normal range of medium-term finance facilities, its Businessloan and Flexible Businessloan schemes. The basic Businessloan scheme is a simple way to borrow between £2,000 and £15,000 for a business. The interest rate remains fixed through the period of the loan so the borrower always knows what is needed each month. The Flexible Businessloan is complementary to term loans and provides a simple way of borrowing more than £15,000. Loans can be repaid over a period ranging from two to 20 years and are available to fund capital and working capital requirements. For the first three years the interest rate is fixed, after which both the business and the bank have the option to review the interest rate arrangements.

Barclays has a loan scheme for holders of self-employed pension plans issued through the bank's subsidiary, Barclays Life Assurance Company. It is planned to extend the loan scheme to holders of pension schemes issued by other life assurance companies, the first of these being the Legal and General Assurance Society. The aim of the scheme is to overcome the fear of being left short of finance which in the past deterred people from investing the maximum possible in pension schemes. The Barclays plan tries to overcome this by offering pension plan holders the opportunities for loan facilities on acceptable terms.

The scheme is designed mainly for self-employed professional practitioners, for whom loans are available for periods of up to 25 years with no security other than life cover. Loans can be granted for house purchase and improvement as well as business purposes. Amounts from £5,000 to a maximum of 15 times the annual pension contribution, plus a percentage of premiums paid, are available. Borrowers may pay interest only with capital repayment on retirement either from money due from the pension plan or through the sale of the business or practice. Alternatively, they may pay by regular instalments. Loans are planned to run until the pension plan matures, usually not later than the age of 65. Interest is charged either at a fixed rate or a variable rate of 2 per cent above Barclays' base rate.

Self-employed people outside the professional sector can borrow up to 10 times the annual pension premiums, plus a percentage of premiums paid up to the point at which the loan is taken.

Premiums of £5,000 must have been paid before a loan application can be made. The purposes and payment terms of loans are the same, except that loans must be fully secured, including life cover. Interest is charged at 2.5 per cent above Barclays' base rate. People applying for loans do not have to be customers of the bank. The pension plan holder does not have to sacrifice the growth potential of the retirement fund by taking advantage of the scheme.

Merchant Banks

Medium-term finance is available from a number of sources other than those so far described, such as the merchant banks listed on pp 71–2. In general, they do not provide finance from their own funds for.more than five years but obviously have sources through which longer-term needs can be met. There are few fixed minimum sums below which they are not interested but on the whole it is not generally worth approaching a merchant bank for less than £50,000 and probably substantially more than that would be a normal sum of money.

Finance Houses

Finance houses can also be a source of medium-term money, usually up to about five years, though the bulk of their business is in leasing and instalment credit, which are described in Chapter 8. Many of the finance houses are owned by the major financial institutions, including the clearing banks, but nevertheless have become a growing force in providing funds to the smaller business in recent years. One reason is that they go out and sell their wares, literally turning up on the doorsteps of small firms and asking the owners if they are in need of money.

This aggressive marketing has enabled the finance houses to make inroads into markets which the banks might normally consider their sole preserve. A further attraction for the small businessman is often the speed at which the finance house will respond provided, of course, that he has done his homework in the first place. Loans can be obtained for plant and machinery or for new factory buildings, for example; interest rates are usually higher than those which could be obtained from a bank but the disadvantage in this instance may be balanced out in other ways.

Foreign Banks

Foreign banks, as well as British banks which are not clearers, are also alternative sources of medium-term finance but they are more likely to be interested in sums of £50,000 upwards and only in proposals from established firms. They may also wish to limit their involvement to companies which are dealing in some way with their native country.

Useful Addresses

Information about medium-term finance schemes run by the banks can be obtained from branches. Addresses of merchant banks which may supply medium-term finance are listed as Members of the Accepting Houses Committee at the end of Chapter 2. Other sources are:

Members of the Finance Houses Association

Abbey National Personal Finance Ltd,
Genesis House,
310–349 Midsummer Boulevard,
Central Milton Keynes MK9 2JE
Tel 0908 691116

Allied Irish Finance Company,
Bankcentre-Britain,
Belmont Road,
Uxbridge,
Middlesex UB8 1SA
Tel 0895 72222

Associates Capital Corporation,
Associates House,
PO Box 200,
Windsor,
Berkshire SL4 1SW
Tel 0753 857100

Avco Trust Ltd,
Avco House,
Castle Street,
Reading,
Berkshire RG1 7DW
Tel 0734 586123

Beneficial Bank plc,
Prudential House,
Wellesley Road,
Croydon CR0 9XY
Tel 01-680 5096

British Credit Trust,
26–28 High Street,
Slough SL1 1ED
Tel 0753 73211

Burton Group Finance Services plc,
Welbeck House,
Bond Street,
Bristol BS1 3LB
Tel 0272 277442

Cattle's Holdings Finance,
PO Box 17, Haltemprice Court,
38 Springfield Way,
Anlaby,
Hull HU10 6RR
Tel 0482 564422

Chartered Trust,
24–26 Newport Road,
Cardiff CF2 1SR
Tel 0222 473000

Citibank Financial Trust Ltd,
St Martin's House,
1 Hammersmith Grove,
London W6 0NY
Tel 01-741 8000

Close Asset Finance Ltd,
Fifth Floor, Tolworth House,
Ewell Road,
Tolworth,
Surbiton,
Surrey KT6 7EL
Tel 01-390 8201

Club 24 Ltd,
Hepworth House,
Claypit Lane,
Leeds LS2 8AP
Tel 0532 440265

Copleys Ltd,
14 King Street,
London EC2V 8EA
Tel 01-626 0130

Credit and Data Marketing Services Ltd,
JM Centre,
Old Hall Street,
Liverpool L70 1AB
Tel 051-235 2475

First National Bank plc,
First National House,
College Road,
Harrow,
Middlesex HA1 1FB
Tel 01-861 1313

Ford Motor Credit Co Ltd,
The Drive,
Warley,
Brentwood,
Essex CM13 3AR
Tel 0277 224400

Forthright Finance,
114–116 St Mary Street,
Cardiff CF1 1XJ
Tel 0222 396131

Forward Trust Group,
145 City Road,
London EC1V 1JY
Tel 01-251 9090

Frizzell Banking Services Ltd,
8 Christchurch Road,
Lansdowne,
Bournemouth,
Dorset BH1 3NQ
Tel 0202 295544

HFC Bank plc,
North Street,
Winfield,
Windsor,
Berkshire SL4 4TD
Tel 0344 890000

Hitachi Credit (UK) Ltd,
Hitachi Credit House,
Stables Courtyard,
Church Road,
Hayes,
Middlesex UB3 2UH
Tel 01-561 8486

Hodge (Julian) Bank Ltd,
31 Windsor Place,
Cardiff CF1 3UR
Tel 0222 371726

House of Fraser plc,
1 Howick Place,
London SW1P 1BH
Tel 01-834 1515

Industrial Funding Trust,
Fifth Floor,
70–74 City Road,
London EC1Y 2BJ
Tel 01-253 7272

JCB Credit Ltd,
The Mill,
Rocester,
Staffordshire ST14 5JW
Tel 0889 590800

Lloyds Bowmaker Ltd,
9–13 Grosvenor Street,
London W1X 9FB
Tel 01-491 3236

Lombard North Central plc,
Lombard House,
3 Princess Way,
Redhill,
Surrey RH1 1NP
Tel 0737 774111

London Scottish Bank plc,
Arndale House,
Arndale Centre,
Manchester M4 3AQ
Tel 061-834 2861

Marks & Spencer Financial Services Ltd,
Michael House,
57 Baker Street,
London W1A 1DN
Tel 01-935 4422

Medens,
Medens House,
Station Way,
Crawley,
West Sussex RH10 1JA
Tel 0293 518877

Mercantile Credit Co Ltd,
Elizabethan House,
Great Queen Street,
London WC2B 5DP
Tel 01-242 1234

Moorgate Mercantile Holdings plc,
Moorgate House,
312 High Road,
London N15 4BX
Tel 01-801 3361

Nationwide Anglia Trust Ltd,
The Old Meeting House,
Lower Dagnall Street,
St Albans,
Hertfordshire AL3 4PG
Tel 0727 32241

North British Finance Group Ltd,
PO Box 82,
Paragon House,
Ferensway,
Hull HU1 3BL
Tel 0482 23815

North West Securities,
NWS House,
City Road,
Chester CH1 3AN
Tel 0244 690000

RoyScot Finance Group plc,
RoyScot House,
The Promenade,
Cheltenham,
Gloucestershire GL50 1PL
Tel 0242 224455

Sears Financial Services Ltd,
PO Box 809,
23 Harbet Road,
London W2 1JL
Tel 01-629 1234

3i plc,
91 Waterloo Road,
London SE1 8XP
Tel 01-928 7822

Security Pacific Holdings Ltd,
308-314 Kings Road,
Reading,
Berkshire RG1 4PA
Tel 0734 61022

SocGen Lease Ltd,
418 Silbury Court,
Silbury Boulevard,
Milton Keynes MK9 2AF
Tel 0908 606050

Trinity House Finance plc,
Trinity House,
Liston Road,
Marlow,
Buckinghamshire SL7 1XW
Tel 062 84 75441

UCB Financial Services Ltd,
Railway Approach,
Wallington,
Croydon SM6 0DY
Tel 01-773 3111

United Dominions Trust,
1 Lyonsdown Road,
New Barnet,
Hertfordshire EN5 1HU
Tel 01-440 8282

Wagon Finance,
Argyle House,
Joel Street,
Northwood Hills,
Middlesex HA6 1NW
Tel 092 74 26199

Wrenwood Group Finance Ltd,
Lancaster House,
Blackburn Street,
Radcliffe,
Manchester M26 9TS
Tel 061-723 1628

Yorkshire Bank Finance,
2 Infirmary Street,
Leeds LS1 2UL
Tel 0532 442511

(Addresses of foreign banks are given in Chapter 9. Other British banks and lending institutions are listed at the end of Chapter 2.)

CHAPTER 4

Long-term Finance

Introduction

It can sometimes be as difficult to draw demarcation lines between long-term finance in its various forms of venture, development and equity capital, and simple long-term loans as it can be to find a precise dividing line between short- and medium-term finance, especially where the various special schemes developed by the banks are concerned. This chapter, therefore, limits itself largely to consideration of the more straightforward long-term loan plans offered by the banks and the facilities offered by Investors in Industry.

Long-term Loans

Long-term loans are usually considered to be debt finance, provided for periods of more than 10 years, for buying fixed assets which can be expected to have a reasonably long life span, such as factory and warehouse buildings – either to buy or build – and substantial items of plant and machinery. Debt finance can also include funds needed to buy other businesses or be used as a more permanent form of working capital, though if it is the latter the firm concerned would probably be better off looking at some form of equity participation on which it would not necessarily be committed to paying interest at regular, inflexible intervals. The smaller firm might also encounter some problems with meeting security requirements for longer-term loans if assets which it holds in the form of property are already committed to supporting its overdraft or different types of bank loans.

Taking a long-term loan will also commit the small firm to fairly detailed planning of its future progress, an exercise which often draws a hostile response from the businessman with his energies concentrated on surviving until tomorrow. On the other hand failing to plan can mean that there is little chance of surviving until tomorrow in any case. Planning can easily be dismissed as crystal ball gazing because of the difficulty of predicting anything far into the future with any degree of accuracy. Plans rarely work out as they

are intended in exactly the form desired but the existence of a plan does make it much easier to cope with problems or with the unexpected diversions from the plan which arise. Where a financial plan has been drawn with the right mixture of short-, medium- and long-term finance the chances of being caught without finance to meet requirements are much reduced.

Inflation in varying degrees is now a permanent part of the economic scene and planning is of special importance during inflationary periods. It is of course possible to misjudge likely trends and many firms have run into problems because of the unforeseen gyrations in the United Kingdom rate of inflation in recent years, being forced to raise working capital to higher and higher levels as turnover has increased sharply in money terms but has remained static or grown only slowly in volume terms. Cash crises have been common in firms which have been basing their finances entirely on profits retained from better times and overdrafts, funding their long-term needs from short-term money.

As long-term loans tend to be more expensive than short-term ones it could be thought that the buying of a long-term asset could be financed by a series of short-term loans, renegotiating on the balance each time a loan expired. That may be all right in theory but renegotiation each time will in itself bring additional costs; it might be that at the time a new loan is needed interest rates are particularly high, or there may be restrictions on bank lending at the time, which mean that the loan cannot be renewed immediately, at least not on terms or from sources which would be acceptable. The need therefore is to match the purchase of a long-term asset with a long-term loan, where there is an element of predictability.

Fixed and Variable Interest Rates

The decision whether to choose fixed or variable rates of interest, where there is a choice, can also be a difficult one. In theory, a company benefits from being able to tap lower rates of interest as and when they are available, but it is not necessarily the case, as for many years short-term rates have consistently risen to ever higher plateaus, and long-term loans taken at what appeared at the time to be high rates of interest have turned out to be remarkably economic. This is not a situation which lenders like and has been a factor in the reluctance of banks to enter into long-term lending, a situation which has only recently started to change.

Variable rates introduce uncertainty for the businessman trying to make an accurate assessment of his future cash needs and demands in terms of interest payments. For the smaller firm, especially if the view is taken that higher interest rates are a permanent feature of the economic scene, a fixed rate is probably preferable if it can be obtained. What may appear to be a higher cost in the short term may in fact turn out to be lower over the long term. It has to be noted, however, that simply maintaining an existing level of trade can require an increasing amount of capital.

Gearing

In assessing needs for the future, two elements of the risk involved have to be considered. First, there is the risk arising from the judgement of future demand: expectations of inflation, unit costs, and so on; second, there is the risk measured by what is known as gearing. Gearing is a measurement of the company's capacity to borrow; in simple terms, a lender may be prepared to lend only £1 for every £1 which the company owner and other shareholders are prepared to put into the business themselves in the form of share capital and retained profits. In the past banks stuck rigidly to this 1:1 gearing ratio but have since become more flexible. Another kind of gearing is that related to the income of a company, namely the proportion of cash flow taken up by the known fixed costs of repaying borrowed capital, renting buildings, and so on. Basically a firm which has a cash flow subject to substantial variation and unpredictability should be wary of becoming highly geared; in a recession it can find itself quickly at the edge of the precipice. On the other hand low gearing can mean that a company does not have the funds available to take advantage of opportunities quickly enough. The right balance of borrowing is therefore important, ensuring that short-term needs are financed from short-term funds and long-term projects from long-term funds.

All the points mentioned so far emphasise the importance of cash flow and cash flow forecasting because many of the problems of a small business arise from obtaining the wrong balance of capital by failing to match the right loans with the right investments. A company which tries to finance a long-term investment with short-term funds strains its cash flow and becomes very vulnerable, whichever way the economy turns; if it turns down the company cannot find the money to pay the immediate bills and if it turns up, it cannot find the money to finance the demand for its goods.

Individual Bank Schemes

Turning now to the individual schemes offered by the banks, the Barclays Business Loan was described in detail in Chapter 3 and is also suitable for long-term requirements as it can run for terms of up to 20 years.

Midland Bank has often been a leader in developing new facilities for the independent business and offers a long-term loan scheme for amounts ranging from £20,000 to £500,000 over periods of 10 to 20 years. There is a choice of fixed or floating interest rates, the variable rate being linked to the bank's base rate. Fees, terms and general conditions are those which the bank judges to be appropriate to the long-term loan market. Security is required, such as good freehold or long leasehold property. Repayment arrangements are usually structured on a regular reducing basis to match the cash flow pattern of the business, although an initial rest period of up to two years may be allowed in certain circumstances. It is expected that most loans will be repaid using the equal instalment method. The scheme is available only to appropriate existing business customers of the bank though inquiries from non-customers are considered.

Most of the other special bank schemes for the longer-term borrower have an element of equity involvement, such as the National Westminster Capital Loan scheme, and that will therefore be described in detail in Chapter 10, though banks in general are now much more prepared to discuss long-term lending.

Investors in Industry (3i)

3i is an important source of long-term lending for small and medium-sized companies in Britain and was formed in 1945 as part of Finance for Industry, owned 15 per cent by the Bank of England and 85 per cent by the English and Scottish clearing banks. It has gained a reputation for always taking an equity stake in companies with which it deals but this is not the case as only about three out of 10 of its cases include an equity involvement, the vast bulk being in the form of term lending. In many cases it may well have liked the idea of an equity stake but when the company owner has refused to part with shares in the firm 3i has still provided funds in the form of loans.

Finance is provided through long-term loans at a fixed rate of interest, payable only on the amount owed. The loan period is normally in the range of seven to 20 years with capital repayments being planned where necessary to start some years ahead to coincide with cash flow projections. 3i says its interest rates are competitive, in the lower range of market rates at the time of negotiation of the loan.

Mortgages

Another form of long-term finance is through mortgages, the concept of which will be familiar to most people; they are taken on the specific security of land or property and run for 20 or so years with the maximum amount loaned being around 65 per cent of the valuation. The costs of preliminary work in drawing up a mortgage, legal fees, surveys, and valuations are paid by the borrower, amounting to around 2 per cent on loans of up to £50,000 and less for larger sums. Interest rates can be either fixed or variable. Building societies do not provide mortgages for industrial purposes but this type of loan can sometimes be obtained through finance houses, from insurance companies and from pension funds. The insurance and pension institutions sometimes negotiate directly with the borrower and sometimes through middlemen such as merchant and other banks. The amounts lent tend to be from £50,000 upwards but that is not an inflexible rule. A policyholder with an insurance company may be able to obtain loans for smaller amounts; some institutions actually have special mortgage schemes designed for smaller companies, the amounts of which can vary between £15,000 and £25,000. The amounts available on mortgage from these institutions are flexible, however, and depend very much on the institution approached and the project involved.

The merchant and other banks listed on pp 71–4 are in many cases able to provide or negotiate long-term finance as are foreign banks, although the latter are usually more interested in the financing of foreign trade. The amounts are flexible but usually of £50,000 upwards and established companies are preferred in most cases.

As might be expected the UK clearing banks have moved strongly into this sector, a typical example being National Westminster with its Flexible Commercial Mortgage scheme for loans between £25,000 and £2 million for up to 25 years. These are available to help businesses of all sizes and professional practices acquire or develop premises for their own use. Flexibility of repayment is offered by allowing either monthly, quarterly, half-yearly or annual instalments, and if the borrowing is £250,000 or less it can be repaid with the proceeds of a suitable endowment or personal pension policy. Customers can choose to have the interest linked to NatWest's base rate, or a fixed rate where the loan is £100,000 or more, or linked to the London Inter-Bank Offered Rate, where the loan is for £250,000 or more. There is a capital repayment 'holiday' option of up to three years. For amounts of up to £1 million the bank will lend up to 75 per cent of the value of the property or 66 per cent above £1 million. In certain circumstances, such as where additional security is available, the bank will provide 100 per cent finance. Other banks offer commercial mortgage facilities, which in many respects are similar to this. Lloyds, for example, provides mortgages for amounts between £15,000 and £100,000 covering 90 per cent of open market valuation, with low start repayment and capital 'holiday' options, with interest rates either fixed or linked to base rate. For amounts above £100,000 it has its Premier Commercial Mortgage.

Company Story

Biscuit making is a highly competitive business but there is room for the specialist who can produce quality goods for outlets other than the mass markets or the superstore chains, as Philip and Dorothy McIvor have proved with Farmhouse Biscuits in the hills near the borders of Lancashire and Yorkshire.

It is a business which has grown from production in the kitchen of their farmhouse near Nelson in Lancashire and a market stall in nearby Blackburn to a company turning over £1 million a year and employing more than 50 people, in the course of which the finance for development has come from retained profits, a mortgage organised by 3i, and funds from the European Economic Community through the European Investment Bank, also arranged by 3i.

The McIvors were originally farmers from longstanding farming families and after marrying in 1961 took over a farm of 110 acres at Twiston up on the moorland around Nelson producing mainly poultry but also sheep and beef cattle. Like all hill farms the living was hard, producing a small income with little margin for difficult times. Those difficult times arose in the bleak winter of 1962–1963 which resulted in the poultry either failing to lay eggs or just dying from the bitter cold.

Their income amounted to about £14 a week and, as the problems showed no signs of easing, they decided to act on a suggestion that they should take a stall in Blackburn market, selling eggs and dressed poultry.

Philip McIvor did not go down to the market for the first day's trading, leaving it to his wife and his mother. 'I was a little cautious about the idea as I'd always been wary about market traders.' They borrowed a couple of trestles and some planks for a makeshift sales counter and had an encouraging start. 'They came home with £14 in cash which made me change my attitude rather quickly.' They graduated from one day to three days at Blackburn and extended their range of products by selling cheese, cakes and home-made biscuits produced by Dorothy and his mother.

Eventually the baking side began to take over, especially as shopkeepers started coming to the stall and asking for the biscuits to sell in their shops so that they would have different attractions from the supermarkets. By 1965 demand had grown sufficiently to enable them to take another market stall at Clitheroe and Mrs McIvor's mother had been drawn in to help increase production. The family were working almost round the clock as they were still running the farm and had to get up early in the morning to tend the stock as well as cope with the expanding business. The biscuits were produced using a small electric cooker and an Aga stove, plus a small electric mixer which regularly broke down.

The first easing of the situation came when Mrs McIvor's parents gave up farming and took a cottage next door to the farmhouse at Higher Oaklands Farm, Barrowford, which the McIvors had bought and which still remains the registered office of the company. A year later they took over the business of a Blackburn trader who had also been producing home-made biscuits.

The oven and mixer from that business were taken up to the farmhouse to form the basis of a rudimentary flow line. There still remained a major physical problem, however, because even though more space was available by using part of the former dairy for the equipment the biscuit paste still had to be rolled out laboriously by hand to the required thickness and then cut into shapes; it had to be done with a heavy iron roller, the use of which had been properly mastered only by Mrs McIvor. They were then producing about 800 to 900 pounds of biscuits a week and at the end of every day's rolling out biscuit paste Mrs McIvor would get water bags under her wrists from the effort involved.

It became obvious that a machine was needed to do the job but finding one was not easy. Philip McIvor continued: 'I looked at the advertisements in a trade magazine and wrote to three companies, one British and two foreign, hoping really to be able to buy a British machine. One of the foreign companies immediately sent information and a representative around to see us; the other sent brochures. We waited and waited but the British company never even bothered to reply.'

The Dutch machine of the first company that approached them seemed to fit their requirements but they needed to see it in action to be absolutely sure that it did all that was needed. They were told that the machine was in a working display at an exhibition in Amsterdam and decided to go to see it. 'We were looking after my father's farm at the time as well as running our own business so we had to get up, milk his cows, and then make the one-and-a-half hour drive to Manchester airport.'

They arrived in Amsterdam and saw the machine at the exhibition; it was working but not actually producing biscuits. The salesman told them of a bakery at The Hague where there was one actually in production; they drove down to The Hague, saw the machine, decided that it did all that was required, and gave their order. 'It cost £1,700, an enormous sum it seemed at the time, especially as nothing we had bought before had cost any more than £80.' They made the flight back to Manchester and raced for home where they still had to look after Philip's father's farm. 'When we got there the cows were all standing there at the gate of the field with their legs crossed. More milk ended up on the field that night than where it should have been. It was years before I dared tell my father what had happened.'

The new machine solved one problem but created another because the oven which they had could not keep up with the productivity of the new equipment. Another £3,000 had then to be invested in a new oven. 'I remember thinking it was a lot, you could have bought a house for less at that time,' says Mr McIvor. But it also meant that baking needed to be done only three days a week and this enabled them to take a little relaxation from the business. By 1972 production of biscuits had risen to one ton a week; then two more ovens were installed, staff increased to 20 and four evening shifts were being worked.

Demand grew at a regular pace, not through advertising, of which Farmhouse Biscuits has never found much need, but through word of mouth and from the biscuits being seen and bought by visitors to the area and to the nearby Lake District.

The products are marketed through distributors spread throughout the country with the biscuits being sold, not in the big stores and supermarkets, but in the smaller specialist shops and outlets such as garden centres. 'We have been approached by Marks and Spencer but business of the kind of volume which they would want would overwhelm us so we are not interested in pursuing that,' says Mr McIvor.

By 1978 the business had grown so much that it was no longer possible to continue working in the farmhouse so the McIvors started looking for a new factory of around 10,000 square feet. 'I fancied a new building with green fields around, being a farmer, but the only one which met those requirements was on offer at £80,000 which was far more than we wanted to pay and they would not reduce to our price. When we did find the right kind of premises they were in fact a former garage in Brook Street in Nelson itself with a floor space of 22,000 square feet, which seemed enormous but has since been outgrown as the business has expanded.'

The price of the premises was £35,000 and it was at this point that Farmhouse Biscuits came into contact with 3i. 'At first they wanted a share stake in the business but I was not prepared to do that after all the hard work we had put into the business.' 3i still offered funds, however, and arranged a mortgage for £28,000 of the purchase price. The company is now producing around four tons of biscuits a week in 11 different varieties with a full range of automated biscuit-making machines and ovens.

Sales rose 20 per cent a year until the recession hit in 1980 but even then it was a slowing down of growth rather than a decline, and by Easter 1981 the recession was over for Farmhouse Biscuits and growth resumed its upward climb. Interest in the farm's products is growing overseas and in 1982 the first substantial order was received from Australia which could develop into a valuable market. 'We have never actually looked for a distributor either at home or overseas, they have always come to us.'

The McIvors then aimed at a turnover of £1.5 million and to enable them to achieve this they spent £100,000 on plant and equipment. The 22,000 square feet former garage which they bought in 1978 has become too small for their needs so they have bought the adjoining premises, trebling their production space. The purchase of this involved a loan of £42,000 through 3i under the European Investment Bank scheme for which 3i is an agent in the UK. The loan was at an interest rate of 14.5 per cent with a capital repayment 'holiday' of 18 months and the loan is being repaid in 12 half-yearly instalments. The two previous slices of finance which Farmhouse Biscuits had from 3i were at different interest rates and both in the form of mortgages from 3i's own funds. The £28,000 slice already mentioned was at 14.25 per cent over 10 years and a further £10,000 was borrowed at 16.25 per cent over eight years to buy another piece of land adjoining the present factory.

Useful Addresses

Information on long-term loan facilities from clearing banks can be obtained from local branches. Merchant and other banks and financial institutions should be approached directly.

3i,
91 Waterloo Road,
London SE1 8XP
Tel 01-928 7822
3i has 18 area offices at Aberdeen, Birmingham, Brighton, Bristol, Cambridge, Cardiff, Edinburgh, Glasgow, Leeds, Leicester, Liverpool, London, Manchester, Newcastle, Nottingham, Reading, Sheffield, and Southampton.

Information on long- and medium-term loans and mortgage finance from insurance companies can be obtained from:

The Secretary,
Business Finance Information,
British Insurance Association,
Aldermary House,
Queen Street,
London EC4N 1TU
Tel 01-243 4477

Information on long-term finance from pension funds can be obtained from:

The Secretary,
National Association of Pension Funds,
Prudential House,
Wellesley Road,
Croydon CR9 9XY
Tel 01-681 2017

Addresses of foreign banks which may offer long-term finance are listed at the end of Chapter 9 on export finance.

CHAPTER 5

Government Sources of Finance

The range of financial assistance available from Government and local authority sources is enormous and a detailed examination of every element would fill a complete book. For that reason it is proposed in this chapter to pick out those which are most likely to be of interest and value to the small businessman and indicate sources of information on more detailed aid schemes. Assistance available through local authorities, several of whom have now established their own development agencies, and various Government agencies, such as the Rural Development Commission, is also described.

It is perhaps unfair to say that the effort and time required in ploughing through the administrative procedures which are attached to most forms of state assistance often render the eventual aid uneconomic, with the problems of getting through the system outweighing the end results. Most public officials in the departments concerned are in fact anxious and willing to disburse the assistance available but it is true that even that willingness can be frustrated by the system itself, designed to ensure that the taxpayers' money is properly and effectively distributed to those entitled to receive it. It is equally true, however, to say that in many cases actually to obtain the money requires a high degree of stamina and determination. Whether the effort involved is worthwhile is a matter for the businessman himself to decide.

Fortunately in the past few years a number of organisations have grown up which provide invaluable help in mapping out a path through the maze. These are, in particular, the local enterprise trusts - their addresses are listed on pp 45-60 - which have increased rapidly in number since the value of the services offered by the pioneers in this field, Enterprise North at Durham and the Community of St Helens Trust in the Merseyside town, became clear. With the assistance of organisations such as these, and the Government's own Small Firms Service, the task of acquiring state aid for the development of a business has become a much more manageable proposition for the smaller firm, which lacks the resources a large organisation can devote to the job.

Very considerable changes to Government schemes of help were introduced in 1988 in what the Government called its Enterprise Initiative, the objective of which was to co-ordinate and give publicity to the range of measures which the state provides to encourage the development of business. There are 10 elements to the Enterprise Initiative: the regional initiative; six business development/consultancy initiatives, including marketing, design, quality, manufacturing systems, business planning, and financial and information systems; the export initiative; the research and technology initiative; and the business and education initiative.

Regional Initiative

The Government's primary aim in reforming regional policy was to cut down deadweight spending associated with automatic aid and so make its policy more cost-effective. The regional development grant has therefore been abolished but regional selective assistance has been retained with the criteria under which it is granted remaining the same. Negotiation of this grant has, however, been tightened for larger firms, with all applications for more than £500,000 having to be referred to the industrial development departments of the Department of Trade and Industry in London. The assisted areas remain the same. A Regional Enterprise Grant has been introduced under which independent firms in development areas with fewer than 25 employees can obtain a 15 per cent grant towards the cost of fixed assets up to a maximum of £15,000, and a grant of 50 per cent for product and process innovation up to a maximum of £25,000; but grants can only be claimed once. The business development initiatives for independent firms with fewer than 500 employees also provide for regionally differentiated grants towards advisory assistance. The Government says it is committed to indigenous regional development and that the main aim of regional policy is to encourage the 'development of indigenous potential within the assisted areas with the long-term objective of self-generating growth in these areas'. The Government claims that spending on regional industrial policy is being held at existing levels but in fact there will be a drop in cash terms in regional aid spending from £466 million in 1987–1988 to about £356 million by 1990–1991.

The Business Development and Consultancy Initiatives (BDI)

These provide for a range of advisory schemes for independent firms with less than 500 employees and are designed to improve the competitiveness of small and medium-sized enterprises by encouraging the use of consultants from the private sector. The business development initiative – with its six elements of marketing, design, quality, manufacturing systems, business planning, and financial and information systems – operates on a national basis. A grant of 66.6 per cent is available in the assisted areas and designated Urban Programme areas towards 5–15 man-days of advice; the grant rate in other parts of the country is 50 per cent. Firms can claim assistance twice under the BDI scheme. Firms considering the initiative can have up to two days of free advice from a counsellor appointed by the Department of Trade and Industry, who will examine the business and make suggestions on how the business development initiative could be of use to the firm. The objective of the scheme is to provide knowledge on how to undertake business planning, marketing, design, and so on, rather than actually to provide finance for these activities in themselves.

Research and Technology Initiative

This brings together a range of existing measures whose purpose is to encourage technological innovation, but the Department of Trade and Industry will only assist those activities which would not otherwise find support in the market place. The Government is especially anxious to encourage collaboration in research and development between firms themselves and between businesses and universities, polytechnics and other research bodies. The Department of Trade and Industry will link firms with experts, give information, and provide grants for up to half the cost of a collaborative project, and will also help in participation in various European Community technology initiatives, including ESPRIT, RACE, and EUREKA.

Business and Education Initiative

This groups a number of measures designed to encourage greater links between education and industry, including externally funded research in higher education institutes.

Export Initiative

Under this initiative the British Overseas Trade Board will assist with advice on foreign tariffs, regulations and marketing, as well as undertake research for firms in particular markets, local representation and standards. Financial support is available for trade missions and participation in overseas trade fairs.

Regional Selective Assistance (RSA)

For firms in assisted areas selective assistance is available to encourage industrial or commercial projects which have a good chance of success and which create or safeguard jobs. Both manufacturing and service industry is eligible for assistance but it is expected that the bulk of the finance required will come from the firm's own resources or other private sources. Schemes must improve productivity or exports and be of identifiable national and regional benefit, and it must be demonstrated that assistance is essential for the project to go ahead. The project grant represents the main form of RSA aid and is related either to the fixed capital costs of the project or the number of jobs it will create. Working capital can be taken into account in deciding the level of grant. Help is also given towards the cost of providing new technology skills to trainees under 25 years old. There is also a training grant of up to 40 per cent of eligible training costs which attracts a matching grant for a further 40 per cent from the European Social Fund, but this does not apply to normal replacement training, continuing training projects, apprentices or those over the age of 25.

In many ways the enterprise initiative is mainly a re-packaging and promotion of existing policies, but one of its effects is to tip the balance in favour of the smaller and medium-sized firm; this means independent firms only, as firms which are part of larger groups are not covered by the provision of advisory assistance. Financial assistance is now focused on the smaller, independent business because there is seen to be a problem in capital markets for such firms.

Government Factories

Government agencies often provide factories in the assisted areas, either of standard design or built to meet the needs of the user. Firms may also buy land to build their own factories. The Government factories range in size from small workshops of 500 square feet to factories of 50,000 square feet or more. Units can be either rented or bought. The rents reflect local market values and in certain circumstances, where it is warranted by the number of jobs being created, a rent-free period can be negotiated. When a factory is bought arrangements can be made to spread payments over 15 years. Selective financial assistance may be available where Government factories are rented or bought but the application for this aid must be made before the arrangements for the factory have been settled. When the amount of the selective assistance is decided any rental concession will be taken into account.

Management of Government factories depends on their location, being the responsibility either of the English Industrial Estates Corporation, the Scottish or Welsh development agencies.

Contracts Preference Schemes

Preferential treatment can be obtained under two schemes: the General Preference Scheme and the Special Preference Scheme. It is given to firms in development areas when they tender for contracts placed by Government departments, nationalised industries and other public bodies.

Under the *General Preference Scheme* firms in the qualifying areas are given opportunities to tender for public contracts for goods and services, and provided that the terms offered, such as delivery date, price and quantity, are the same as those offered by other businesses, then contracts are awarded to those in the qualifying areas rather than elsewhere.

Government purchasing departments and the Post Office – though not other nationalised industries and public bodies – operate the *Special Preference Scheme*. When a firm outside the development areas obtains a contract from these sources, businesses within the qualifying areas may be given the opportunity of undertaking 25 per cent of the order at a price which would result in no additional cost to the buyer.

Any firm which wants to benefit from these two schemes should ask for its name to be included on lists kept by the purchasing organisations. Further information and a booklet, 'Government Contract Preference Schemes', can be obtained from regional offices of the Department of Trade and Industry or its Investment and Development Division.

Grants for Converting Rural Buildings

Villages often lack suitable buildings where new firms can settle and provide job opportunities to secure the future of country communities. Derelict barns, redundant chapels, disused dairies, abandoned military establishments, old railway stations, mills and factories can, however, be converted for use by small firms as craft workshops, research laboratories, or premises for services or light manufacturing industries.

The Rural Development Commission, whose business service now includes what used to be known as the Council for Small Industries in Rural Areas, provides grants towards the cost of converting redundant buildings in its priority areas. These rural development areas are in: Cambridgeshire, Cheshire, Cleveland, Cornwall and the Isles of Scilly, Cumbria, Derbyshire, Devon,

Dorset, Durham, East Sussex, Gloucestershire, Hereford and Worcester, Humberside, Isle of Wight, Kent, Lancashire, Lincolnshire, Norfolk, Northamptonshire, Northumberland, North Yorkshire, Nottinghamshire, Shropshire, Somerset, South Yorkshire, Staffordshire, Suffolk, and West Yorkshire.

Applications may be made by individuals, partnerships, co-operatives, or companies. Converted buildings can be intended for use by applicants themselves or for leasing to others. Grants usually cover 25 per cent of the actual costs of conversion work and professional fees. Minimum eligible expenditure is £1,000 and the maximum usually £50,000. Projects with total costs of more than £50,000 may be considered on their merits. Eligible work can cover improvement, alteration or repair to the fabric of permanent buildings, the reasonable provision of heating, lighting, power supply, water supply, sewerage, and access to premises. Modest extensions to existing buildings may be considered if they provide facilities such as toilets or office space.

Any application for a grant must be made and approved before work starts and must be supported by drawings and costings of work to be done and building and planning consents must be obtained. If during a five-year period after payment of a grant the building is sold or its use changed, RDC will be entitled to reclaim a proportion of the grant on a sliding scale. The Rural Development Commission receives about 300 applications for conversion grants every year. Further information can be obtained from RDC head office or regional offices.

Crafts Council Loans and Grants

Grant and loan schemes have been devised by the Crafts Council to help the artist craftsman or woman at various career stages. Quality of work is the principal criterion for offering financial aid, although other factors are taken into account. Grants are available for craft projects of national significance within England only, or for projects of mainly regional significance within England where the amount required is unlikely to be available from the relevant Regional Arts Association. Craft Commissions Scheme grants are available up to 50 per cent of the total cost of commissioning craft works for buildings or sites readily accessible to the general public.

Grants are also available to individual crafts people working within London for exhibitions and for 50 per cent of the cost of equipment or workshop improvements, as well as for 'purposeful' travel, marketing and promotion and attendance at seminars and conferences. Grants are also available for craft organisations for projects within London.

Crafts people may apply for grants in connection with setting up their first workshop. Applications can be made either before the workshop is established or at any time during the first two years. Applicants should not be employed outside the workshop for more than two days a week. An equipment grant is paid of up to 50 per cent of the cost of equipment for establishing the workshop; a maintenance grant provides financial assistance towards running the workshop in the first months of the business.

Established crafts people who want to employ a trainee can apply for grant aid to help provide a living wage during the initial months of employment. The grant is usually for one year but in some cases may be extended for a second year at a reduced rate. The employer is expected to provide training in all aspects of the particular craft, together with business experience. Graduates in a crafts discipline or people already with some training intending to set up a workshop or already pursuing careers as crafts people may apply for assistance to enable them to spend time in one or more established workshops undertaking intensive training and gaining workshop experience.

A craftsman or woman who has been in business for at least two years may apply for a loan of up to £5,000 to enlarge a workshop, improve facilities or buy additional equipment. The loan is repayable monthly over five years. There is also a bursary scheme which enables crafts people who have been working for seven years or more to take a sabbatical period in which to reassess their work or undertake a specific project.

For those crafts people in England and Wales further information can be obtained from the Crafts Council, and for those in Scotland from the Small Business Division of the Scottish Development Agency.

Government Agencies

There is now a wide range of Government agencies in different parts of the country, the whole or part of whose job is to help in the development of smaller firms. They can very often provide funds on advantageous terms or at least help in the preparation of a case to be put to a conventional source of finance, such as a bank. The role of the British Technology Group is dealt with in Chapter 11 on financing technology.

Agencies in England

Rural Development Commission

The objective of the Rural Development Commission is to stimulate the economy in rural areas of England by encouraging industrial development in those areas through the provision of small factory and workshop units in certain special investment areas (SIAs). In 1988 the Rural Development Commission was formed by a merger between the Development Commission and its main agency, the Council for Small Industries in Rural Areas; the role of CoSIRA is now performed by the Business Services Division of the RDC and in fact operates from the same Head Office. The commission also encourages voluntary or self-governing bodies providing wide-ranging services which improve the social and cultural life of rural communities. Factory construction is undertaken for the commission by the English Industrial Estates Corporation to improve job opportunities and check rural depopulation.

The commission is the agent for disbursing the Development Fund, voted annually by Parliament, and is responsible to the Department of the Environment.

The Business Services Division offers a local source of information and assistance with a wide variety of problems affecting small rural businesses through its local representatives, called Small Industries Organisers, working in every English county, backed up by a voluntary committee. There is also a professional but practical, down-to-earth consultancy and advisory service providing expertise in management and technical skills; training courses in a range of skills for both experienced craftsmen and new entrants to industry; help with funding propositions to be presented to sources of finance and loans for buildings, equipment and working capital. No charge is made for the assistance and information provided by the local organiser and fees for the technical or business management services are modest.

Normally small manufacturing and servicing businesses are eligible for help provided that not more than 20 skilled people are employed - there is no limit to the number of unskilled who may be employed - and the firm is located in an English rural area or country town usually with a maximum of 10,000 inhabitants. Small tourism enterprises providing overnight accommodation are also eligible in certain areas, including small hotels, guest houses, bed and breakfast establishments, motels and holiday chalets. The service does not extend to agriculture, horticulture, the professions or the retail trades.

The Division can provide loans from its own resources, the maximum being £15,000 and the minimum £250 with repayment periods for loans on buildings of up to 20 years and for loans on plant, equipment or working capital up to five years. Interest rates are decided by the Treasury and vary with the length of the loan.

The Rural Development Commission has supplemented its own resources by developing close links with several of the clearing banks, including National Westminster, Barclays, Lloyds, Midland, and the Co-operative, which have resulted in the offer of loans on special terms to rurally based small businesses. Sums between £2,000 and £250,000 may be borrowed for buildings and plant or for working capital, with repayment terms of up to 20 years. Applications for loans on these special terms must be made through the RDC's Business Services Division, which can also help with assistance in drawing up a business plan.

For established businesses the Division expects the major part of the funding to be arranged with the banks, 3i, or other lending sources, reserving its own funds for new firms and businesses in the first year or two of development to augment the financing of a project.

Small Firms Service

The facilities of the Department of Employment's Small Firms Service are available throughout the country but largely in the urban areas, while in Scotland and Wales the facilities are provided through the Scottish and Welsh Development Agencies. The Small Firms Service does not itself provide funds but acts as an information and counselling service through a nationwide network of Small Firms Centres, which can be contacted individually or through a national freefone number. Inquirers should dial 100 and ask the operator for Freefone Enterprise.

The service acts as a 'signpost' and small firms can obtain information on any business problem including finance, diversification, industrial training, exporting, planning, industrial relations, marketing, and technological advances. It puts firms in touch with Government departments, chambers of commerce, sources of finance, local authorities, or other advisers appropriate to their need. Firms approaching the counselling service can discuss their problems confidentially with an experienced businessman. Information is provided free; the first session of counselling is also free but for subsequent sessions, up to a maximum of 10 days in any one year, a small charge is made.

Agencies in Scotland

Scottish Development Agency (SDA)

The purpose of the Scottish Development Agency is to promote the economic development of Scotland, develop employment, industrial efficiency and international competitiveness, and improve the environment. It tries to achieve these objectives by providing loans, guarantees, share capital, industrial and financial partnerships, factories, and management advisory services. It has a Small Business Division to deal directly with the smaller firms in the country. It is especially interested in firms or individuals already based in Scotland or prepared to set up there and which want to enter new markets or develop new techniques, companies expanding in Scotland or firms in Scotland which have short-term financial problems but long-term viability.

The SDA arranges loans at competitive rates of interest with repayment terms varying from short periods to 20 years. Security is usually required though there is no upper limit on the amount borrowed.

The agency's Small Business Division handles applications from firms in manufacturing or service industries employing up to 100 people for amounts from £500 to £50,000. Instead of making direct investments the agency may provide guarantees on suitable terms so that businesses can borrow from other sources. The SDA also builds and manages factory units ranging in size from 500 square feet workshops to factories of 100,000 square feet or more, including advance, modernised or tailor-made factories. These premises can be rented, leased or bought and rent-free periods may also be given. Advisory services covering a general counselling service, training facilities, and help with marketing and exporting, are also provided.

Highlands and Islands Development Board (HIDB)

The other major development agency in Scotland is the Highlands and Islands Development Board, the purpose of which is to assist the economic and social development of the Highlands and Islands region by providing finance and other help to firms in the manufacturing and service industries, agriculture, fisheries and tourism. Financial aid is available in the form of loans, interest relief grants, participation in share and stock holding, removal grants and special grants for building and other purposes.

The HIDB can fund up to half of the cost of a commercially viable project and the rest has to come from the company's own resources or borrowing from other sources. The amount of aid from the board is reduced where a firm or project is receiving other Government financial aid, such as regional development grants.

Concessionary interest rates are usually available on loans, together with rest periods on repayments and even interest-free periods. Loans are provided for plant, equipment, or working capital for periods of up to 10 years and for construction or purchase of buildings for up to 20 years, with security being required. The board may also give an interest relief grant to reduce the interest cost of borrowing from another source; this is an alternative to a loan, not additional to it. Purpose-built factories and workshops as well as plant and machinery can be leased through the board, which also offers advisory services to businesses within the Highlands and Islands region.

Agencies in Wales

Welsh Development Agency

The Welsh Development Agency was set up to further the economic development of the country, improve employment, industrial efficiency, international competitiveness, and the environment by making loans, providing guarantees, share capital, factories and management advisory services. It provides medium- to long-term loans of five to 10 years at competitive fixed interest rates, with security. It does not, however, provide short-term finance.

The Small Business Unit handles applications from small firms, providing advice on a wide range of management, marketing and technical problems, as well as loans of up to £50,000. It also provides guarantees as an alternative to direct investment so that firms can borrow from commercial sources.

Factory units which the agency builds and manages range from 1,500 square feet upwards and can be rented, taken on long lease, or bought. Rent-free periods are also available.

Mid-Wales Development

The objectives of Mid-Wales Development, which acts in Wales in much the same way as the RDC in England, are to promote the economic and social development of mid-Wales, countering depopulation and encouraging repopulation, the development of manufacturing industry, and helping towns and villages with special problems. Information and guidance is given to companies wanting to relocate in mid-Wales, and the agency has a Business Advisory Service to help establish businesses in the area and provide continuing aid on subjects such as management accounting, marketing and technical matters.

It provides loans for established businesses which have well-defined projects, firms entering the area for the first time, and new firms with experienced management. The board does not provide finance where other suitable funds are available, and projects must be directed towards improving the productivity, profitability, competitiveness and efficiency of a company. Manufacturing industry is preferred and the board should be approached before a firm starts work on a project.

Equipment loans are provided for up to 10 years and building loans for up to 20 years with a minimum contribution of 20 per cent being expected from the applicant's own resources. For working capital loans of up to five years, applicants must contribute 50 per cent from their own resources. All these loans are at commercial rates of interest.

Loans of up to £50,000 are also provided at reduced interest rates provided the project results in the creation of sufficient new jobs and the business does not employ more than 20 skilled people, much as with RDC loans. These loans can be as much as 3 per cent cheaper than the other loans. The board provides premises throughout its area ranging from starter units of 500–750 square feet on 12-month licences to larger factories on 25-year leases, which may include a rent-free period. Among other services are marketing support to enable firms to take part in exhibitions and trade fairs, seminars and general training programmes. It has, for example, held courses for retail shopkeepers in order to try to improve the efficiency of, and thereby maintain in existence, small village shops.

Development Corporation for Wales

This third agency for Wales aims to promote the interests of existing businesses in the country and encourage the establishment of new ones. It sponsors and organises overseas trade missions, gives information on industrial opportunities in Wales, and gives a range of free and confidential advice. It is financed by WDA, the Development Board for Rural Wales, Welsh industry, commerce and local authorities.

Agencies in Northern Ireland

Northern Ireland is considered as a special case and has a vast range of incentives to encourage industry, including automatic grants and selective assistance. Benefits which are not related to the number of jobs created include capital grants, training grants and key worker grants.

Capital grants of 50 per cent of eligible costs of new building, machinery and equipment, used for manufacturing purposes, are similar to regional development grants and do not count as income for tax purposes. Training grants are available for training personnel at various levels. Cash grants are available for key workers transferred to Northern Ireland to reimburse them for many of the expenses incurred.

Selective aid is available to manufacturing and service businesses whose projects are particularly attractive because of the number of jobs they create, such as when new products are introduced. Industrial development grants of 40 to 50 per cent of the qualifying costs of new buildings, machinery and equipment are provided but the rates of grant depend on the location chosen and the number of jobs which result. Start-up grants are provided towards working capital needs, such as setting-up and initial operating costs; they are negotiated on the basis of overall capital requirements, location and number of jobs. Further grants during the build-up years are available for managerial costs, including salaries.

Interest relief grants may be obtained to reduce the cost of commercial loans when funds to finance new projects are raised through non-government sources. Grants are provided for up to seven-year terms, the first three years at broadly commercial rates followed by four years at 3 per cent a year. Research and development grants of 40 to 50 per cent are available for labour and material costs of basic research, related design work, building and testing of prototypes, final design and production drawing costs. Some consultancy costs can also qualify. Total assistance cannot exceed £250,000 for any one project. A wide range of Government factories is also available, often at concessionary rents and with rent-free periods. Where a factory is bought on a negotiated payment basis the amount to be repaid can be reduced by a grant of up to 45 per cent of the cost.

Full information can be obtained from the Department of Commerce in Belfast or from the Ulster Office in London; addresses are given on p 116.

Local Enterprise Development Unit (LEDU)

Sponsored by the Department of Commerce, the Local Enterprise Development Unit has specific responsibility to promote the setting up and growth of small manufacturing and service industries employing not more than 50 people. It provides financial aid in the form of grants and loans geared to the needs of the individual project, making available Government factories and sites, and giving business advice in marketing, technology, accountancy, and design. It does not usually deal with industries unsuited to small-scale operations or with wholesale, retail, distribution, tourist and transport businesses. Addresses of the four regional offices are given on p 116.

Local Authorities

There is a wide range of assistance available for industry from local authorities and great variations from area to area, so it is essential to inquire from the appropriate local authority about the specific assistance available. This section will therefore look at the overall pattern of aid available, and then highlight a number of particular examples of initiatives in different parts of the country. Many local authorities have set up full-scale economic development corporations, or are planning to do so.

Inner Urban Areas

Local authorities at county and borough district levels in a number of areas are able to participate more fully in the economic development of their areas through the Inner Urban Areas Act 1978. They can declare 'improvement areas' of either an industrial or commercial character, in which they may make loans or grants for conversion and improvement of industrial or commercial buildings; they can make loans of up to 90 per cent on commercial terms for up to 30 years for acquiring land and carrying out building and site works; they can give grants and loans, limited to a maximum of £1,000, towards the administrative and other costs of establishing common ownership or co-operative enterprises but they cannot help with capital needs or running costs under this Act.

Seven inner city partnership areas have special areas which enable them to exercise three extra powers: these are: (i) grants to help with rents paid by firms taking new leases for the first years of a tenancy; (ii) interest-free loans for up to two years for site preparation, including installation of services; (iii) interest relief grants for small firms which employ less than 50 people for loans on land and buildings. Interest relief grants relieve the burden of interest on a loan. Basic assessment of interest rates is at a commercial rate; assistance relieves that burden and effectively reduces the rate of interest.

Authorities will want to be sure that projects will benefit the area, create or preserve jobs, or improve property or the environment. Aid will not be given if the project can be funded satisfactorily from other sources and that which is provided will be the minimum needed for the project to go ahead.

Districts containing inner city partnership special areas are: Birmingham, the London areas of Greenwich, Lewisham, Newham, Southwark, Tower Hamlets, Hackney, Islington and Lambeth, Liverpool, Manchester and Salford, Newcastle upon Tyne and Gateshead.

Districts where there are inner area programmes are: Bolton, Bradford, Hammersmith, Kingston upon Hull, Leeds, Leicester, Middlesbrough, North Tyneside, Nottingham, Oldham, Sheffield, South Tyneside, Sunderland, Wirral, and Wolverhampton.

Other designated districts in England are: Barnsley, Blackburn, Brent, Doncaster, Ealing, Haringey, Hartlepool, Rochdale, Rotherham, St Helens, Sandwell, Sefton, Wandsworth, Wigan; in Scotland: Dumbarton, Clydebank, City of Glasgow, Hamilton, Inverclyde, Monklands, Motherwell, Renfrew, City of Dundee; in Wales: Blaenau Gwent, Cardiff, Newport, Rhondda, and Swansea.

Derelict Land Clearance Areas

Local authorities in the assisted areas and derelict land clearance areas in England (such as disused coal mining areas) are eligible for 100 per cent grants of the approved cost of reclaiming derelict land; elsewhere grants of 50 per cent are paid and the scope of the grants has been extended to the private sector so that individuals or public companies who want to reclaim derelict land for development can also qualify for 50 per cent grants. The Department of the Environment administers these grants and applications must be made before any work starts. Responsibility for reclamation in Scotland and Wales rests with their development agencies.

Enterprise Zones

The Government has established a number of enterprise zones to see how far industrial and commercial activity can be encouraged by removing certain tax burdens, and relaxing or accelerating planning controls. The zones will be designated for 10 years and are not part of regional policy, nor directly connected with other existing policies such as those for inner cities or derelict land, though the sites will benefit from any aid available under those policies. Nor are the zones specifically aimed at small businesses, though obviously small firms can benefit as much as any others.

The benefits are: exemption from development land tax, 100 per cent capital allowances for corporation and income tax purposes for industrial and commercial buildings, exemption from general rates on industrial and commercial buildings, simplification of planning procedures, abolition of industrial development certificates, exemption from the scope of industrial training boards, favourable treatment of requests for customs warehouses and relaxed criteria applying to private customs warehouses, and reduced demands from Government for statistical information. These incentives apply to both new and existing businesses in the zones.

Further information can be obtained from the Department of the Environment or from the authorities in the local areas.

Urban Development Corporations

The Government has set up seven urban development corporations, in the Black Country of the West Midlands, Teesside, Cardiff, Trafford Park and Liverpool in the north-west, Tyne and Wear and London docklands. The aim is to regenerate these areas in a way that will attract private sector development, and the corporations have powers to make loans and grants.

New Towns

Many of the new town development corporations have taken a particular interest in encouraging the development of smaller firms, by building small premises, sometimes with communal services such as telephone answering, typing facilities or conference rooms. They have often set up Small Business Advisory Services, giving a wide range of assistance on matters such as marketing and management generally, as well as helping to formulate business plans which can help firms to obtain finance from commercial sources. Some new town authorities also offer low-cost facilities for an entrepreneur to develop a product or project before putting it on the market or launching an independent business.

Individual Initiatives by Local Authorities

Many individual initiatives have been taken by local authorities to try to stimulate industrial development in their areas, including large local authorities such as the Greater Manchester Economic Development Corporation and the West Midlands Development Corporation, as well as a number of smaller ones. This does not pretend to be an exhaustive description of all the schemes available, but rather an indication of what is there to be used.

The Greater London Enterprise Board, set up by the former Greater London Council, has survived the abolition of the Metropolitan Authority but in a rather different form. It now likes to be known as Greater London Enterprise, takes a much more hard-headed business approach to projects, and is more likely to take equity investments in companies than provide loans and grants as it used to do. An indication of its new approach is the setting up of the London Enterprise Venture Fund, with funds of £3 million. This makes investments in the range of £40,000 to £500,000, with the majority being in the £40,000–£100,000 range; this is primarily equity capital for capital growth and it will take 50 per cent of ordinary share capital, usually putting its own director on the board. It invests in start-ups as well as product development and aims for 40 per cent return plus on start-ups and 30 per cent plus on others. It is looking for exit routes in the normal way; since it is dealing with smaller than average venture capital investments the fund is interested in selling on its investments to development capital/later stage investors as well as making trade sales, or seeing the companies floated on the stock markets. One of the similarities with the previous organisation is that it operates from the same address.

Other organisations originally set up by local authorities, such as the West Midlands Enterprise Board, Greater Manchester Economic Development Corporation, and the West Yorkshire Enterprise Board (now known as Yorkshire Enterprise), have not only survived the abolition of their Metropolitan Authority parents but are flourishing. The West Midlands Board (WMB), for example, is a major provider of investment capital in the region and not only manages funds for other organisations but is also very much involved in the management buy-out scene. It has also launched venture capital funds and has linked with the merchant bankers, Lazards, in a unit trust designed to attract pension fund capital into the West Midlands, which it has done successfully. In general, the WMEB offers a mixture of equity and long-term loan finance in sums ranging from £100,000 to £750,000, mainly in firms employing 50–1000, but it is also interested in smaller firms who are able to show that in two or three years they will expand their workforces to this level. It is mainly interested in manufacturing companies. Merseyside Enterprise Board has also set up a unit trust to provide equity investments of £50,000 to £300,000. Yorkshire Enterprise offers a range of funding for companies in its region and has also embarked on joint ventures with such local authorities as Humberside County Council to provide risk capital for the smaller firm; the joint company, called Humberside County Enterprises, provides equity and loan finance of £25,000 to £250,000. Greater Manchester Economic Development Corporation also provides equity and short- and medium-term loans (in co-operation with the Co-operative Bank) in sums of £25,000 to £250,000. The South Yorkshire Residuary Body, which took over from the old South Yorkshire County Council, provides – through the County Superannuation Fund – financial packages of £100,000 to £1 million.

The City of Sheffield provides cash under a number of schemes, such as that aimed at developing new technology firms. Under its product development grant scheme grant aid can cover up to 100 per cent of costs up to a maximum of £10,000. Cash help, in return for a small royalty, can be used to cover materials, equipment, fees, marketing and promotional material. The city also provides business development and marketing services, which include a management development programme grant, marketing advice, market analyses, and advice on organisation planning and management development. There is also a premises grant scheme to help small independent firms employing 25 or less to acquire premises with a grant towards rates and rent or purchase price. Sheffield is one of the authorities involved with the Co-operative Bank in its special Loan Guarantee Scheme described on pp 31–2.

The London Borough of Hammersmith and Fulham produces a useful booklet describing its range of schemes for the smaller firm. These include a marketing grant of up to £2,000, though more often grants of up to £1,000 are provided which represent a proportion of the total outlay involved, usually 50 per cent. There is also a business development loan of up to £5,000 but this is only available where there is a matching loan from a bank or other lending institution and it is intended to be in addition to rather than in substitution for other conventional forms of finance. Technology and innovation grants are also made.

The city of Nottingham provides a wide variety of assistance, including premises, enterprise workshops, an advanced business centre, as well as industrial improvement grants. The city also provides interest relief grants on loans obtained from 3i of up to 7 per cent in the first year, 5 per cent in the second year, and 3 per cent in the third on loans from £15,000 to £200,000.

A very useful booklet on local authority assistance in London has been produced by the London Research Centre and the London Chamber of Commerce, while National Westminster Bank's Official Sources of Finance and Assistance to Industry provides a comprehensive list of what is available from local authorities.

In South Tyneside the municipal borough council has joined forces with the Bunzl company to provide commercial development capital funding to local businesses through a joint company called South Tyneside Investments. Funds of £10,000 to £75,000 are available to start-ups and expanding businesses where more traditional forms of finance are not available or appropriate, and are available as equity, preference shares or loans. In County Durham the County Council and the Co-operative Bank have established the Durham Enterprise Loan Fund which will provide £2,000 to £5,000 to businesses at 1 per cent above base rate, with interest-only repayments in the first six months. The funds are aimed at businesses employing fewer than 10 people.

In North-east Scotland, the Grampian Regional Council provides financial aid through its Small Business Enterprise scheme, which was started in 1978 and is administered by the North East Scotland Development Association.

Loans may be available for up to 20 years towards part of the cost of building, acquiring, adapting, or improving premises for industrial activities. Prevailing rates of interest apply and loans are secured on property, the maximum loan being 75 per cent of the property valuation. Interest-free loans towards the cost of buying plant, machinery and other equipment may be available for up to five years. They can be up to £7,500 in areas of relatively high unemployment, or up to £5,000 elsewhere. As an alternative it may be possible to obtain a loan guarantee from Grampian Regional Council for up to £5,000 towards the cost of buying plant, machinery and equipment.

Loans of more than £7,500 and £5,000 may also be available for up to five years towards the cost of buying plant, machinery and equipment. The loans are at prevailing rates of interest, secured on property, with a maximum of 75 per cent of the valuation of the property. Under certain conditions, working capital loans may be available for up to two years, again at prevailing interest rates and secured on property, the maximum loan being £15,000 or 75 per cent of the property value.

A grant may also be available for up to nine months towards the initial payment of rent on industrial premises. Grants of up to £1,000 are available for management and technical training, product research and development, and market development if sales are to be outside the Grampian Region, as well as towards the cost of assessing the commercial viability of an industrial co-operative.

Much of this aid is available in other areas but in Grampian has been packaged into an attractive incentive scheme, in which the application procedure itself helps to identify the viability of a business proposal.

These various examples illustrate the active involvement of local authorities in promoting and encouraging the development of small businesses in their areas and also indicate the varied forms which schemes can take. It is therefore essential to contact the local industrial development officer or planning department of the local authority to find out just what schemes are being operated in particular areas.

Useful Addresses

Information on aid in the Assisted Areas can be obtained from the following numbers:
01-215 4021, *or*

North East
(Newcastle upon Tyne) 0632 324722

North West
(Manchester) 061-236 2171

Yorkshire and Humberside
(Leeds) 0532 443 171

East Midlands
(Nottingham) 0602 506 181

West Midlands
(Birmingham) 021-632 4111

South East
(London) 01-730 9678

South West
(Bristol) 0272 272 666

Scotland
(Glasgow) 041-248 2855

Wales
(Cardiff) 0222 825 111

Northern Ireland
(Belfast) 0232 233 233

Department of Trade and Industry Industrial Development Departments are listed at the end of Chapter 6 pp 129–30.

Regional Small Firms Information Centres
All can be contacted by dialling 100 and asking for Freefone Enterprise.

Eastern Region,
1 Carlyle House,
Carlyle Road,
Cambridge CB4 3DN

East Midlands Region,
Severns House,
Middle Pavement,
Nottingham NG1 7DW

London and South-eastern Region,
Ebury Bridge House,
2–18 Ebury Bridge Road,
London SW1W 8QD

Northern Region,
Centro House,
3 Cloth Market,
Newcastle upon Tyne NE1 1EH

North-west Region,
26–28 Deansgate,
Manchester M3 1RH

Liverpool,
Graeme House,
Derby Street,
Liverpool L2 7UJ

Sub-office for Liverpool,
1 Old Hall Street,
Liverpool L3 9HJ

South-west Region,
5th Floor,
The Pithay,
Bristol BS1 2NB

West Midlands Region,
9th Floor,
Alpha Tower,
Suffolk Street,
Queensway,
Birmingham B1 1TT

Yorkshire and Humberside Region,
1 Park Row,
City Square,
Leeds LS1 5NR

Southern Region,
Abbey Hall,
Abbey Square,
Reading RG1 3BE

Northern Ireland:

Department of Commerce,
64 Chichester House,
Chichester Street,
Belfast BT1 4JX

Ulster Office in London,
11 Berkeley Street,
London W1X 6BU

Scotland:

SDA,
21 Bothwell Street,
Glasgow G2 6MR

and

SDA,
Rasebery House,
Haymarket Terrace,
Edinburgh EH12 5EZ

Wales:

16 St David's House,
Wood Street,
Cardiff CF1 1ER

The nearest Small Firms Centre can be contacted by telephoning the operator on 100 and asking for Freefone Enterprise.

Local Enterprise Development Unit Offices

Ledu House,
Upper Galwally,
Purdy's Lane,
Belfast BT8 4TB
Tel 0232 491031

Northern area,
17 The Diamond,
Londonderry BP48 6BR
Tel 0504 67257

Southern area,
5 Downshire Place,
Newry
Tel 0693 2955

Western area,
14 Mountjoy Road,
Omagh
Tel 0662 45763

Tourist Boards

English Tourist Board,
4 Grosvenor Gardens,
London SW1 0DU
Tel 01-730 3400

Scottish Tourist Board,
23 Ravelston Terrace,
Edinburgh EH4 3EU
Tel 031-332 2433

Wales Tourist Board,
Brunel House,
2 Fitzalan Road,
Cardiff CF2 1UY
Tel 0222 49990

Government factories

English Industrial Estate Corporation,
Team Valley Industrial Estate,
Gateshead,
Tyne and Wear NE11 0NA
Tel 0632 876071

Information about Scotland and Wales can be obtained from the Scottish Economic Planning Department and the Welsh Office respectively; their addresses are at the end of Chapter 6 p 130.

Government agencies

Rural Development Commission,
11 Cowley Street,
London SW1P 3NA
Tel 01-222 9134

Rural Development Commission
Business Services,
141 Castle Street,
Salisbury,
Wiltshire SP1 3TP
Tel 0722 336255

Development Board for Rural Wales,
Ladywell House,
Newtown,
Powys SY16 1JB
Tel 0686 26965

Development Corporation for Wales,
Pearl Assurance House,
Greyfriars Road,
Cardiff CF1 3AG
Tel 0222 371641

Highlands & Islands Development
Board,
Bridge House,
27 Bank Street,
Inverness IV1 1QR
Tel 0463 34171

Scottish Development Agency,
120 Bothwell Street,
Glasgow G2 7JP
Tel 041-248 2700

Welsh Development Agency,
Treforest Industrial Estate,
Pontypridd,
Mid-Glamorgan CF37 5UT
Tel 044 385 2666

Derelict Land Clearance Areas

Department of the Environment,
2 Marsham Street,
London SW1P 3EB
Tel 01-212 3551

Enterprise Zones

Belfast Enterprise Zone Office,
Clarendon House,
9-21 Adelaide Street,
Belfast BT2 8DJ
Tel 0232 248449

Clydebank Enterprise Zone,
Clydebank District Council,
Clydebank District Council Offices,
Clydebank G81 1PG
Tel 041-952 0084

Corby Enterprise Zone,
Douglas House,
34 Queen's Square,
Corby NN17 1PA
Tel 053 66 62571

Delyn Enterprise Zone,
Enterprise House,
Aberpark Place,
Clwyd CH6 5AY
Tel 03526 4004

Dudley Enterprise Zone,
Industrial Development Unit,
Dudley Metropolitan Borough,
Council House,
Dudley,
West Midlands DY1 1HF
Tel 0384 55433

Glanford (Flixborough) Enterprise Zone,
Glanford Borough Council,
Station Road,
Brigg,
Humberside
Tel 0652 52441

Hartlepool Enterprise Zone,
Hartlepool Borough Council,
Civic Centre,
Hartlepool,
Cleveland FS24 8AY
Tel 0429 665522

Invergordon Enterprise Zone,
62 High Street,
Invergordon IV18 0DH
Tel 0349 853666

London Enterprise Zone,
London Docklands Development Corporation,
West India House,
Millwall Dock,
London E14
Tel 01-515 3000

Londonderry Enterprise Zone,
3 Water Street,
Londonderry BT48 6BQ
Tel 0504 263992

Middlesbrough: Britannia Enterprise Zone,
Middlesbrough
Tel 0642 222279

Milford Haven Waterways Enterprise Zone,
Preseli District Council,
Cumbria House,
Haverfordwest,
Dyfed
Tel 0437 4551

Newcastle City Council,
Economic Development Unit Policy
Service Department,
Civic Centre,
Newcastle NE1 8QN
Tel 0632 328520 ext 5046

N E Lancashire Enterprise Zone,
Stephen House,
Bethesda Street,
Burnley,
Lancashire BB11 1PR
Tel 0282 37411

N W Kent Enterprise Zone,
Medway Development Offices,
Mountbatten House,
88 Military Road,
Chatham,
Kent ME4 4TE
Tel 0634 826233

Rotherham Enterprise Zone,
Industrial Development Unit,
Norfolk House,
Walker Place,
Rotherham S60 1QT
Tel 0709 72099

Scunthorpe Enterprise Zone,
Industrial Development and Enterprise Agency,
Scunthorpe Borough Council,
Civic Centre,
Ashby Road,
Scunthorpe,
South Humberside
Tel 0724 862141

Speke Enterprise Zone,
Liverpool Development Agency,
11 Dale Street,
Municipal Buildings,
Liverpool L2 2ER
Tel 051-227 3911

Swansea Enterprise Zone,
63-75 Samlet Road,
Llanlet,
Swansea SA7 9AG
Tel 0792 50821

Tayside Enterprise Zone,
Industrial Development Office,
Angus District Council,
Market Street,
Forfar
Tel 0307 65101 or 0382 29122

Telford Enterprise Zone,
Hasledene House,
Central Square,
Telford Centre,
Telford TF3 4TL
Tel 0952 502277

Trafford Park Enterprise Zone,
Borough Council,
Birch House,
Talbot Road,
Old Trafford,
Lancashire
Tel 061-872 2101

Tyneside Enterprise Zone,
Gateshead MBC,
Town Hall,
West Street,
Gateshead MA8 1B
Tel 0632 771011

Wakefield Enterprise Zone,
City of Wakefield MDC,
Newton Bar,
Wakefield
Tel 0924 370211

Wellingborough Enterprise Zone,
Director of Development,
Borough Council of Wellingborough,
Council Offices,
Tithebarn Road,
Wellingborough,
Northants NN8 1BN
Tel 0933 229777

Workington (Allerdale) Enterprise Zone,
Mobet Trading Estate,
Workington CA14 3YB
Tel 0900 65656

General inquiries

Department of the Environment,
2 Marsham Street,
London SW1P 3EB
Tel 01-202 8416

Urban Development Corporations

London Docklands Development Corporation: see address under Enterprise Zones, London Enterprise Zone.

Merseyside Development Corporation,
3rd Floor,
Graeme House,
Derby Square,
Liverpool L27 SU
Tel 051-227 4111

Industrial Development Associations

North-east Scotland Development Association,
8 Albyn Place,
Aberdeen AB1 1YH
Tel 0224 56491

North of England Development Council,
Bank House,
Carliol Square,
Newcastle upon Tyne NE1 6XE
Tel 0632 610026

North-west Industrial Development Association (Norwida),
Brazennose House,
Brazennose Street,
Manchester M2 5AZ
Tel 061-834 6778

Yorkshire & Humberside Development Association,
10 Woodhouse Square,
Leeds LS3 1AD
Tel 0532 444639

Local Authority Development Corporations

Greater London Enterprise Board,
63-67 Newington Causeway,
London SE1 6BD
Tel 01-403 0300

Greater Manchester Economic Development Corporation,
Barnard House,
Piccadilly Gardens,
Manchester M1 4DD
Tel 061-247 3819

West Midlands Enterprise Board,
Wellington House,
31-34 Waterloo Street,
Birmingham B2 5TJ
Tel 021-236 8855

Yorkshire Enterprise,
Elizabeth House,
Queen Street,
Leeds,
West Yorkshire LS1 2TW
Tel 0532 420266

New Towns

Inquiries should be addressed to the New Town Development Corporation.

England:

Aycliffe,
Churchill House,
Newton Aycliffe,
Darlington,
Co Durham DL5 4LE
Tel 0325 312521

Basildon,
Gifford House,
Basildon,
Essex SS13 2EX
Tel 0268 553261

Central Lancashire,
Cuerden Hall,
Bamber Bridge,
Preston PR5 6AX
Tel 0772 38211

Corby,
Chisholm House,
9 Queen's Square,
Corby,
Northants NN17 1PA
Tel 05366 3535

Milton Keynes,
Wavendon Tower,
Wavendon,
Milton Keynes MK17 8LX
Tel 0908 74000

Northampton,
Cliftonville House,
Bedford Road,
Northampton NN4 0AY
Tel 0603 34734

Peterborough,
PO Box 3,
Touthill Close,
City Road,
Peterborough PE1 1UJ
Tel 0733 68931

Peterlee,
Lee House,
Yoden Way,
Peterlee,
Co Durham SR8 1BB
Tel 0783 863366

Redditch,
Holmwood,
Plymouth Road,
Redditch,
Worcs B97 4PD
Tel 0527 64200

Skelmersdale,
Pennylands,
Skelmersdale,
Lancs WN8 8AR
Tel 0695 24242

Telford,
Priorslee Hall,
Priorslee,
Telford,
Salop TS2 9NT
Tel 0952 613131

Warrington/Runcorn,
PO Box 49,
New Town House,
Buttermarket Street,
Warrington,
Cheshire WA1 2LF
Tel 0925 51144

Washington,
Usworth Hall,
Stephenson,
District 12,
Washington,
Tyne and Wear NE37 3HS
Tel 0632 463591

Other inquiries about new towns should be made to:

Commission for New Towns,
Glen House,
Stag Place,
London SW1E 5AJ
Tel 01-828 7722

Scotland:

Cumbernauld,
Cumbernauld House,
Cumbernauld,
Scotland G67 3JH
Tel 02367 21155

East Kilbride,
Atholl House,
East Kilbride G74 1LU
Tel 03552 41111

Glenrothes,
New Glenrothes House,
Glenrothes,
Fife KY7 5PR
Tel 0592 754343

Irvine,
Perceton House,
Irvine,
Ayrshire KA11 2AL
Tel 0294 214100

Livingston,
1 Kirk Lane,
Livingston,
West Lothian EH54 7AD
Tel 0589 31177

Wales:

Cwmbran,
Gwent House,
Town Centre,
Cwmbran,
Gwent NP4 3XJ
Tel 06333 67777

Mid-Wales (Newtown),
Ladywell House,
Newtown,
Powys SY16 1JB
Tel 0686 26965

Northern Ireland:

Antrim,
7 Church Street,
Antrim BT41 4BE
Tel 023841 3148

Ballymena,
Thomas Street,
Ballymena BT43 6BA
Tel 0266 3655

Craigavon,
Marlborough House,
Central Way,
Craigavon BY64 1AD
Tel 0762 41144

Londonderry,
19D Limavady Road,
Londonderry BT47 1JY
Tel 0504 46521

CHAPTER 6

Money from the European Economic Community

There is potentially an enormous amount of money which small firms in the United Kingdom can draw from the various institutions of the European Economic Community to finance their businesses. Use of these sources has been increasing as awareness of their availability has grown, along with the fact that they often carry lower rates of interest than comparable funds in the UK, together with the increased attention which those institutions themselves have given to publicising their wares.

The two main sources of funds from Europe are the European Coal and Steel Community (ECSC) and the European Investment Bank (EIB). The ECSC provides funds for projects in areas where coal mines and steel plants are closing and is stepping up the range of schemes it has for financing the smaller firm. The EIB, which is the EEC's bank for long-term finance, has in the past been more usually associated with the financing of public works and infrastructure development, such as building roads, but it is increasingly emphasising its facilities for the private sector, especially small firms. Facilities from the EIB were until recently mainly available through the Department of Industry in England, the Scottish Economic Planning Department, the Welsh Office Industry Department, and the Northern Ireland Commerce Department, but are now available through private sector institutions such as 3i and some of the clearing banks, who act as the agents of the EIB.

Some of the clearing banks and Government agencies such as the Welsh and Scottish development agencies also act as agents in the UK for the ECSC funds. Financial help is available through the European Social Fund for projects mainly related to training and re-training, for example of displaced agricultural or textile workers, but this assistance is indirect in that it is channelled through the employment authorities in the countries concerned and it is not necessarily possible to identify whether the aid is from the EEC or from the individual Government.

Coal and Steel Closure Area Funds

Turning first to the finances available from the European Coal and Steel

Community, these are the main sources of relatively low-cost funds for industrialists investing in projects in coal and steel closure areas; the demarcation lines of the areas surrounding the coal mines and steel plants are drawn quite widely and although a doomed mine or steel plant may seem some distance away it is often worth checking whether your business is in a qualifying area. The ECSC also makes grants as well as loans and it should be remembered that qualifying projects can be diverse; industrial projects can include works and installations which contribute to increasing the production, reducing the production costs, or improving the marketing of coal and steel products. Companies receiving the loans may therefore not necessarily be coal or steel undertakings themselves but could even include companies converting a system to make use of coal instead of another fuel.

The funds of most interest to small firms will be those known as conversion loans which are available for investment projects offering employment prospects suitable for redundant steel workers or coal miners. This does not automatically mean that the workers taken on must previously have worked in those industries but the jobs must be suitable for such workers and reasonable efforts made to make them available to those workers displaced. Aid is given only for investment projects and not for general cash needs or working capital requirements.

The maximum loan is for 50 per cent of the cost of fixed asset investments and loans can be negotiated for periods of up to 20 years. Interest rates depend on and fluctuate with world interest rate levels (though once a loan is agreed the interest rate is fixed at the level prevailing at the time for the duration of the loan), but can be reduced by a rebate of 3 per cent per year for the first five years for industrial projects of recognised priority status. The interest rebate is available only on part of the loan equal to approximately £12,500 per job suitable for ex-coal or steel workers and is unique to coal or steel areas. It should also be noted that another reason for the lower cost of ECSC loans is that when a loan is negotiated the interest rate will be below the general market rate applying at the time, usually about 3 per cent below. As in some cases the secondary rebate already mentioned can apply to the total amount of the loan, the cost of ECSC money can even be described as cheap compared with other sources. A further advantage of these loans is that the rest period on capital repayments extends to the end of the fourth year so the borrower does not have to start paying back the capital until the fifth year.

Applications for the generally more substantial industrial loans can be made direct to the EEC Commission Directorate-General for Credit and Investments in Luxembourg but smaller firms would almost certainly be interested only in the conversion loans for which they have to approach the Department of Trade and Industry in London or its regional offices or one of the financial institutions which acts as an ECSC agent.

In addition to the Scottish and Welsh development agencies, ECSC loans in the UK are available through 3i, Barclays Bank, National Westminster, Bank of Scotland, Clydesdale Bank, Royal Bank of Scotland and the Co-operative Bank.

An example of the use of ECSC money for expansion is JPM (Automated

Machines) in Cardiff which used a loan of £195,000, backed up by £50,000 of 3i money, to develop a new factory for the production of its gaming and amusement machines, enabling the company to expand its workforce from 90 to 275 employees. Another illustration, which shows composite financial structuring, is Abrahams and Co, a Newcastle-based firm specialising in the production of glassware and metal gift ware; it used ECSC funds of £120,000 and regional development grants of £69,000 to complement its own investment of £120,000 to expand production facilities, enabling it to increase its workforce by 50 per cent.

Barclays is using the 'global loan' – basically a line of credit – for what it calls its Job Creation Loan scheme. Barclays is the leading bank for ECSC loans with some 44 per cent of the market. Just over three of 10 of its loans have gone to South Wales, 14 per cent to North Wales, 13 per cent to Yorkshire and Humberside, 10 per cent to the North-east, 28 per cent to the East and West Midlands, 2.4 per cent to the North-west and 1.6 per cent to Scotland. In 1978 when the loans first became available, a mere £800,000 was taken up but this has grown to more than £30 million today. Barclays did not enter the scheme until 1982 but since then it has arranged nearly £50 million worth of cheap money for small British firms. By far the largest volume has gone to existing small firms with turnovers in the region of £1 million to £5 million. More emphasis is now being placed on smaller firms as ECSC now pays a larger rebate subsidy in cases of companies employing less than 500 people. The total employment created in companies helped by Barclays' lending of ECSC finance is around 7,000. In recent years the cost of borrowing cheap ECSC money has been as low as 8 per cent and this figure reduces further by the availability of the rebate subsidy, which is currently 3 per cent for small to medium-sized companies. The smallest ECSC loan processed by Barclays is £5,000 but generally it only considers applications in excess of £15,000. The money is available under Barclays' normal lending criteria to both existing firms and start-ups to fund up to 50 per cent of capital spending on projects in qualifying areas. The loan period is up to eight years at fixed interest rates.

The business concerned must employ no more than 50 employees at the time it makes its application and must be located near a qualifying coal or steel closure. The bank also points out that if the business is unable to raise the other 50 per cent necessary to get an expansion plan off the ground it can itself offer 'top up' loans from its normal loan sources at normal rates. Other financial institutions offering ECSC money, such as 3i and the Co-operative Bank, would obviously also be able to offer additional funds from their own resources where these were needed and the project and company suitable.

Any company wishing to borrow ECSC funds should therefore approach either the regional offices of the Department of Trade and Industry, or the Department of Commerce in Northern Ireland, the Welsh or Scottish Development Agencies – whose terms are similar to those for the Barclays scheme – Barclays Bank branches, Co-operative Bank branches, and the area offices of 3i. Considerable help in obtaining these funds can also be had from BSC (Industry) and British Coal Enterprise, the job creation arms of British Steel and British Coal, whose services are discussed more fully later in this chapter.

An example of how ECSC funds can help in providing jobs comes from a company set up with the assistance of the Scottish Development Agency. Some 25 Scottish workers out of 60 who lost their jobs in 1981 when Munro and Junor NEI Peebles Ltd closed their factory at Bellshill, Lanarkshire, found jobs as a result. Two directors, Sam Cullen and John Tillman, and a manager, Stewart Cuthbertson, pooled their redundancy money to form a new business and received backing from the ECSC and SDA with £15,000 in the form of low interest loans. The deal was the first to be approved under agreements which allowed the SDA to channel £5 million of ECSC funds to Scottish industry as loans. The new business makes electrical engineering components and carries out shopfitting from an SDA factory at Wishaw, under the name of M and J Services. Many of the previous company's customers promised orders for the new company, enabling it to hire 22 of the former workers from the Munro and Junor company.

European Investment Bank

The other major European source of funds is the European Investment Bank, which operates on a non-profit making basis and is therefore able to offer loans at or near the rates prevailing in capital markets. It operates through an agency agreement with the UK Government, which usually handles the larger loans, and by providing global loans to financial institutions. National Westminster, Barclays, Clydesdale, Royal Bank of Scotland, 3i and the Midland Bank have made agreements with the EIB in Britain, and they lend EIB funds to the individual customers who approach them. EIB finance is intended for small and medium-sized industrial and tourism investments. Applications for agency loans go directly to the regional offices of the Department of Trade and Industry in England, the Scottish Economic Planning Department, the Welsh Office Industry Department, the Northern Ireland Commerce Department or the Tourist Boards in the case of tourism investments. Applications for finance under the global loan schemes go directly to the area offices of 3i or bank branches.

Funds provided are restricted to not more than half of the new fixed asset investment and are normally available only for companies with fewer than 500 employees and less than £16.5 million in fixed assets. Projects must be in assisted areas and help their development by creating or safeguarding employment; industrial projects must qualify for selective assistance under Section 7 or 8 of the Industry Act 1972, or the Industries Development Act (Northern Ireland) 1966. Under present arrangements loans go from £15,000 to £4.25 million under the Government agency scheme and from £15,000 to £50,000 under the 3i and bank schemes. Repayments are normally over seven to eight years with a capital repayment 'holiday' of up to two years after which payments are made up of equal half-yearly instalments of capital and interest. Security requirements are negotiated directly with the lending agency.

EIB finance is normally provided in foreign currencies but applications to borrow under these schemes will automatically be considered for exchange risk cover. The borrower pays for this cover by a charge which in the past was expressed as a flat rate percentage of 1 or 2 per cent, depending on the location of the borrower's project. This premium is for covering the risk of fluctuations in exchange rates as most small firms are unwilling to take foreign currency loans without this safeguard. The cover means that small businesses take on a repayment liability which is fixed in sterling terms.

Until 1984 firms in non-assisted areas could benefit from the lower cost finance available from institutions in the European Economic Community but the Government has now withdrawn exchange risk cover for funds provided to firms outside the assisted areas. Most of National Westminster Bank's lending, for example, under European Investment Bank schemes had been to non-assisted areas and other banks were also experiencing heavy demand from these areas. The Government was, however, making a substantial loss on providing this exchange risk cover and decided to restrict it to firms in assisted areas – the designation of which has also changed substantially.

The funds were provided at rates of interest as much as two percentage points below those available under non-scheme lending. It is still possible – theoretically – for EIB funds to be provided in non-assisted areas but the exchange risk cover would have to be provided by the banks; they would then cover the cost with an additional charge. The premium would be as much as 2 or 3 per cent, which would eliminate the margin of lower interest rates and make the exercise pointless. In assisted areas the Government still provides exchange risk cover under both the EIB and European Coal and Steel Community schemes.

With the Department of Trade and Industry, the EIB and ECSC try to provide funds in the most favourable mix of currencies, one of the reasons why the overall cost is usually below the borrowing rates prevailing in the UK commercial banking sector. The currency 'cocktail' is converted by the DTI so that the liability of the borrower is in sterling, with the Department providing cover against adverse exchange rate movements during the period of the loan – the problems of which are obvious at a time of volatility in exchange rates, especially when the pound is on the wrong end of the changes. The participating banks and 3i will be the small company's point of contact for these schemes.

European Social Fund

As far as funds from the European Social Fund are concerned, under the present rules training and re-training schemes operated by private firms must be already supported by a public authority. The amount of grant aid may be restricted to no more than that provided by the public authority. Inquiries should be made through the Department of Employment.

British Steel Corporation (Industry)

British Steel Corporation (Industry) is a wholly owned subsidiary of the British Steel Corporation, with its own independent board, and has worked since its formation in 1975 to introduce new long-term job opportunities in the areas affected by rationalisation, aimed at making BSC itself economically viable. In 1984 these became known as the BSC (Industry) Opportunity Areas, and the company's main priority now is to help business enterprise with potential for growth in these areas. Its work involves close co-operation with local and central Government, the EEC, and other organisations as part of a network of support. Together with enterprise agencies it provides training and other back-up help and facilities to help achieve positive results in business regeneration and job creation. It tries in particular to remedy, through training and advice, the major problem which afflicts many small, growing enterprises, namely the lack of management skills. BSC (Industry) can help with finance, and finds in practice that an infinite range of possibilities is available and that each case has to be talked through on its own terms in order to organise the most appropriate package of help, bringing together the promoters and commercial funds with the grants and incentives available and, where required, cash from BSC (Industry) itself. The intricate maze of assistance available both from the EEC and local and central Government makes the helping hand of organisations such as enterprise agencies, BSC (Industry) and British Coal Enterprise essential.

A BSC (Industry) loan might typically be for two to three years at around base rate terms but equity can be considered where most appropriate. Below £25,000 it does not usually ask for security but it does expect a high level of commitment from the promoters of the business and looks for a proportion of commercial financial backing. More than £21 million has so far been invested in this way by the organisation in job-creating ventures totalling around 2,700, which have helped to recover about half of the jobs lost in BSC restructuring. A recent new business initiative launched by BSC (Industry) is its Accelerated Business Development Scheme, designed to meet the two most crucial requirements of growing businesses – finance and management skills. A training needs assessment is undertaken by a training specialist at no cost to the company; once the training programme identified and agreed between BSC (Industry) and the company has been successfully completed, the interest payable on the BSC (Industry) loan is waived for up to one year. Those businesses that are supported are usually existing successful ones who need the extra help to take advantage of growth opportunities. The loans, based on BSC (Industry)'s normal criteria, are between £25,000 and £150,000, with fixed interest around base rate. BSC (Industry) can also help with premises, having pioneered the managed workshop concept in 1979 with the conversion of part of the old Clyde Ironworks, near Glasgow, and the opening of Clyde Workshops. The workshops make small areas of space available, ranging in general from 100 to 2,000 square feet, to new enterprises and small businesses on an easy in, easy out licence basis, offering licensees management advice and assistance when required. Today, with an investment of more than £6.5 million, BSC (Industry) owns nine such sites around the country, in which around 1,000 businesses have started, about one-third of which have moved into more permanent premises as they have become established. Around 300 businesses are using BSC premises at any one time.

A recent independent study by the Small Business Research Trust found that more than 80 per cent of the firms assisted by BSC (Industry) were expanding both in terms of turnover and of employment. The average number of employees had risen by 25 per cent, from around 15 before receiving help to just over 19 afterwards. Most of the jobs were created by manufacturing firms while service sector companies were the smallest in terms of employment. Three out of five businesses had approached BSC (Industry) early in their search for help and 43 per cent felt that the help received had speeded the development of their businesses. Of these 47 per cent cited loans and allied help while 24 per cent thought help with the start-up process was the most significant contribution. Two out of three had received financial assistance from BSC (Industry) and three out of 10 said that money from other sources had depended on BSC (Industry)'s agreement to fund them. BSC (Industry) itself has been self-funded since 1984 and the interest and repayments it gets from clients are used to fund more projects.

British Coal Enterprise

British Coal set up its job creation subsidiary to increase job prospects in coal mining areas. Its help is not limited to British Coal employees but the projects which it supports must result in permanent jobs in coal mining areas. Every month British Coal Enterprise uses £1.5 million of its £40 million funding to invest in around 75 projects, helping to create 800 new job opportunities. Financial help is usually provided in the form of a loan; the amount would normally be geared to the job-creating element of a project, usually based on a figure of up to £5,000 for each new job created, and would not normally exceed 25 per cent of the total financial requirement of the project. Loans can be arranged relatively quickly, at favourable rates of interest, and form smaller loans usually without security. Of equal help, the organisation puts firms in touch with other sources of finance, such as regional development grants, local authorities, financial institutions, the private sector, the EEC and enterprise agencies.

Company Story (1)

It is possible to extract money from the maze and actually get a business off the ground as two firms guided by BSC (Industry) show. David Conner and William Carlin were made redundant from their jobs as plant engineer and electrical foreman at the BSC subsidiary of Pipework and Engineering Development at Tollcross, Glasgow, at the ages of 56 and 40 respectively. They decided to form an electrical and mechanical engineering company together with five other BSC workers made redundant at the same time. The agency was approached at an early stage and provided help with a business plan and arranging a bank facility. When a factory was chosen it helped with the provision of plant and machinery. The first factory was about 500 square feet, which the firm quickly outgrew and, as a result, had to move into a 4,000 square feet factory.

Company Story (2)

In another steel closure area, Blaenau Gwent in South Wales, more than 30 companies were set up in the late 1970s, one of which was Taylormade Upholstery, a furniture company which took a factory in 1978. The founder of the company, Phil Taylor, the former England rugby international, made a cautious start but then trade began growing rapidly, even though the staff needed re-training as the skilled machinists in the area had no previous experience of making upholstery. The company was only making upholstery at the start but by 1980 was able to expand into producing furniture frames as well, with BSC (Industry) assisting with the leasing of woodworking machinery. The workforce grew to 60 and experience then led to a further expansion in 1981 (when more than 100 three-piece suites a week were being produced) following a consultancy study provided by the agency. The company moved into the production of high quality furniture, taking over a new factory, which led to further significant increases in the workforce.

Conclusion

In order to benefit, small firms have not only to make use of money available from banks and financial institutions through individual schemes but also from the agencies which exist to match those incentives effectively with other opportunities.

Useful Addresses

Department of Trade and Industry,
Industrial Development Departments

England:

Kingsgate House,
66–74 Victoria Street,
London SW1E 6SJ
Tel 01-828 3400

East Midlands Region,
Severns House,
20 Middle Pavement,
Nottingham NG1 7DW
Tel 0602 56181

Merseyside sub-office,
1 Old Hall Street,
Liverpool L3 9HU
Tel 051-236 5756

Northern Region,
Stanegate House,
2 Groat Market,
Newcastle upon Tyne NE1 1YN
Tel 0632 24722

North-west Region,
Sunley Building,
Piccadilly Plaza,
Manchester M1 4BA
Tel 061-236 2171

South-eastern Region,
Charles House,
375 Kensington High Street,
London W14 8QH
Tel 01-603 2060

South-west Region,
The Pithay,
Bristol BS1 2NQ
Tel 0272 291071

West Midlands Region,
Ladywood House,
Stephenson Street,
Birmingham B2 4DT
Tel 021-632 4111

Yorkshire & Humberside Region,
Priestley House,
3–5 Park Row,
Leeds LS1 5LF
Tel 0532 443171

Location & selective financial aid inquiries:

South-west Industrial Development Office,
Phoenix House,
Notte Street,
Plymouth PL1 2HF
Tel 0752 21891

Scotland:

Scottish Economic Planning Department,
Industrial Development Division,
Alhambra House,
45 Waterloo Street,
Glasgow G2 6AT
Tel 041-248 2855

Wales:

Welsh Office Industry Department,
Government Buildings,
Gabalfa,
Cardiff CF4 4YL
Tel 0222 62131

North Wales Area Office,
Government Buildings,
Dinerth Road,
Colwyn Bay LL28 4UL
Tel 0492 44261

Northern Ireland:

Department of Commerce,
Chichester House,
64 Chichester Street,
Belfast BT1 4JX
Tel 0232 34488

London Office,
Department of Commerce Representative,
Northern Ireland Government Office,
11 Berkeley Street,
London W1X 6BU
Tel 01-493 0601

Government agencies

Scottish Development Agency,
120 Bothwell Street,
Glasgow G2 7JP
Tel 041-248 2700

Welsh Development Agency,
Investment Department,
Treforest Industrial Estate,
Pontypridd,
Mid Glamorgan CF37 5UT
Tel 044 385 2666

European Economic Community (EEC)

European Investment Bank,
Liaison Office for the UK,
23 Queen Anne's Gate,
London SW1H 9BU
Tel 01-222 2933

EIB,
PO Box 2950,
100 Boulevard Konrad Adenauer,
Luxembourg-Kirchberg
Tel Luxembourg 4379-1

Global loans from EIB from:

Midland Bank,
Poultry,
London EC2P 2BX
Tel 01-606 9911
(and from branches)

3i,
91 Waterloo Road,
London SE1 8XP
Tel 01-928 7822
(and area offices)

ECSC

Barclays Bank,
Corporate Business Department,
5th Floor,
Bucklersbury House,
3 Queen Victoria Street,
London EC4P 4AT
Tel 01-626 1567

Co-operative Bank,
1 Balloon Street,
Manchester M60 4EP
Tel 061-832 3456

British Steel Corporation (Industry) Ltd
Ground Floor,
Canterbury House,
2–6 Sydenham Road,
Croydon CR9 2LJ
Tel 01-686 2311

Scotland
BSC Industry Regional Office,
41 Oswald Street,
Glasgow G1 1PA
Tel 041-221 3372

Northern
BSC Industry Regional Office,
Templetown,
Knitsley Lane,
Consett,
County Durham DH8 7PG
Tel 0207 591000

Yorkshire and Humberside
BSC Industry Regional Office,
4–8 East Parade,
Sheffield S1 2ET
Tel 0742 700933

Wales and West Midlands
BSC Industry Regional Office,
5th Floor,
Clarence House,
Clarence Place,
Newport,
Gwent NP9 7AA
Tel 0633 244001

Managed workshops

Coatbridge
Coatbank Way,
Coatbridge,
Lanarkshire ML5 3AG
Tel 0236 33448

Clyde
Fullarton Road,
Tollcross,
Glasgow G32 8YL
Tel 041-641 4972

Consett
Berry Edge Road,
Consett,
County Durham DH8 5EU
Tel 0207 509124

Hartlepool
Usworth Road Industrial Estate,
Usworth Road,
Hartlepool,
Cleveland TS25 1PD
Tel 0429 265128/235648

Normanby Park
Normanby Road,
Scunthorpe,
South Humberside DN15 8QZ
Tel 0724 849457

Corby
Central Works Site,
Corby,
Northants NN17 1YB
Tel 0536 64215

Port Talbot
Addison Road,
Port Talbot,
West Glamorgan SA12 6HZ
Tel 0639 887171

Blaenau Gwent
Unit 22,
Pond Road,
Brynmawr,
Gwent NP3 4BL
Tel 0495 311625

Cardiff
Unit A,
Lewis Road,
East Moors,
Cardiff CF1 5EG
Tel 0222 471122

British Coal Enterprise

Scotland
British Coal Enterprise Ltd,
Longannet Operations Centre,
Longannet Mine,
Kincardine-on-Forth,
Clackmannanshire FK10 4AL
Tel 0259 30485

Western
(Coalfield areas of North West England, North Wales, Staffordshire, Shropshire and West Midlands (excluding Coventry))
British Coal Enterprise Ltd,
Anderton House,
Lowton,
Warrington,
Cheshire WA3 2AG
Tel 0942 672404

South Midlands
(Coalfield areas of Leicestershire, South Derbyshire, and Warwickshire (including Coventry))
British Coal Enterprise Ltd,
Snibston Colliery Offices,
Ashby Road,
Coalville,
Leicestershire LE6 2LN
Tel 0530 813143

South Wales
British Coal Enterprise Ltd,
NSF Offices,
Cardiff Road,
Nantgarw,
Nr Cardiff CF4 7YH
Tel 044385 2511

North East
(Coalfield areas of Northumberland, Tyne & Wear and Durham)
British Coal Enterprise Ltd,
Coal House, Team Valley,
Gateshead,
Tyne & Wear NE11 0JD
Tel 091-487 8822

Yorkshire
British Coal Enterprise Ltd,
Carcroft Enterprise Park,
Station Road,
Carcroft,
Doncaster DN6 8DD
Tel 0302 727228

North Midlands
(Nottinghamshire and North Derbyshire Coalfield)
British Coal Enterprise Ltd,
East Midlands Regional Offices,
Huthwaite,
Sutton-in-Ashfield,
Notts NG17 2NP
Tel 0623 554747

South East
(Coalfield areas of Kent)
British Coal Enterprise Ltd,
65 Burgate,
Canterbury,
Kent CT1 2HJ
Tel 0227 6147

CHAPTER 7

Factoring

A major complaint of the small businessman is the difficulty of getting customers, especially if they are large companies, to pay their bills on time, a task which becomes even more difficult than usual during a recession when everyone holds on to cash as long as possible. One way of speeding up the flow of cash into the business is to make use of the facility known as factoring, which is an arrangement to sell trade debts in order to raise money. The modern version of this old practice includes not only the provision of finance but also services such as sales accounting and collection and credit management. In the past it acquired a bad reputation when unscrupulous factoring companies adopted strong-arm tactics with debtors. It was also regarded by some customers as an indication that the company using such facilities was in financial difficulties. In fact any firm which is financially shaky is unlikely to be taken on the books of any reputable factoring company, nor would such a company resort to tactics which would be likely to damage it.

The Association of British Factors (ABF)

An indication that factoring is both an acceptable and accepted form of business is given by the rapid growth which has taken place in recent years, with volume expanding from less than £1 billion a decade ago to more than £7 billion today. More than 5,500 companies now use factoring, of which the majority have turnovers of less than £5 million, while around 1,500 of them are small businesses with turnovers of less than £250,000 a year. All the Big Four UK clearing banks now have factoring interests and factoring members of the Association of British Factors - one of the two trade associations in the industry, the other being the smaller Association of Invoice Factors - and Factors Chain International, which covers 70 factoring members in the world's commercial centres, are increasing. There is only one major factor remaining outside the ABF, Kellock.

The industry is growing at more than 20 per cent per year and, as recent research by the Midland Bank subsidiary, Griffin Factors, shows, the business base has been widening considerably from its traditionally strong areas of engineering and textiles. New growth sectors such as staff and advertising agencies are now entering the factoring market, and service companies now account for nearly 15 per cent of the industry's client base. Modern manufacturing, such as electronic component companies and the increasingly diverse printing and publishing industries, are major contributors to the factors' manufacturing client base. As a whole, manufacturers account for 44 per cent of factoring business and distributors and transport companies for another 40 per cent.

An indication that the growth is showing no signs of slackening is contained in the results of ABF members for the first half of 1988, which showed the highest ever six-monthly increase. Total business volume of the 10 members of the association rose by 28.5 per cent to £4.17 billion, compared with £3.2 billion in the corresponding period of the previous year. Factoring business covering UK sales remained the largest sector, increasing by 26 per cent to £2.05 billion; of this non-recourse business, where credit protection is provided, rose 22 per cent to £1.25 billion, and resource factoring, where the client continues to take the credit risk, totalled £791 million, a rise of 31 per cent. Invoice discounting, a simpler form of business, rose by a dramatic 35 per cent to £1.82 billion, while international factoring rose by 10 per cent to £246 million. The value of bad debts absorbed by factors on behalf of their non-recourse clients actually fell by 9 per cent and the average debt collection time was reduced by two days to 61 days, which as Tom Hutson, the ABF chairman, points out, saves clients some 3 per cent overall in finance costs. The principal use for the cash was to pay suppliers for best discount, though it was also used for paying labour and expanding the stock range.

Members of the ABF are largely subsidiaries of clearing banks or major financial groups while those of the Association of Invoice Factors are smaller independent companies. The banks moved into the business a few years ago when the Bank of England restricted their lending and, as factoring is not lending as it does not increase a firm's debts, they found it a useful source of new business.

Factoring as a Source of Short-term Finance

Factoring is basically a source of short-term finance, easing cash flow and increasing working capital so it should not be used for such purposes as buying machinery because equipment does not usually produce a sufficiently quick return. It should be remembered that a company with very seasonal trade could have problems if it relied too much on factors providing it with instant invoices; the problems could arise when the season ended and the flow of invoices slowed. Factoring is not a substitute for proper cash management but an element of it whose benefits and disadvantages need to be carefully assessed. Remember that a factor does not lend money on future sales but only on invoices for approved sales already completed. In theory therefore a factor has no vested interest in the survival of a company but in practice that is obviously a short-sighted view and any factor who displays that kind of attitude is not worth dealing with.

Factoring and Expanding Firms

Factoring is most likely to be suitable for firms which are expanding rapidly with sales growing quickly. It provides a fast and flexible source of finance as money is provided against sales as soon as they are invoiced; the availability of money is linked to sales and it is up to the client to decide whether to take advantage of the facilities arranged. Once a company has arranged facilities with a factor it is not obliged to use them. Cash flow becomes to some extent predictable as the factor will pay the client against sales factored either as each invoice is settled or on an agreed future date representing the average time taken by the client's customers to pay.

The terms which can be negotiated with factors vary widely and can be organised to suit a range of particular needs. Where a factor makes payments immediately to a client against the sales invoices of that client then the company can receive up to 80 per cent of the value of the approved trade debts; the balance is paid when the customer pays the factor, or after an agreed period even if the customer has not actually paid the bill. *Non-recourse factoring* is where the factor takes responsibility for the debt and agrees not to go back to the client for reimbursement in the event of the customer failing to pay. The factor gives 100 per cent protection against bad debts on all approved sales, having first taken considerable care to ascertain as far as possible the creditworthiness of the customer – so it is not a method of unloading shady customers.

It is not necessary to have a large turnover in order to make use of a factor. It can be as little as £1,000 a month, with no upper limit, though by its very nature it is not really open to a business just starting up as such a business will not have the necessary portfolio of customers and sales invoices which can be factored. Once it is trading, however, factoring can help to accelerate its growth. The charge for finance provided against invoices is geared to base rates and can be between 2 and 3 per cent above either bank base rate or finance house base rate. It is not necessarily a cheap way of raising finance but that cost has to be weighed against the benefits which will be achieved through the cash that is released to be used in the growth of the company.

Factors' Services

This financial aspect of factoring bridges the gap between the delivery of goods and the receipt of payment, keeping the cash flow moving. But factors provide other services which can be equally useful in enabling a growing firm to keep pace with expansion. One of these services is sales accounting and collection, with the factor assuming responsibility for the sales ledger administration. Many factors have advanced computer systems and trained credit control personnel which enable them to carry out these functions often more efficiently and cheaply than can be done by an in-house operation, freeing a company's staff for such tasks as the highly important but frequently neglected one of management accounting or for developing actual sales.

The functions undertaken by the factor can include assessment of the creditworthiness of potential or actual customers, maintaining the sales ledger, sending out statements and reminders, and then collecting the money owing. The factor deals directly with debtors so all the client has to do is send off the invoices to the factor and wait for the funds to come back in accordance with the terms negotiated. These services are provided either on a non-recourse basis with responsibility for bad debts remaining with the factor or on a recourse basis where in the event of a bad debt the client bears the loss. Even where facilities are on a non-recourse basis action is not usually taken against a bad debtor without the matter first being discussed with the client, so that the question of loss of goodwill can be examined.

These services are not provided free, of course, and in addition to the charge for finance – which may be lower where other services are being taken – there is a service fee, varying between 0.75 and 2.5 per cent of gross turnover. This percentage will be affected by considerations such as volume of sales, the markets in which a company operates, the average value of invoices and the number of customers, and the risks involved if a non-recourse service is being provided.

Export Factoring

Factoring is not limited to sales made in the home markets but can be very useful when a company is developing an export business where the problems of administration and collection can be considerable. Exporters can take advantage of the full service and finance facilities offered by factors, some of whom specialise in this field. They often have overseas office networks, associated companies or banking links which enable them to assess creditworthiness or collect payments more easily than an individual small firm. Some factors also offer arrangements for minimising exchange risks involved in exporting as well as looking after export sales ledger administration in the same way as a home sales ledger.

Receivables Financing

A rather more limited service offered by many factors is called *receivables financing* or *invoice discounting*. This is useful for firms which want to realise only a proportion of the funds locked up in book debts or whose cash flow is subject to considerable variations because of seasonal trade or other reasons. It is a service usually provided only for firms which have a strong administration of their own.

Essentially the facility provides cash by the sale to the factor of all debts or batches of selected debts on a flexible basis. Receivables financing is confidential and the client remains responsible for his own sales accounting and collection of debts. Credit risks and other services associated with full factoring are not part of the agreement. The main charge for this kind of facility would be the cost of the money made available though in some cases a service charge is also made.

Remember that with factoring the factor accepts the debts that he is prepared to take, which are not necessarily the same as the debts which the client would like him to have. The factor will investigate the potential client as thoroughly as any of the customers whose debts he is being asked to take. Factors are not bad-debt collection agencies or a lifebelt for bad management; in fact the factor is backing management and assessing its ability to sell its products to buyers who will pay for them.

Briefly, factoring is a source of finance for growing businesses, a financial tool which can increase profits, turnover, and jobs, and a simple method of exchanging book debts for cash on an agreed regular basis – enabling a client to take advantage of any discounts which his own suppliers may offer for prompt payment, for example.

Lloyds Bank Factoring Guarantee Scheme

Lloyds Bank, in conjunction with the factoring subsidiaries of Lloyds Bowmaker, Alex Lawrie Factors and International Factors, has a novel factoring guarantee scheme. Under this scheme, branches of Lloyds Bank introduce customers, who in the main are small and medium-sized companies, to one of the two factoring companies. Assuming a positive assessment, the factor guarantees the customer's bank overdraft up to 65 per cent of approved trade debts. Additionally, Alex Lawrie or International may fund customers a further 15 per cent, giving them the opportunity to obtain finance totalling up to 80 per cent of their debtor book. The scheme enables Lloyds' customers to combine the flexibility of a bank overdraft – where interest is calculated on a daily basis and only on the amount outstanding – with the traditional services of a factoring company, including of course maintenance of sales ledgers, provision of regular statements and instigation of all action necessary to recover debts.

Company Story (1)

Stakehill Engineering of Bolton in Lancashire was formed in the early 1970s, making products for the materials handling industry. The managing director, Malcolm Rawlinson, developed the business steadily and after being in business for about two years saw a product he believed had potential for development.

The product, specialised pallet fittings for the motor industry, had been developed by an American, Stanley Genei. In the opposite kind of move from that which usually happens – British innovations being developed in the United States – Mr Rawlinson set out to develop an American innovation in Britain. Like all the best innovations the pallet fitting is deceptively simple in conception. It is in essence a corrugated strip of metal coated with a special plastic material; the idea is that when these strips are fitted on to a pallet, parts such as car doors can be transported with a minimum amount of damage.

Pallet fittings such as these were already used extensively in the United States and their value had been proven. Mr Rawlinson took the British and European licence for the product and was assured of orders from several British motor manufacturers. At that time his turnover was around £60,000 a year and clearly, in order to finance the substantial orders from the motor manufacturers, he needed a considerable injection of funds. He was not prepared to give away a stake in the business in return for finance from an outside investor and so he went to his bank for backing. He presented his detailed business plan and cash flow projections which were showing 'an ever climbing demand for working capital'.

'Attitudes all those years ago were different from what they are now and the bank took the view, "Where are you going to get your working capital?; because you're not going to get it from us." ' says Mr Rawlinson.

The prospects for developing the idea looked clouded until his accountant suggested factoring, a source of finance which he had not previously considered. A factor was approached and very quickly gave a positive decision. From then on Stakehill invoices were sent to Alex Lawrie Factors who, the day after receiving them, sent 70 per cent of their value less a service fee back to the company, providing Stakehill with the essential working capital for growth. The balance of the invoices less interest charges was paid as soon as the customers, who included all the major United Kingdom motor manufacturers, such as Ford, British Leyland, and Vauxhall, paid their bills. The rate of interest charged was 2.5 per cent above the Finance Houses Association rate.

Mr Rawlinson admits that the finance obtained in this way was not cheap 'but very early on in running my own business I realised that probably the most important part of my job was in maintaining the cash flow'. Use of the factor provided Stakehill with the cash flow which enabled it to service its blue chip customers even though the bank had not felt able to help. In spite of his experience then Mr Rawlinson has stayed with the same bank, which has seen the firm grow from a turnover of £60,000 a year to around £2 million with a list of customers which includes the major motor manufacturers in Europe as well as the UK.

Even though the motor industry throughout Europe has been going through problems Mr Rawlinson sees growth for his products with the increased internationalisation of production in the industry. The movement of parts not just from one factory to another but from one country to another with different stages of the assembly process being carried out separately is commonplace now. This system, however, makes such items as body panels vulnerable to damage and rectifying damaged panels is both time-consuming and expensive. As motor manufacturers increasingly look for ways of tightening up on costs, the huge reduction in the number of processes involved makes these pallet fittings very attractive. They have potential uses in other industries, such as those producing domestic appliances like washing machines.

Company Story (2)

Terry Gilbert, managing director of Compact Envelope Company, was concerned, not about the lack of business, but its growing volume. Sales of envelopes for the year would be £200,000, sales debt was £40,000, stock another £45,000 and there was no cash left. Sales and stock were increasing but there was a decreasing amount of cash available to service this success. Sales for the following year were projected at £400,000 but there was no way a 100 per cent increase in business could be financed. He asked his bank for an increase in his overdraft facility from £25,000 to £80,000; the bank asked for collateral but the company could not provide it. Mr Gilbert then decided to investigate factoring facilities. 'I was amazed at how simple it was to start and how few problems occurred. As soon as the contract was signed and the system installed, it was as if some magic hand had lifted a great weight from our shoulders.'

'Not only can we pay our suppliers on time, we can invariably negotiate settlement terms. Cash in hand means we are in a much stronger position to bargain for even better prices. In our own case we can now have 75 per cent of debts outstanding, in cash, on the very day we despatch our invoice, giving us currently on call over £100,000 instantly. Yet we pay no more for this facility than we would have paid our own bank. Second, we've no more worries about credit control. As a quickly expanding business we were putting on four or five new customers a week. Some were so big we never bothered to check their credit. Others we'd never heard of – how much bad debt risk were we open to? So having International Factors check new clients' credit and setting credit limits was a godsend.'

Running the sales ledger involved hours chasing overdue accounts instead of selling the products. With an increase to £400,000 sales a full-time credit controller/money chaser would have been needed, with no guarantee that the cash would flow as quickly as necessary. Using a factor overcame this problem. As far as bad debt was concerned, provided the company stayed within the realistic credit limits set by International Factors, all debts were paid no matter whether the customer reneged. With the factor controlling cash collection on a day-to-day basis the payment period also improved from 73 to 63 days.

Two clients objected to dealing with the factor; one later ceased trading himself and the other the company put on direct billing 'and discovered that they were very slow payers; they had no doubt realised that the factoring company would not have given them the leeway we might have done . . .'; they are no longer clients.

The company exceeded its target of £400,000 and analysed all the costs, finding that it had paid £6,700 for factoring services. 'If we had employed a full-time credit controller it would have cost us more than this in total. We no longer had to worry about bad debts. We knew exactly what our cash flow situation would be at any time. Last but by no means least is the unquantifiable value of never having to chase clients for money and never being short of cash.' That controlled cash flow also enabled the company to keep its prices at the same level in the following year, giving it a competitive advantage over its rivals.

Useful Addresses

Association of British Factors,
Information Office,
Hind Court,
147 Fleet Street,
London EC4A 2BU
Tel 01-353 1213

Member companies:

Alex Lawrie Factors Ltd,
Beaumont House,
Beaumont Road,
Banbury,
Oxfordshire OX16 7RN
Tel 0295 272272

Barclays Commercial Services Ltd,
Arbuthnot House,
Breeds Place,
Hastings,
East Sussex TN34 3DG
Tel 0424 430824

Century Factors Ltd,
Southbrook House,
25 Bartholomew Street,
Newbury,
Berkshire RG14 5LL
Tel 0635 31517

Credit Factoring International Ltd,
Smith House,
PO Box 50,
Elmwood Avenue,
Feltham,
Middlesex TW13 7QD
Tel 01-890 1390

Griffin Factors Ltd,
21 Farncombe Road,
Worthing,
Sussex BN11 2BW
Tel 0903 205181

H & H Factors Ltd,
Randolph House,
46-48 Wellesley Road,
Croydon,
Surrey CR9 3PS
Tel 01-681 2641

International Factors Ltd,
PO Box 240,
Sovereign House,
Queen's Road,
Brighton,
Sussex BN1 3WZ
Tel 0273 21211

RoyScot Factors Ltd,
Exchange Court,
3 Bedford Park,
Croydon,
Surrey CR0 2AQ
Tel 01-686 9988

Security Pacific Business Finance (Europe) Ltd,
126 Dyke Road,
Brighton,
Sussex BN1 3TE
Tel 0273 21177

UDT Commercial Finance Ltd,
Boston House,
The Little Green,
Richmond,
Surrey TW9 1QE
Tel 01-940 4646

Association of Invoice Factors,
Northern Bank House,
109-113 Royal Avenue,
Belfast BT1 1FF

Member companies:

Anpal Finance Ld,
PO Box 37,
Kimberley House,
Vaughan Way,
Leicester LE1 9AZ
Tel 0533 56066

Gaelic Invoice Factors,
10 West Nile Street,
Glasgow G1 2PP
Tel 041-248 4901

Larosta Ltd,
296 Kingston Road,
London SW20
Tel 01-543 3322

London Wall Factors,
15 South Molton Street,
London W1Y 1DE
Tel 01-629 9891

Ulster Factors,
113 Royal Avenue,
Belfast BT1 1FF
Tel 0232 24522

Non-member of either association:

Kellock Ltd,
Abbey Gardens,
4 Abbey Street,
Reading RG1 3BA
Tel 0734 585511

CHAPTER 8

Leasing

This chapter deals not only with the rapidly expanding practice of leasing, which is essentially a contract which gives a company possession and use of a particular asset in return for payment of a rental charge over a period of time, but also with other short- to medium-term methods of raising finance, such as hire purchase, block discounting, contract hire, and sale and leaseback. All these methods of financing the acquisition of goods, plant and equipment are of value to the growing business in that they enable the firm to plan cash flow with a greater degree of certainty than would otherwise be possible and conserve working capital resources for use in meeting more immediate demands on the company's funds. In short they help to provide the flexibility which companies need to take advantage of trading opportunities when they arise.

Leasing is not a new idea, as the Equipment Leasing Association, the principal trade association for the sector, points out in its explanatory booklet 'Equipment Leasing'. It was widely used in Britain in the middle years of the last century in the coal and rail industries, but it was not until the end of the 1940s in the United States that the growth which has brought it to its present influential position in the financial world began and it was not until the end of the 1950s that it started to develop in the UK. It now accounts for more than 30 per cent of externally funded investment in industry and 20 per cent of total manufacturing investment compared with 10 per cent in 1979 and only 5 per cent in 1975.

The Different Forms of Leasing

There are several different forms of leasing: finance leasing, operating leasing, sales-aid leasing. Contract hire (described on pp 147–8) is a form of leasing, and so are rental, hiring and plant hire; the difference is that in these cases the leasing companies buy the equipment and keep it in stock, lending it out on a short-term basis. This can range from catering equipment to excavators and cranes, or even the power tools hired to the general public.

With these, as with leasing proper, the leasing company (the lessor) retains

ownership of the asset concerned, which never becomes the property of the company to which it is leased (the lessee) though arrangements may be made for the asset to be sold to the lessee at an agreed price when the lease expires. This distinct separation of ownership and use is essential to the concept of equipment leasing and emphasises its difference from other systems of payment by instalment. Leasing companies in the ELA are not sellers or makers of equipment, they are financial institutions who lease equipment which their customers want to use. The equipment concerned is actually chosen by the lessee.

Finance leasing can also be called *full payout leasing* and is a contract involving payment over a period of time of such sums as will cover the capital outlay of the leasing company – the lessor – and provide for that company's borrowing costs and profit. The company using the asset is usually responsible for its maintenance. Leases can be extended and rentals are usually reduced substantially during an extension period.

An *operating lease* is one in which cost of the asset bought is not wholly covered during the period of the lease and the leasing company does not rely entirely on the rentals received during that period for its profit but expects to recover the balance of costs and profits from selling or leasing the asset again after the end of the first leasing period. This kind of lease usually involves goods where technological or other changes mean that the company using the asset, such as cars or computers, does not want the asset for its full working life or where there is a good secondhand market for the goods.

Sales-aid leasing usually involves a connection between the leasing company and the manufacturer or seller of the goods. In this situation the leasing company or the seller offers a leasing package as an alternative form of finance, a sales incentive, on the particular goods being distributed. Sales-aid leasing can involve either finance or operating leasing.

Leasing is available to the smallest company or partnership as much as to the large or multinational company, though small firms have probably not made as much use of the facilities as they could have done. Some leasing companies concentrate on a particular sector of the market or type of equipment while others divide their activities by value. Some act as brokers in much the same way as an insurance broker, while much vehicle leasing is carried on through subsidiaries of the distributors. Some leasing companies are actually subsidiaries of manufacturers and specialise in the manufacturer's products. Most of the finance leasing, however, is carried on through ELA members.

By leasing, a company can have the use of equipment while paying for it out of revenue and the payments are charged against revenue for tax purposes; the company's gearing is not increased, however, because leasing is not considered as borrowing; in fact as it brings new working capital into the company, it actually reduces gearing when older assets are replaced. In evaluating a leasing contract a firm has to consider how it can use the funds which otherwise would remain locked up in a piece of machinery bought outright.

Any capital allowances available on the purchase of the plant or equipment are claimed by the leasing company and are usually reflected in lower rentals at the start of the leasing contract, a factor which can be of particular advantage to a capital intensive firm which might otherwise have to wait for the benefits because earnings would not initially be sufficient. Regional development grants are payable for machinery used in development areas and where appropriate these would be claimed by the leasing company and again should benefit the lessee by showing up in lower rentals at the start of the contract. The lessee may, however, still be able to claim selective assistance in respect of leased plant and equipment under the Industry Act, 1972.

For the using company there are the benefits gained from not having to spend time battling through the bureaucratic maze to obtain regional grants and the fact that the benefits will be received immediately the contract starts instead of the company having to suffer from the delays which often occur in payment of grants.

Using this system enables a company to calculate its cash flow more easily because payments have to be made at regular intervals and in known amounts. As long as the company pays on time the leasing firm cannot change the payments or cancel the lease, even if economic conditions change during the term of the lease. The using company is immediately able to work out the real cost of an asset over its period of use without having to take into account such factors as grants, allowances and depreciation, simplifying calculations and book-keeping. Some leasing companies offer terms in which rentals vary with tax changes or money costs but for the using firm which wants certainty the fixed-term contract is more commonly available.

Leasing also usually provides finance for the whole of the cost of an asset, unlike some forms of assistance where the amount provided only matches that found by the company itself. There is a high degree of flexibility in negotiating the terms of a lease so that if an industry is subject to seasonal variations in cash flow the payments can be organised to reflect this, such as a farmer making major payments after harvest time when the bulk of his income will be received. Inflation must be considered as the lessee will be obtaining immediate use of the asset but payments are met out of future earnings so that real costs will be falling over a period of time where payments are fixed in money terms. On the other hand, the leasing company is also making an assessment of future inflation in the level of the rental; the question then is whose guess on the trend of inflation is the right one. The using company should also remember that it will be responsible for costs such as maintenance and insurance.

Leases usually run for three or five years; three years for office equipment is fairly common though an average of five years for most leased equipment can be expected. This makes decisions on replacing obsolete equipment easier; when a piece of machinery has been bought outright there is a tendency to hold on to it after its real economic life is over in the often mistaken belief that it is 'costing nothing'; what it may be costing is lost opportunities and lost profits. When equipment is leased that temptation is removed and a company is more likely to equip itself with what it really needs to meet future demands.

It is just as easy, however, to become over-committed to leasing as it is to any other form of financing and it should be used as part of a properly balanced mixture of finance. Although it does not represent new borrowing to a company and does not involve charges on other assets for security it is a financial commitment which the using company must be in a position to meet as it becomes due. The uses to which the equipment is going to be put and the income it can generate or help to generate have to be carefully considered, even though leasing removes the need to tie up capital in fixed assets.

Costs vary considerably, just as the items which can be leased vary from small equipment costing a few pounds to that costing many tens of millions of pounds. It will obviously cost less to lease office furniture or telephone answering equipment than commercial vehicles, textile machinery or machine tools. As clearing banks all have leasing subsidiaries it is useful to have a quote from your own bank as a benchmark for judging the quotations of others – but make sure that the quotations themselves are comparable.

Insist on quotes of so many £ per £1,000 so they all have a common base; where a quotation is based on interest rates the real costs can be subject to considerable variations. Make sure also that the terms being quoted are at fixed rates if that is what you are looking for and not subject to variations for one reason or another, such as corporation tax or movements in interest rates.

Hire Purchase

The principle of hire purchase is familiar to most people and there is little difference between hire purchase taken by the private individual and that taken by a company, partnership or sole trader, the additional advantage to the business user being that the firm can benefit from any capital allowances or investment grants available as well as obtaining tax relief on the interest paid. Hire purchase offers finance at a fixed rate of interest over a known period, and documentation is usually standard so that the finance can be obtained fairly quickly subject to a check on the creditworthiness of the borrower. There are normally no fees to pay and security is limited to the equipment bought which is less onerous than a charge on the firm's assets.

Technically, the finance house approached for the facility buys the particular item of equipment to the firm's specification and then leases or hires it to the business against an initial down-payment of 20 or 25 per cent followed by regular fixed amounts over an agreed term. The equipment remains the property of the finance house until the firm pays a nominal purchase fee at the end of the agreed period. The hiring company of course has beneficial ownership of the item during the payment period.

Virtually any movable piece of equipment or vehicle can be bought in this way, ranging from office equipment to lathes, from shop-fittings to cars or vans for maintenance or sales people, with repayments being spread over the working life of the equipment so that the equipment is actually paying for itself while it is being bought.

Until the Finance Act, 1984 it was possible to write off 100 per cent of capital investment in the year of acquisition, but this allowance has been abolished.

The cost of this form of instalment finance varies considerably from one finance house to another and it is essential to shop around to find the most advantageous terms. As banks and other financial groups are extensively involved in finance houses it is often possible to use a rate quoted by a bank-owned company as a benchmark for the others, as a bank-owned company will often quote a more competitive rate. These 'finer' rates will usually be offered only where the bank introduces the custom to its own finance house so it can be useful to make the first approach through your own bank manager and then compare other rates quoted by a bank-owned company as a benchmark for the others, as it may not be volunteered; finance companies prefer to quote flat rates because they look less. Unfortunately they take no account of the reductions in the sum borrowed as repayments are made. A simple way of calculating a true rate is to double the flat rate and then deduct 0.5 per cent – so if a flat rate of 12 per cent is quoted the true rate will be 23.5 per cent, that is 12 × 2, minus 0.5 per cent. This gives a much more accurate assessment of the real cost of buying an item of equipment on hire purchase.

Credit Sale

The term 'hire purchase' is often used today as a general description for many forms of credit sales, although strictly speaking hire purchase and credit sales are different. Credit sale may be offered as an alternative to hire purchase and actually gives full ownership of the goods to the buyer at the start. The borrower has to give the lender a written promise to repay the cost, plus interest, and this represents the security to the lender. It does not mean that the borrower can avoid making the regular payments which he has agreed to pay off the debt; such an action, if deliberate, would be fraud.

In short, hire purchase or credit sale finance is useful because of the flexibility of repayment, which can help cash flow, the lack of legal charges, and the relative ease with which it can be obtained.

Contract Hire

This is another popular and well-known form of financing over a period the use of equipment which the company probably could not afford to buy outright. It is almost always related to vehicles and such an agreement is made between the finance house, the vehicle dealer, and the hiring company. The company pays a rental either monthly or quarterly in advance but does not have to pay a deposit and has no option to buy the goods at the end of the contract. Generally an agreement will contain a maintenance contract, which means that the dealer will maintain the vehicles at regular intervals and provide a replacement for any period that a hired vehicle is out of action. The company can keep up its image by always having a fleet of modern cars, vans or trucks as the vehicles in the fleet can be replaced at agreed intervals of, say, two or three years depending on the needs of the hirer.

The regular payments mean that costs can be budgeted accurately, especially as the hirer will not have to worry about such matters as maintenance or replacement costs. When the agreement expires the dealer buys the vehicles back at a price agreed in the original contract. There are several factors which go into assessing the rental charge under a contract hire agreement: the difference between the cost of buying the vehicles and their sale price when the agreement ends; the flat rate hiring charge on the net cost of the vehicles during the hiring term; the cost of the maintenance agreement; and an interest charge based on the price at which the vehicles are bought back also spread over the hire term.

Block Discounting

This is a facility offered by finance houses to retailers who are involved in providing instalment credit and in renting goods to the general public, such as televisions, to enable them to preserve their working capital. In effect the finance house buys from the retailer blocks of instalment credit agreements, thus releasing to the retailer the working capital otherwise locked up. In most cases the retailer continues to collect the instalments on behalf of the finance house and the customer knows nothing of the transaction. Block discounting is in many ways another version of a simple form of factoring.

For the retailer the advantage is that he can obtain cash amounting to between half and three-quarters of any balance on outstanding instalment or rental agreements with customers, capital which can be used to offer more flexible terms and so improve competitiveness or to take advantage of any discounts offered by suppliers for prompt payment. Capital is no longer locked up in items of stock, such as furniture or carpets which may have been sold on 'easy payment' terms over a period of time. Any firm wanting to take advantage of block discounting should be able to offer the finance house a reasonable volume of agreements in whatever line of retailing it specialises in.

The cost of block discounting is subject to considerable variation and will be influenced by factors such as the kind and quantity of business but is usually based on a flat rate charge of the sum advanced. Some finance houses deduct the charge – the discounting cost – from the amount of the advance agreed while others pay the full amount and levy the charge separately.

Sale and Leaseback

Property and sometimes substantial items of capital equipment are usually the subject of sale and leaseback agreements, which are a method of raising permanent capital for a company – perhaps to avoid having to sell a share of the equity to an outsider. While having superficial attractions, they can have many drawbacks and should only be considered with the greatest possible care and the best advice. What happens is that the company concerned sells a piece of its property to a financial institution, such as a pension fund, and then leases it back on a long-term lease for which it pays a rental charge reflecting the value of the building. That rental charge will be subject to upward rent reviews at regular intervals. The selling company usually receives the full value of the building in cash, unlike a mortgage where only a proportion of the value is realised.

Unlike a mortgage (see pp 92–3), however, sale and leaseback does not increase the capital employed in a company, in fact it can be said that it reduces it. It also reduces the company's ability to borrow at a later stage because an asset which could otherwise be used as collateral for loans has been lost. The firm commits itself to that particular building for a considerable length of time and problems can arise, for example, if the firm wants to make alterations to the building because of the development of the business.

The amount of cash which can be raised by this method is generally more than through a mortgage but the eventual costs of sale and leaseback throughout the term of the lease in real terms can be high. Calculations must be precise when working out whether this is a suitable method of raising funds.

As a rule of thumb it should probably only be considered as a last resort and after careful consultation with an accountant, especially as there may be tax implications to such a move. Insurance companies are a possible source of sale and leaseback finance as are pension funds. Further information about these two sources can be obtained from finance houses which are members of the Finance Houses Association listed on pp 84–6, the British Insurance Association and the National Association of Pension Funds whose addresses are on p 97.

Start-up Leasing Scheme for Young Firms

This is a special start-up leasing scheme for small enterprises, including sole traders, partnerships and limited companies. Sometimes new and young businesses have faced problems in obtaining equipment on lease because leasing companies have insisted on clients having a record of three years' trading before they will offer any kind of lease. This has been a particular disadvantage to new firms, who could probably benefit most from leasing, given the inevitable cash flow problems of the initial stage. Subject to status, new firms can now lease, through Tudor Leasing, most kinds of equipment needed for business, including plant and machinery for all industries, construction equipment, catering appliances and office machinery and furniture. Normally, three rentals need to be paid as a deposit, interest rates are fixed, and payment terms can be from one to three years. When the lease comes to an end the lessee can have the option of using any residual value in the equipment against new products. Further information can be obtained from:

Tudor Leasing Ltd,
50 St John's Street,
Bury St Edmunds IP33 1SP
Tel 0284 701482

Useful Addresses

Equipment Leasing Association,
18 Upper Grosvenor Street,
London W1X 9PB
Tel 01-491 2783

Member companies:
Anglo Leasing plc,
2 Clerkenwell Green,
London EC1R 0DH
Tel 01-253 4300

ANZ Merchant Bank,
65 Holborn Viaduct,
London EC1A 2EU
Tel: 01-489 0021

Arbuthnot Leasing International Ltd,
131 Finsbury Pavement,
Moorgate,
London EC2A 1AY
Tel 01-628 9876

Atlantic Computer Systems plc,
Winchmore House,
Fetter Lane,
London EC4A 1BR
Tel 01-583 9481

BAII Leasing Ltd,
1 London Bridge,
London SE1 9QU
Tel 01-378 7070

Banque Paribas,
68 Lombard Street,
London EC3V 9EH
Tel 01-929 4545

Barclays Mercantile Industrial Finance Ltd,
Elizabethan House,
Great Queen Street,
London WC2B 5DP
Tel 01-242 1234

Baring Brothers & Co Ltd,
8 Bishopsgate,
London EC2N 4AE
Tel 01-283 8833

BNP Finance Ltd,
8-13 King William Street,
London EC4P 4HS
Tel 01-626 5678

Boston Leasing Ltd,
39 Victoria Street,
London SW1H 0ED
Tel 01-799 3333

British Credit Trust,
34 High Street,
Slough SL1 1ED
Tel 0753 73211

BUHAL Leasing Ltd,
15 Austin Friars,
London EC2N 2DJ
Tel 01-628 4499

Canadian Imperial Bank of Commerce,
Cottons Centre,
Cottons Lane,
London SE1 2QL
Tel 01-234 6000

Capital Leasing,
4 Melville Street,
Edinburgh EH3 7NZ
Tel 031-453 1919

Carolina Leasing,
26 Austin Friars,
London EC2N 2EH
Tel 01-588 9133

Chartered Trust,
24-26 Newport Road,
Cardiff CF2 1SR
Tel 0222 473000

Chase Leasing Ltd,
3 Shortlands,
London W6 8RZ
Tel 01-747 4524

CIS Computer Leasing Ltd,
Quadrant House,
The Quadrant,
Richmond upon Thames,
Surrey TW9 1DJ
Tel 01-948 8344

City Leasing,
23 Great Winchester Street,
London EC2P 2AX
Tel 01-588 4545

CLF Holdings plc,
The Quadrant,
4 Clifton Street,
London EC2A 4BT
Tel 01-247 5463

Concord Leasing (UK) Ltd,
Concord House,
61 High Street,
Brentford,
Middlesex TW8 0AA
Tel 01-568 3321

Continental Illinois National Bank & Trust Co Chicago,
162 Queen Victoria Street,
London EC4V 4BS
Tel 01-236 7444

Dataserv Ltd,
Queen Anne's Court,
Windsor,
Berkshire SL4 1DG
Tel 0753 868133

DNC Leasing Services Ltd,
20 St Dunstan's Hill,
London EC3R 8HY
Tel 01-621 1111

Eastlease Ltd,
8 Surrey Street,
Norwich NR1 3ST
Tel 0603 22200 ext 2555

Elco Leasing,
41 Tower Hill,
London EC3N 4HA
Tel 01-480 5000

First Co-operative Finance Ltd,
1 Balloon Street,
Manchester M60 4EP
Tel 061-832 3300

Forward Trust Group Ltd,
145 City Road,
London EC1V 1JY
Tel 01-251 9090

Girobank plc,
10 Milk Street,
London EC2V 8JH
Tel 01-600 6020

GKN Sankey Finance Ltd,
PO Box 6,
Dudley Street,
Bilston,
West Midlands WV14 0JF
Tel 0902 405261

Guinness Mahon Leasing Ltd,
PO Box 442,
32 St Mary-at-Hill,
London EC3P 3AJ
Tel 01-623 9333

Hambros Bank Ltd,
41 Tower Hill,
London EC3N 4HA
Tel 01-480 5000

Hewlett-Packard Finance Ltd,
Miller House,
The Ring,
Bracknell,
Berkshire RG12 1XN
Tel 0344 424898

Hill Samuel Leasing Co Ltd,
100 Wood Street,
London EC2P 2AJ
Tel 01-628 8011

Humberclyde Finance Group Ltd,
Chailey Court,
Winchester Road,
Basingstoke,
Hampshire RG21 1UE
Tel 0256 841863

IBJ Leasing (UK) Ltd,
Bucklersbury House,
Walbrook,
London EC4N 8BR
Tel 01-489 8806

IBM United Kingdom Financial
Services Ltd,
PO Box 41,
North Harbour,
Portsmouth,
Hampshire PO6 3AU
Tel 0705 321212

Japan Leasing (UK) Ltd,
107 Cheapside,
London EC2V 6DT
Tel 01-600 5756

Kleinwort Benson Ltd,
20 Fenchurch Street,
London EC3P 3DB
Tel 01-623 8000

Landhurst Leasing plc,
6-7 Queen Street,
London EC4N 1SP
Tel 01-236 8702

Lazard Equipment Leasing Ltd,
21 Moorfields,
London EC2P 2HT
Tel 01-588 2721

Lease Plan UK Ltd,
Thames Side,
Windsor,
Berkshire SL4 1TY
Tel 0753 868268

Lloyds Leasing,
57 Southwark Street,
London SE1 1SH
Tel 01-403 1600

Lombard North Central plc,
Lombard House,
3 Princess Way,
Redhill,
Surrey RH1 1NP
Tel 0737 774111

Manex Leasing Ltd,
Pembroke House,
40 City Road,
London EC1Y 2AX
Tel 01-251 9261

Milestone Leasing Ltd,
Warnford Court,
Throgmorton Street,
London EC2N 2AU
Tel 01-638 4191

Samuel Montague Leasing Services Ltd,
10 Lower Thames Street,
London EC3R 6AE
Tel 01-260 9000

North West Securities Ltd,
NWS House,
City Road,
Chester CH1 3AN
Tel 0244 690000

Norwich Union Insurance Group
(Equipment Leasing) Ltd,
PO Box No 4,
Surrey Street,
Norwich NR1 3NG
Tel 0603 622200

OKO Finance Ltd,
2 Throgmorton Avenue,
London EC2N 2AP
Tel 01-256 5861

Orient Leasing (UK) Ltd,
391 Strand,
London WC2R 0LT
Tel 01-831 1455

Orion Leasing Holdings Ltd,
Royal Bank of Canada Centre,
71 Queen Victoria Street,
London EC4V 4DE
Tel 01-489 1177

PB Leasing Ltd,
Aviation House,
129 Kingsway,
London WC2B 6NH
Tel 01-404 5555

Rea Brothers Leasing Ltd,
Alderman's House,
Alderman's Walk,
London EC2M 3XR
Tel 01-623 1155

Royal Bank Leasing Ltd,
RoyScot House,
The Promenade,
Cheltenham GL50 1PL
Tel 0242 224455

Saturn Asset Finance Ltd,
PO Box 180,
Ferroners House,
Shaftesbury Place,
London EC2Y 8AJ
Tel 01-248 4235

Scandinavian Leasing Ltd,
2-6 Cannon Street,
London EC4M 6XX
Tel 01-236 6090

Schroder Leasing Ltd,
Townsend House,
160 Northolt Road,
Harrow,
Middlesex HA2 0PG
Tel 01-422 7101

SocGen Lease Ltd,
418 Silbury Court,
Silbury Boulevard,
Milton Keynes MK9 2AF
Tel 0908 606050

Sovereign Leasing plc,
Central Buildings,
211 Deansgate,
Manchester M3 3NW
Tel 061-834 1582

Stakis Finance Ltd,
90 West Nile Street,
Glasgow G1 2QH
Tel 041-333 0848

Standard Chartered Merchant Bank,
33-36 Gracechurch Street,
London EC3V 0AX
Tel 01-623 8711

Storebrand Finans Ltd,
Storebrand House,
140 High Street,
Esher,
Surrey KT10 9PY
Tel 0372 69131

3i plc
91 Waterloo Road,
London SE1 8XP
Tel 01-928 7822

TSB England & Wales Asset Finance Ltd,
100 Wood Street,
London EC2P 2AJ
Tel 01-628 8011

Union Discount Finance Leasing Ltd,
39 Cornhill,
London EC3V 3NU
Tel 01-623 1020

United Dominions Trust Ltd,
Holbrook House,
116 Cockfosters Road,
Cockfosters,
Hertfordshire EN4 0DY
Tel 01-449 5533

United Financial Services Ltd,
126 Jermyn Street,
London SW1Y 4UQ
Tel 01-925 2844

US Leasing Ltd,
Gateway House,
322 Regent's Park Road,
London N3 2LP
Tel 01-349 4834

Wang Equipment Services Ltd,
100 Great West Road,
Brentford,
Middlesex TW8 9HL
Tel 01-568 9200

SG Warburg & Co (Leasing) Ltd,
33 King William Street,
London EC4R 9AS
Tel 01-280 2222

Yorkshire Bank Lease Management Ltd,
2 Infirmary Street,
Leeds LS1 2UL
Tel 0532 442511

CHAPTER 9

Export Finance

Introduction

Exporting is not necessarily fun but it can be profitable. At the very least it can provide a useful balance in the trading pattern of any company as a source of orders when home markets are sluggish. Though overseas countries have suffered recession, the timing of its impact varied in the different markets which meant that there were opportunities somewhere abroad when there was no demand at home. About half of Britain's export trade is carried out by large companies, though there is considerable indirect input by small firms who supply goods and components which are included in exports by larger companies, such as the General Electric Company or British Leyland. There is plenty of room for an increase in direct exports by small firms, especially if they live up to their reputation for flexibility and an ability to take advantage of a market opportunity more quickly than a large company with its established procedures and bureaucracy.

There is perhaps a tendency for small firms to be alarmed at the potential difficulties (real or imagined) of selling abroad, such as finding markets in the first place, establishing the creditworthiness of potential customers, documentation in shipping the goods, and then actually getting paid, a point where considerable delays can occur especially as credit terms are longer than in the home market. The vast bulk of Britain's export trade, however, is carried out on either a cash basis or on short-term credit. Even so, there has been a recent increase in smaller firms moving into export markets, particularly the vast tariff-free 'home' market of the European Economic Community and some other Western European countries.

This chapter, however, is not about exporting as such but about export finance which means funding the gap between the shipment of goods and the receipt of the payment for them from the overseas buyer. Every other country in the world offers its business community a wide range of incentives to obtain export orders resulting in offers of generous credit terms which have to be matched by us. Few countries admit to providing export subsidies but most do in one form or another and British exporters should therefore take advantage of whatever assistance is available to them.

The range of financial facilities available is enormous, from bank overdrafts, loans and bill finance – the idea of which was described in Chapter 2 on short-term finance – to documentary letters of credit, bank guarantees and insurance from the Export Credits Guarantee Department, to the schemes for smaller exporters run by several of the banks, the Midland being the first bank to have a specific scheme for smaller exporters though other banks offer a full range of export finance facilities. It is possible to finance the whole process by negotiation, through production and shipment to eventual payment as well as obtaining assistance for the very early stages of researching a market and breaking into it.

British Overseas Trade Board (BOTB)

It is perhaps as well to start with the finance available to help with researching the market in the first place. That can be obtained through the British Overseas Trade Board (BOTB), which is basically an export promotion agency of the Government though it consists of businessmen as well as Government officials.

Most of the aid it offers is not of a specifically financial nature but more in terms of an information service which can be worth more than money if it avoids the waste of resources in futile exercises. Probably the four main areas of initial interest to the smaller firm are: export market research, which enables firms acting on an individual basis to get financial assistance of up to one-third of the total cost; the market entry guarantee scheme, which is specifically designed to help small and medium-sized firms break into new overseas markets; the joint ventures scheme for overseas trade fairs, where small firms can take advantage of very advantageous rates offered, especially where they are exhibiting for the first time; and finally outward missions, a facility which can be of substantial help to the smaller firm. Full details of BOTB services and advice on specific markets can be obtained from the board, whose address and various telephone numbers are given on p 164–5. The four areas already mentioned, however, are described briefly here.

Export Marketing Research Scheme

This is designed to encourage UK firms to undertake overseas market research as an essential part of their export effort. It provides a free professional overseas marketing research advisory service and financial support for export marketing research and in certain cases for subsequent management consultancy services. The scheme is open to exporters and potential exporters whose goods or services are produced in the UK; priority is given and the highest grants paid to firms with little or no previous experience of export marketing research.

In approved cases the BOTB makes grants towards the cost of market research studies in overseas countries. It pays up to 33⅓ per cent of the total cost of commissioning professional consultants to undertake market research overseas. It pays up to 33⅓ per cent of the total cost of employing professional management consultants to advise on setting up or reorganising a firm's export department, if this has been one of the principal recommendations in a BOTB financially assisted export market research study carried out by professional consultants. It will pay up to half of certain essential travel costs plus a daily allowance for time necessarily spent overseas for market research studies undertaken by a suitably qualified and experienced researcher on a firm's staff, provided the research is of a standard equal to that of a professional consultant or agency.

When a new export marketing research department is set up, BOTB will pay up to one-third of the cost of salary, certain overseas travel costs, and a daily allowance for time spent by one newly appointed and suitably qualified researcher on overseas research projects during the department's first year. Groups of unconnected firms which jointly commission a professional market research study may be eligible for a grant of up to half of the total cost. Trade associations carrying out in-house research or commissioning consultants on behalf of their members can qualify for a grant of up to two-thirds of the total cost. A grant can also be obtained for up to a third of the cost of buying multi-client studies and other published research, though this does not include directories, market overviews, or the renewing of subscriptions.

The total cumulative amount of grant available overall to any one firm is £20,000 but there is no restriction on the number of projects which can be supported within this limit. The limit for groups of unconnected firms - such as a number of independent furniture makers or boat-builders or trade associations - is a total of £30,000 or £40,000 respectively. For management consultancy overall financial support is limited to £5,000. An offer of a grant has to be accepted within a month and the grant is paid after the research has been completed. Estimated costs for in-house projects must be agreed with the board before the project is started and research projects already commissioned, under way, or completed are not eligible for grants.

No grants are payable for research undertaken in EEC countries but the board can make available professional market research studies on export prospects for specific products or services in these countries. A consultation charge is made for this service. The board operates a free advisory service on the best methods of researching overseas markets. Applications for assistance under the export marketing research scheme and full details of requirements can be obtained from the BOTB's Export Marketing Research Section.

Commissioning Research

Research on overseas markets can be commissioned from consultants or agencies at varying degrees of cost but for the smaller firm it is worth mentioning that high quality research at an economic cost can be obtained from a non-profit seeking consultancy recognised by both the BOTB and the London Chamber of Commerce which works on the basis of expenses plus a contribution to overheads.

This consultancy is called Scanmark and was set up in 1974 by the School of

Management and Languages at Buckinghamshire College of Higher Education. Scanmark is actually a team of postgraduates in the final year of an export marketing course who, over the years, have carried out more than 100 research projects in 20 different countries for small businesses launching their first product, large companies moving into new markets, export houses, and even other market research companies. For research in the United States, Canada, and Mexico, Scanmark has what it sometimes calls its 'spring sale'.

They are able to offer market research at remarkably low rates because, as part of a long-standing reciprocal arrangement, the team visits Cleveland State University in Ohio where it bases itself for three weeks making full use of all the facilities of the business school there to carry out research projects for British companies. All intercontinental flights have been paid for, taking BOTB rebates into account, but the cost of research is far lower than if carried out by a commercial market research organisation.

Many of the group already have experience in commerce and all are postgraduates with first degrees in subjects such as languages and business disciplines who plan to start careers in export marketing within a few months. Individual companies speak highly of the organisation: one producer of squash rackets says it cracked the US market for him; a producer of car park control equipment received, for five days' work in Spain by the group, a list of all car parks, competitors, future plans for Madrid car parking, possible agents, an assessment of the market and a recommended course of action.

Europe is the usual choice for projects while the Middle East has been popular recently. Projects have included field research for woodworking machinery in China and for steam engine valves in South America. Firms do not use Scanmark because they cannot afford anything better – clients in the past have included companies of the stature of Wilkinson Sword, Max Factor, Chubb, The Daily Mirror Group, and Racal. The address of Scanmark is given on p 165.

Overseas Trade Fairs

The BOTB provides space and a shell stand, or other appropriate display facilities, at attractive rates to firms taking part in group displays of United Kingdom products at overseas trade fairs. For events taking place outside Western Europe the board additionally provides assistance towards each firm's travel costs. Under the joint venture scheme a number of firms in an industry participate in a collective presentation of UK goods or services at a specialised trade fair overseas. The minimum number of firms acceptable in a joint venture is normally ten. Proposals for joint ventures should be made as early as possible and no later than nine months before the opening of the event.

Charges for participation on inside space in a joint venture tend to increase year by year, so contact the Fairs and Promotions Branch in London or a BOTB Regional Office. For fairs at which the cost to the board for space and display facilities is very high charges are determined individually with the aim of recovering half of estimated costs. In accordance with a published scale, the

BOTB makes a contribution towards the cost of travel to and from the UK for two representatives of each firm taking part in a joint venture, British pavilion, or all-British exhibition outside Western Europe, on sight of air ticket counterfoils. When claiming travel aid firms are expected to use British carriers where possible and make claims within three months of the event.

Full details can be obtained from the Fairs and Promotions Branch of the BOTB. The same branch will also give details of the outward trade missions scheme under which the board provides assistance to groups of exporters visiting overseas markets either to explore and assess the prospects for their goods or services or to reinforce their overseas marketing effort. Financial assistance is usually limited to one representative of each company in the missions, which have to be sponsored by an approved trade association, chamber of commerce, or other approved non-profit making body. Proposals for outward missions have to be made at least six months before the proposed date of departure. Each participant approved for support may claim a contribution towards his costs after the event.

The BOTB provides a considerable number of other services for exporters, full details of which can be obtained through the board publicity unit.

Export Houses

Having gone this far a potential exporter may still not want to get involved in all the details of documentation, shipment and payment and one way of getting round this problem is to make use of an export house. These firms offer a range of services which are of particular use to the small and medium-sized company. There are basically three types of export house: the export merchant who buys the goods outright and then sells them in the overseas market on his own account, so the manufacturer receives payment in sterling as if from a domestic customer; the export manager or agent, whose export house handles all the details of exporting goods which remain the property of the seller; and finally what is known as a confirming house, which is actually working for the overseas purchaser but which ensures that the exporting manufacturer receives payment when the goods are shipped. Most export houses tend to specialise either in a type of product or a particular market area though some of the larger ones will offer a complete range of services. The specialised knowledge of an export house can be particularly valuable for the smaller firm as such houses should be in close contact with banks throughout the world and be aware of individual banks' interests in particular markets. Banks will move in and out of markets, or different countries, frequently. The banks will have set up their own credit limits for particular countries and once those limits have been reached they will not commit themselves further. Once contracts in that country have been fulfilled and the bank is no longer at risk it will have a credit facility available for new contracts. The export house should know what is available and where and so be able to arrange a tailor-made package of finance and credit facilities for the exporter. Use of an export house can be valuable in arranging facilities quickly and in a form acceptable to the eventual customer.

Exfinco (The Export Finance Company Ltd)

It is also possible to improve cash flow and secure more orders from overseas customers by using the services of such companies as Exfinco. The company makes what it calls a 'Standing Offer' to buy from the exporter, at the time of shipment, the full credit insured value of the goods, which is generally 90 per cent of the invoice value, less a discount, and pay the balance, less the value of credit notes or other adjustments, at a fixed time from the date of invoicing. This fixed time, called the average credit period, applies to all invoices, whether the customer pays earlier or later than that time. The average may be, for example, 85 days from the date of invoice, regardless of the actual payment terms on any one invoice. Cash flow is improved because of the ability to forecast shipment dates and values for the months ahead. The selling of the goods and contact with the customer remain with the client. The exporter must, however, have an acceptable short-term credit insurance policy as security, as in the event of non-payment by the customer a credit insurance claim will be made and settlement paid to Exfinco. Further information can be obtained from:

The Export Finance Company Ltd,
Exfinco House,
Sanford Street,
Swindon
Wiltshire SN1 1QQ
Tel 0793 616333

The Essex Export Agency

Another organisation which has been set up to help potential and actual exporters is the Essex Export Agency, a joint venture between Essex County Council and the British Overseas Trade Board. The agency does not offer finance as such but provides advice on all aspects of exporting, which includes finance as well as marketing, methods of payment, documentation, transportation and insurance, export seminars, overseas missions, and organising courses. Further information can be obtained from:

The Essex Export Agency,
Chelmer Court,
Church Street,
Chelmsford,
Essex CM1 1NH
Tel 0245 283030

Export Credits Guarantee Department (ECGD)

The Export Credits Guarantee Department (ECGD) provides credit insurance for UK exporters and merchants against the risks they face in trading overseas, the two main factors being the creditworthiness of customers and economic and political stability. The ECGD is frequently criticised for being inflexible and over-cautious but even so it provides credit insurance for more than a third of Britain's exports.

The Government does not itself provide finance for exports even though ECGD itself is a Government department, but when an exporter insures with ECGD the credit risks taken in selling to an overseas customer, the bank is far more likely to provide the finance needed by the exporter to carry out the order. ECGD not only provides a number of schemes for credit insurance but also bank guarantees which enable a company to obtain finance from its bank at favourable rates of interest. Banks are said to be reluctant to provide finance unless the deal has been covered by ECGD, a situation which is probably not entirely true, but such a reliance obviously puts pressure on the department and can cause delays in response about which complaints are sometimes made.

ECGD Credit Insurance

The bulk of the credit insurance provided by ECGD is on what is described as a comprehensive short-term guarantee, which will cover trade by an exporter in goods sold on credit terms of up to six months. The risks usually covered under this policy are for non-payment for goods exported in a number of specific circumstances; the exporter will be covered for 90 per cent of his losses if the buyer fails to pay for goods accepted within six months of the due date or if the buyer becomes insolvent; the exporter is covered for 90 per cent of losses arising through resale of the goods, less 20 per cent, when the buyer does not accept, without a reasonable cause, the goods which have been sent to him; where the cause of the loss is war, revolution, export restrictions imposed, and occurs before the goods are sent, the exporter is covered for 90 per cent of invoice value, increased to 95 per cent when these events happen after the goods have been sent.

The exporter who holds a comprehensive policy does not have to inform ECGD of each individual contract negotiated – though it is surprising how many do and clog the system with unnecessary paperwork – unless there is a delay in payment. The exporter has to work with a discretionary credit limit agreed when the policy is taken out for normal trading activities during a period of 12 months. Where a contract involves a significant amount of credit to a new customer or extra credit to an existing customer, the ECGD will expect to be told. Goods are covered normally from the date they are shipped but a manufacturer can, for an additional premium payment, cover his risks from the date the contract is signed. In this case the goods must be exported within 12 months. There are two elements to the cost: an annual payment on the issue or renewal of a policy together with a flat rate premium which has to be paid every month and is based on the value of the business which is done under the terms of the policy.

Where risks can be insured through the normal commercial market ECGD will not usually provide cover; this includes such factors as fire or anything which is under the control of the exporter himself, such as the refusal of the buyer to accept or pay for goods which are faulty. This can also include a situation where export restrictions are imposed, but of which the exporter should reasonably have been aware were imminent or likely and so could have avoided the problem himself.

If an exporter wants to give credit terms of more than six months but less than five years he can obtain a supplemental extended terms policy, which in effect is an endorsement to the comprehensive policy. Each contract must be approved individually by ECGD under this policy and the premiums are paid on each case approved, not on a general basis. Manufacturers, merchants and confirming houses can also obtain a policy to cover situations where goods do not necessarily pass through the UK but are delivered directly from one country overseas to another, with a maximum cover of 90 per cent, and the range of risks which ECGD is prepared to accept is limited. There are specific policies available to cover exports which involve high value capital goods, major capital projects, and services where there is no continuing pattern of business but in general these will probably not concern the smaller exporter.

In all these cases the level of the premium will depend largely on the grading of the market by ECGD, that is the level of risk it sees itself taking, because of the political or economic stability of the country concerned, for example. Whenever an export contract is being negotiated and there is a likelihood of credit terms being needed ECGD should be consulted at the earliest possible stage to avoid the problem of decisions having to be delayed because cover is not available. Where a comprehensive policy is held individual notification is required only when a contract is out of the ordinary or the terms beyond the limits already negotiated.

One other service which should be mentioned is the cover available to give protection between the period of tender and contract where exporters are quoting prices in foreign currency. This covers against loss through unfavourable movements in exchange rates between the date of the tender and the date the contract is accepted by the overseas customer.

Credit Insurance from Other Sources

While ECGD is the main provider of credit insurance on export business in the UK it is not the only one and there are a number of commerical credit insurance companies. Cover can be negotiated to suit individual needs but only for commercial risks, and bank guarantees are not provided.

It is not obligatory to use the facilities of the Export Credits Guarantee Department when exporting goods from the UK and many recoil in alarm at the prospect of filling in all the necessary forms, though considerable assistance in completing the documentation can be obtained from banks, who invariably maintain specialist departments or subsidiaries to handle export finance. Firms which decide that ECGD cover is not for them are faced with the prospect of financing the credit necessary to win orders from overseas buyers themselves, that is, using whatever bank borrowing facilities each company has and which can easily come under pressure from demands arising from the general running of the business. The company will need working capital to finance the production of the goods intended for export as well as the inevitably extended period of credit to the overseas buyer.

Such a method of financing exports will impose a number of restrictions on the company as it will not be protected in the event of non-payment by the customer and the amount of business which can be financed in this way will be limited, thereby holding back the development of other overseas business. The next step is to finance the export business through the use of *bills of exchange*, which were described in Chapter 2 on short-term finance (pp 67–8). Where security can be provided, the bank may be prepared to advance a proportion of the face value of the bills presented by the exporter, who will still be liable to pay the bank if the overseas customer fails to pay the bill when it becomes due. The bank would usually undertake to collect the amounts due, only coming back to the exporter in the event of default.

The bank may agree to buy bills payable on sight or at the end of a term up to a limit agreed beforehand and for periods of up to 180 days. When the bills are collected the payments go towards repaying the advance from the bank, together with any collection costs incurred by the bank and the amount of interest due. The bank will still be able to demand payment from the exporter if the buyer fails to pay. When goods are sold overseas and financed either through the exporter's overdraft with his own bank or through a bill of exchange the banks are far more likely to provide finance if the company holds an ECGD policy, so even when a company does not want such cover it may be forced to take it.

Letters of Credit

A further method of covering against the difficulties of securing payment from overseas customers is to use documentary letters of credit, either irrevocable or revocable, though the second form is little used for the simple reason that the buyer can cancel or amend it at any time until payment, negotiation or acceptance has been made by the bank, thus largely defeating the object of the exercise. The only letter of credit which is usually worth having is an irrevocable one, which is the safest and quickest way of obtaining payment for goods. Like all easy methods, however, it has its drawbacks.

Under a documentary letter of credit the buyer arranges with his own bank to give instructions to a correspondent bank in Britain to pay the exporter when documents are presented in the specified time and in accordance with the terms of the letter of credit. This letter of credit has to be raised with each individual export order and avoids any bad debt risk.

When an irrevocable letter of credit is used there can still be a problem even though the obligations of the various parties to it cannot be altered without the agreement of everyone. This happens when the letter is unconfirmed; it means that the buyer opens an irrevocable letter with his local bank in favour of the British exporter and the local bank then instructs its correspondent bank in the UK to tell the British company both that the credit has been set up and its terms. The British company, however, has to rely entirely on that overseas bank and even on the political situation in the country where it is located. A great deal of business is carried out in this way and usually without any problems, but if an exporter wants to be absolutely certain of payment he can ask his own bank in the UK to confirm the letter of credit, for which a charge will be made. When a letter is confirmed the confirming UK bank will make payment no matter what happens to the overseas buyer, the overseas bank, or the country concerned. All documents presented in connection with a documentary letter of credit must be precisely in accordance with the terms set out; if they are not exactly as they should be then the bank has no discretion to make payment and can act only in accordance with the prescribed terms. It is therefore essential to be absolutely certain of every detail of the terms from the start and any confusion should be clarified immediately the advising bank tells the company that a letter of credit has been set up and what its terms are. Confirming banks accept term bills of exchange under letters of credit for periods of up to 180 days; the exporter can sell the bill to any bank for cash when it is confirmed.

One disadvantage of a letter of credit is that it obliges the overseas customer to raise credit facilities with his own bank at his own expense, an involvement which could well set limits on the extent to which an exporter can develop a market. The exporter becomes vulnerable when a competitor, either from this country or elsewhere, is able to provide the goods and offers extended credit terms which do not result in the buyer having to use his own credit facilities. Insisting on an irrevocable letter of credit may assure the exporter of payment but it can also mean the difference between winning and losing an order, a consideration which the exporter will have to weigh in the balance. It is therefore useful to have a range of facilities which can be drawn upon to meet different circumstances as they arise.

Hire Purchase, Leasing, Factoring

Another way of financing export orders is the use of hire purchase or leasing, particularly where capital equipment is involved (see Chapter 8). If a buyer can have or wants to take the goods on hire purchase or lease the exporter can arrange a package either through British banks or finance houses which have international connections. A further method is to make use of export factoring services, which were described in Chapter 7, a method which is especially valuable where business is conducted on open account terms and in foreign currency. Factoring can provide 100 per cent protection against the buyer becoming insolvent, as well as political and other risks, in addition to the sales accounting being handled by the factor. Where a factor converts the value of foreign currency invoices to sterling on the day they are received there is also protection against loss through exchange rate movements.

Special Bank Schemes for Smaller Exporters

Several banks now have specific schemes for smaller exporters, including the Midland, Barclays, Lloyds and Co-operative banks, enabling an exporter who has not had ECGD cover for 12 months to overcome the problem of being unable to obtain back guarantees. The schemes are very similar to one another so it is proposed to describe in detail only one of them, that offered by the Midland. In association with its export house subsidiary, British Overseas Engineering and Credit Company, the bank has devised a scheme to provide post-shipment finance which does not usually affect any existing facilities the customer may have with the bank. The criteria for acceptance in the scheme are that bank customers, either new or longstanding, should have:

(a) an export turnover of not more than £1 million a year;
(b) no ECGD comprehensive cover in their own name;
(c) export trade with buyers whose creditworthiness is satisfactory to the bank;
(d) exports supported by bills of exchange drawn on the buyer or promissory notes issued by the buyer;
(e) credit and payment arrangements ranging from sight to six months and subject to a maximum of £25,000 for each bill or note, or the foreign currency equivalent.

There is no minimum amount for transactions.

Procedures are simple, with only a brief agreement document being completed at the outset. All the customer has to do to obtain finance is to deliver the bills or notes to the bank, together with the shipping documents and a simple lodgement form similar to that used for ordinary foreign collections. Lloyds Bank's Smaller Exports Scheme is primarily for companies with an export turnover of less than £1 million a year who do not have an ECGD policy. The bank's factoring subsidiaries, Alex Lawrie and International, provide export debt insurance cover of up to 100 per cent and finance up to 85 per cent of the value of each invoice, with no minimum or maximum value to invoices. A factoring fee is charged and interest rates are similar to overdraft rates, in the range of 1 to 3 per cent over base rates. The bank's Finance for Exporters scheme is aimed at those firms with more than £1 million per year export turnover and provides, without recourse, finance of up to 90 per cent against approved export debtors. Barclays' Smaller Export Scheme provides 100 per cent loan finance, less charges, to customers with an annual export turnover of less than £2 million against the presentation to the bank of export documentation.

Summary

Export finance facilities then are available to a limited extent from the British Overseas Trade Board, the Export Credits Guarantee Department, the clearing banks (whom it is probably best to approach through local branches), merchant banks and discount houses listed on pp 71–4, export houses (see below), factoring companies (pp 140–1), and finance houses (see later). Another source of export funds are British overseas and other banks, and foreign banks with branches in the UK. Some are interested only in large companies but many will consider proposals from smaller firms, especially where they have a particular interest in developing trade and arranging export finance with certain countries, usually their home country.

Useful Addresses

British Overseas Trade Board (BOTB)
1 Victoria Street,
London SW1H 0ET
Tel 01-215 7877

Market branches:

Australia: 01-215 5318
China and South Asia: 01-215 5252
Japan: 01-215 5625
East Europe: 01-215 5258
Europe: 01-215 5336
Middle East: 01-215 5501
North Africa, Caribbean and Latin America: 01-215 5358
North America: 01-215 5647
North-East Asia: 01-215 5625
South-East Asia: 01-215 3261
Sub-Saharan Africa: 01-215 3338

Export Marketing Research Scheme:

BOTB,
Export Marketing Research Section,
1 Victoria Street,
London SW1H 0ET
Tel 01-215 5277

Overseas Trade Fairs; Outward Missions:

BOTB,
Fairs and Promotions Branch,
Dean Bradley House,
52 Horseferry Road,
London SW1P 2AG
Tel 01-215 5222

Regional Offices:

South-east Region,
BOTB,
Ebury Bridge House,
Ebury Bridge Road,
London SW1W 8QD
Tel 01-730 9678

In other regions the following all act as BOTB Regional Offices: export sections of the Department of Trade and Industry in Birmingham, Bristol, Leeds, Manchester, Newcastle upon Tyne, and Nottingham, the Welsh Office in Cardiff, the Scottish Office in Glasgow, and the Department of Commerce in Belfast.

Export Credits Guarantee Department,
Aldermanbury House,
London EC2P 2EL
Tel 01-382 7000

Commissioning Market Research

Scanmark,
School of Management,
Buckinghamshire College of Higher Education,
Queen Alexandra Road,
High Wycombe HP11 2JZ
Tel 0494 22141 ext 35

Export Houses

British Export Houses Association,
69 Cannon Street,
London EC4N 5AB
Tel 01-248 4444
(The Association publishes a directory listing its membership of more than 200.)

Foreign Banks

Algemene Bank Nederland NV,
61 Threadneedle Street,
London EC2P 2HH
Tel 01-628 4272

Allied Arab Bank,
97-101 Cannon Street,
London EC4N 5AD
Tel 01-283 9111

American Express International Banking Corporation,
Winchester House,
77 London Wall,
London EC2
Tel 01-583 6666

American National Bank and Trust of Chicago,
15 St Swithin's Lane,
London EC4N 8AN
Tel 01-626 6121

Amex Bank,
PO Box 171,
120 Moorgate,
London EC2P 2JY
Tel 01-588 6480

Amsterdam-Rotterdam Bank NV,
101 Moorgate,
London EC2M 6SB
Tel 01-638 2700

Banco de Bilbao,
100 Cannon Street,
London EC4N 6EN
Tel 01-623 3060

Banco Espanol en Londres SA,
60 London Wall,
London EC2P 2JB
Tel 01-628 8714

Bank Brussels Lambert (UK),
St Helen's,
1 Undershaft,
London EC3P 3EY
Tel 01-283 3361

Bank für Gemeinwirtschaft AG,
Bucklersbury House,
83 Cannon Street,
London EC4N 8HE
Tel 01-248 6731

Bank Hapoalim BM,
8-12 Brook Street,
London W1Y 1AA
Tel 01-499 0792

Bank Leumi (UK),
PO Box 2AF,
4-7 Woodstock Street,
London W1A 2AF
Tel 01-629 1205

Bank of America NT and SA,
25 Cannon Street,
London EC4P 4HN
Tel 01-236 2010

The Bank of California NA,
PO Box 72,
13 Moorgate,
London EC2P 2NX
Tel 01-606 8771

Bank of Credit and Commerce
International SA,
100 Leadenhall Street,
London EC3A 3AD
Tel 01-283 8566

Bank of New South Wales,
Walbrook House,
23 Wallbrook,
London EC4N 8LD
Tel 01-626 4500

The Bank of New York,
147 Leadenhall Street,
London EC3V 4PN
Tel 01-626 2555

The Bank of Nova Scotia,
62-63 Threadneedle Street,
London EC2P 2LS,
Tel 01-638 5644

Banque Belge,
4 Bishopsgate,
London EC2N 4AD
Tel 01-283 1080

Banque de L'Indochine et de Suez,
62-64 Bishopsgate,
London EC2N 4AR
Tel 01-588 4941

Banque de Paris et des Pays-Bas,
33 Throgmorton Street,
London EC2N 2BA
Tel 01-588 7557

Banque Nationale de Paris,
8-13 King William Street,
London EC4P 4HS
Tel 01-626 5678

Beneficial Trust Ltd,
Prudential House,
Wellesley Road,
Croydon CR0 9XY
Tel 01-681 1133

The British Bank of the Middle East,
PO Box 199,
99 Bishopsgate,
London EC2P 2LA
Tel 01-638 2366

Canada Permanent Trust Co (UK),
1 Finsbury Square,
London EC2A 1AD
Tel 01-638 9046

Canadian Imperial Bank of Commerce,
55 Bishopsgate,
London EC2N 3NN
Tel 01-628 9858

Carolina Bank,
14A Austin Friars,
London EC2N 2EH
Tel 01-628 4821

Chase Manhattan Bank NA,
Woolgate House,
Coleman Street,
London EC2P 2HD
Tel 01-600 6141

Chemical Bank,
180 The Strand,
London WC2R 1ET
Tel 01-379 7474

Citibank NA,
336 The Strand,
London WC2R 1HB
Tel 01-240 1222

Commercial Bank of the Near East,
107-112 Leadenhall Street,
London EC3A 4AE
Tel 01-283 4041

Commonwealth Trading Bank of Australia,
8 Old Jewry,
London EC2R 8ED
Tel 01-600 0822

Continental Illinois National Bank,
162 Queen Victoria Street,
London EC4V 4BS
Tel 01-236 7444

Credit Industriel et Commercial,
74 London Wall,
London EC2M 5NE
Tel 01-638 5700

Dai-Ichi Kangyo Bank,
P & O Building,
Leadenhall Street,
London EC3V 4PA
Tel 01-283 0929

Detroit Bank and Trust Co,
PO Box 151,
9-12 Basinghall Street,
London EC2P 2LL
Tel 01-606 2325

Deutsche Bank AG,
6 Bishopsgate,
London EC2P 2AT
Tel 01-283 4600

First Interstate Bank of California,
36-39 Essex Street,
London WC2R 3AS,
Tel 01-353 4211

First National Bank in Dallas,
16 St Helen's Place,
London EC3A 6BY
Tel 01-638 4111

First National Bank in St Louis,
62-63 Queen Street,
London EC4R 1AD
Tel 01-236 9571

First National Bank of Boston,
5 Cheapside,
London EC2P 2DE
Tel 01-236 2388

First National Bank of Chicago,
1 Royal Exchange Buildings,
Cornhill,
London EC3P 3DR
Tel 01-283 2010

First National Bank of Minneapolis,
35-39 Moorgate,
London EC2R 6EH
Tel 01-628 6671

First Pennsylvania Bank NA,
5 Trump Street,
London EC2V 8HP
Tel 01-606 4571

Girard Bank,
83-84 Queen Street,
London EC4N 1SQ
Tel 01-248 7001

Havana International Bank,
20 Ironmonger Lane,
London EC2V 8EY
Tel 01-606 0781

Hongkong and Shanghai Banking Corporation,
PO Box 199,
99 Bishopsgate,
London EC2P 2LA
Tel 01-638 2300

Hungarian International Bank,
95 Gresham Street,
London EC2V 7LU
Tel 01-606 5371

Irving Trust Company,
36-68 Cornhill,
London EC3V 3NT
Tel 01-626 3210

Manufacturers Hanover Trust,
7 Princes Street,
London EC2P 2AX
Tel 01-600 5666

Mellon Bank NA,
15 Trinity Square,
London EC3N 4AP
Tel 01-488 2434

National Bank of Abu Dhabi,
90 Bishopsgate,
London EC2N 4AS
Tel 01-626 8961

National Bank of Detroit,
28 Finsbury Circus,
London EC2M 7AU
Tel 01-920 0921

National Bank of Nigeria,
2 Devonshire Square,
London EC2M 4XR
Tel 01-247 5561

Northern Trust Company,
38 Lombard Street,
London EC3V 9BR
Tel 01-623 1101

Overseas Union Bank,
61-62 Coleman Street,
London EC2P 2EU
Tel 01-628 0361/4

Qatar National Bank SAQ,
135-141 Cannon Street,
London EC4N 5AH
Tel 01-283 3911

Republic Bank of Dallas NA,
1 Moorgate,
London EC2R 6HT
Tel 01-606 4831

Saitama Bank,
30 Cannon Street,
London EC4M 6XH
Tel 01-248 9421/6

Seattle-First National Bank,
120 Moorgate,
London EC2M 6TE
Tel 01-638 4981

Security Pacific National Bank,
2 Arundel Street,
London WC2R 3DE
Tel 01-379 7355

Société Générale,
105-108 Old Broad Street,
PO Box 513,
London EC2P 2HR
Tel 01-638 4040

Société Générale Bank,
Pinners Hall,
Austin Friars,
PO Box 61,
London EC2P 2DN
Tel 01-628 8661

Syndicate Bank,
2A Eastcheap,
London EC3M 1AA
Tel 01-626 5501

Texas Commerce Bank,
44 Moorgate,
London EC2R 6AY
Tel 01-638 8021

United Overseas Bank,
2 South Place,
London EC2M 2PR
Tel 01-628 3504

Wells Fargo Bank NA,
80 London Wall,
London EC2M 5DN
Tel 01-588 6361

Westdeutsche Landesbank Girozentrale,
41 Moorgate,
London EC2R 6AE
Tel 01-638 6141

CHAPTER 10

Venture and Development Capital

Venture capital is a description which probably means all things to all men in Britain though there are more than a few cynics who say that most of the money goes into fairly safe options and is not ventured at all. On the other hand, the situation could be approaching where there is an over-supply of such capital with too much money chasing too few good ideas and, more importantly, stretching the managements of the venture providers too thinly. This point is important because of the 'hands on' style of operation of today's venture capitalists; in other words they become actively involved with the companies in which they invest, and if they are involved in too many the quality of that participation will be diminished and could lead to problems with investments which might not otherwise have occurred.

Whatever the truth of it and whatever such finance is called, there seems to be plenty of it about at present and many financiers, especially merchant banks, eagerly getting into the act. There are probably about 100 venture capital companies in Britain now, ranging from those backed by major financial institutions like the Prudential, with their Pruventure and Prutec operations, to American venture capitalists spreading their interests to the United Kingdom. About half of them are members of the British Venture Capital Association, which can fairly be described as the representative body of the venture capital industry in this country. Its members alone have about £500 million invested in the UK with a further £150 million in liquid resources available for suitable new investments. A recent entrant into the field is merchant banker, J Henry Schroder Wagg, who announced plans to set up a £15–20 million fund modelled on its successful venture trust in the United States. The fund was marketed mainly to institutional investors, relying on contacts developed by the US fund, Schroder Venture Trust.

This fund aimed at a $25 million minimum subscription level but attracted $37.5 million. The UK fund in fact attracted £25 million, well above its target. Another indication that there are funds looking for a home in the UK was given by Advent Capital raising £36 million, the largest individual fund raising exercise of any venture capital fund in Britain. The relative ease with which the capital was raised is in stark contrast with the problems which some of the funds set up under the Business Expansion Scheme have been having in attracting capital, and particularly as the funds raised by the venture capital companies do not qualify for BES tax relief. The growth in the venture capital market has accelerated recently but has been developing over the last five or six years, before which there were few in the field, with 3i being the principal provider for many years. So far there have not been many major losses among the investments which have failed, though the £8 million crash of the Welsh based computer firm, Dragon, did not fill many hearts with joy, especially Prutec which had a substantial stake there. Even so there appears to have been no diminution in the enthusiasm for investing in the smaller firm, though the use of the word 'small' probably has to be taken with a pinch of salt as minimum investments tend to be measured in chunks of £100,000 and upwards.

An encouraging attempt to bring the benefits of equity investment to firms looking for sums of under £50,000 has been launched, however, by the Rank Xerox Pension Fund who are overcoming the assessment and monitoring administration problems associated with relatively small investments by channelling their funds through two major enterprise agencies, the London Enterprise Agency and Entrust, and the Tyne and Wear Enterprise Trust. It is aimed specifically at those seeking less than £50,000, and £500,000 has been made available initially. A further £500,000 will be available for subsequent financing of small businesses. Equity participation will be in the 20 to 50 per cent range with the majority being below 40 per cent. It is anticipated that investment will be for a period of five to seven years with the object of finding an exit route offering a capital gain in that time-scale; the normal exit route will be through a quotation for the shares, a sale of the company or a buy-back arrangement.

It is perhaps too early to make judgements but there are those who feel that some of the organisations now dabbling in the venture capital field could get their fingers singed, running into problems when the companies in which they have invested face difficulties. The ones with the best chance of succeeding will, as in other areas, probably be the funds with the ability to provide proper appraisal and effective monitoring. For the smaller sums of money the increased use of enterprise agencies, as in the Rank Xerox Pensions Small Business Fund, could well be the route to achieving this in the future.

The Differences between Venture Capital and Development Capital

These may not be immediately easy to see but there are several, though there are probably almost as many definitions as to what constitutes one or the other as there are companies and institutions which now set out to provide it. The basic difference is the stage of development at which the funds go into the company and the kind of company involved rather than the type of finance, equity capital or long-term debt which is supplied. It is perhaps possible to describe venture capital as that which is supplied to start-ups or firms up to

four years old, usually of an innovatory nature, so that they can develop a financial base which will enable them to develop their products to their full potential. Development capital could properly be described as that which is required by established companies with good trading prospects and a history of profitable trading over a period of years, probably with pre-tax profits of £50,000 a year or more, which need an injection of capital for further expansion.

It cannot really be said that venture capital has earned much money in recent years for those involved in providing it, though there are obviously exceptions, the number of which may grow in the future as investments made over the past year or two, using more sophisticated techniques of assessment of potential than perhaps have been used in the past, come to fruition. Much depends on the number of good quality ideas which are generated in the first place. The fact that more ideas are being put to lending or investing institutions does not necessarily mean that they are good ones; companies specialising in funding management buy-outs, for example, are finding it increasingly difficult to find acceptable prospects, that is, acceptable management buy-outs, even though more and more people are coming forward with proposals.

Company Evaluation

Evaluating the commercial prospects of new businesses has always been a difficult, expensive and time-consuming process, which is why in the past the smaller prospect often had difficulty in finding a backer; the amount of time needed was simply not justified by the result. The Government has made attempts to overcome the problem for small firms by using the counselling facilities of its Small Firms Service (see pp 115–16) for carrying out appraisals on behalf of large institutions such as the Post Office Staff Superannuation Fund and the Norwich Union Life Insurance Society. On the basis of those appraisals the institutions chose which prospects they wished to investigate further and invest in.

The problems of evaluating a team which probably has no track record of working together as a management or who are technically rather than managerially qualified are increased when the company wants to develop an innovation or exploit an area of new technology. Any new business by its very nature involves people deeply committed to their project, who have a strong feeling of independence and are reluctant either to give away a share of the business or to tolerate possible interference from the outside investor. For the financial institution there is the problem that such an investment will be difficult to realise for some considerable time and there may be further demands for capital before any income is produced. And as most institutions need a regular, running yield on their investments to pay shareholders, pensioners, or policyholders, the tendency has been and still is to provide development capital for established profit earners.

Providers of Funds

In spite of this, there has been an increase in the number of venture capital providers, involving banks, insurance companies, pension funds, institutions such as 3i, and even a number of large industrial companies. An example is Rainford Venture Capital, backed by Pilkington's, the glass company of St Helens, Merseyside, and partners which include 3i, Prudential Assurance, BP, and others. This company seeks to back new and young firms which in three to five years can grow into multi-million pound businesses by taking a minority equity stake for an investment of £50,000 to £250,000. It has made a number of investments and although initially has limited itself to St Helens it plans to widen its geographical scope and increase the amount of finance available.

Another way for businesses to get in touch with potential investors individually is to make use of the various 'marriage bureau' facilities which have been developed. These charge fees and have the advantage that the businessman can deal with an individual rather than an institution and possibly work out arrangements that include not only financial participation but also assistance with some aspect of management, probably on a part-time basis, which would ease the demands on his own time. These bureaux range from the well-established one run by the London Enterprise Agency to the publication of the Institute of Directors called *Business Investment Digest* and attempts by 3i to use its 18 area offices to match local businessmen with funds available. The counselling service of the Government's Small Firms Service is often able to effect introductions of this nature as the counsellors are themselves local businessmen with a wide range of contacts. The local enterprise trusts can be useful starting points in the quest for capital.

European Investors

Investors from Europe are interested in the British scene and one company, Capital Partners International, was established for the purpose of channelling money from European investors into promising British firms, providing amounts from £10,000 to £350,000, usually in the form of an equity stake, though it can arrange loans as part of the package. The equity stake can be in the region of 30 to 40 per cent and a seat on the board will be required.

Insurance and Pension Company Funds

There are companies backed by insurance companies and pension funds, such as Development Capital (DC), which are interested in investing in the more substantial smaller companies. DC's first activity, the Small Business Capital Fund, was established as long ago as 1969 with backing from the Co-operative Insurance Society as its means of direct investment in the private sector. SBCF backs the new and start-up company, investing from about £75,000 to £250,000, taking an equity stake of 25 to 40 per cent. The objective is long-term capital growth and the fund expects to realise its investment in five to eight years. A non-executive director is usually involved with the company and the fund expects any products with which the firm is involved to be already fully developed and about to be put into manufacture. DC has access to more substantial funds for companies which are already well-established and producing profits of upwards of £100,000. Among its other interests is the management of the venture capital subsidiary of Williams and Glyn's Bank, National and Commercial Development Capital.

This is far from being an exhaustive coverage of all the many private companies providing venture and development capital for the smaller business but it begins to give some idea of the range available, especially as in addition are the established investment trusts who will provide funds to unquoted firms, although they are usually more interested in investing in publicly quoted companies. They will normally be more interested in the larger companies but represent a possible source of funding for others. Pension funds invest directly and further information can be obtained through the National Association of Pension Funds. Names and addresses of the many sources of venture and development capital are listed on pp 182–4.

Banks

The banks have moved into the venture and development capital field, often establishing subsidiaries for the purpose. Barclays, for example, set up Barclays Development Capital to make equity investments of £100,000 or more in firms with a net value of between £250,000 and £10 million and takes a stake usually in the range of 10 to 30 per cent but not more than 49 per cent.

Midland Bank set up a range of companies within its Industrial Equity Holdings group to deal with a variety of situations in addition to its Venture Loan scheme described in Chapter 3 on medium-term finance. The three main companies are Midland Bank Industrial Finance (MBIF), Midland Bank Industrial Investments (MBII), and Midland Bank Venture Capital (MBVC). MBVC concentrates on investments in the £5,000 to £100,000 range in new or recently formed companies, particularly with a technological content. Companies should have a successful or expanding record or potential to support their application. While most investments in new developments or start-ups fall into the range of MBVC, exceptionally, where the investment required is more than £100,000, MBII or MBIF may also invest in them. Products should have been developed to the stage where commercial exploitation can start, though MBVC may support the research and development stage. MBIF and MBII investments are usually for £50,000 upwards.

The bank's companies may appoint a non-executive director to the board of the business and their stake will always be a minority one. Midland requires its return in the form of a running yield – that is, dividends rather than capital gains, though it is possible to arrange for a deferment of payment of dividends for a period.

Midland is also involved in two other companies providing funds in the form of equity stakes: Moracrest, where it is in partnership with British Gas Central Pension Fund and Prudential Assurance, and Meritor, where its partner is the Rolls-Royce Pension Trust. Moracrest looks for investments of £200,000 to £500,000 and will take a minority stake of 10 to 40 per cent as well as putting a non-executive director on the board. Meritor invests £100,000 to £250,000 and takes a stake of 10 to 49 per cent as well as appointing a non-executive director.

National Westminster Bank is shortly to introduce another new development in this field with its new Capital Loan scheme which is to be launched through National Westminster Growth Options Ltd. Loans will be available from £25,000 to £200,000 for up to ten years, with capital repayment holidays possible up to four years and in appropriate cases interest can be rolled up for two years. The loans will be subordinated to creditors in the event of default and will be unsecured except for directors' guarantees which would normally be taken for 25 per cent of the difference between the director's stake in the company and the amount of the loan. In addition, an option is taken to subscribe for shares in the company, normally up to a maximum of 25 per cent of the equity. The terms of the option will be agreed at the outset and are dependent on the underlying proposition, the period of the loan and the financial situation of the company.

Lloyds Bank has formed a subsidiary, called Pegasus Holdings, to provide equity capital for profitable businesses. It supports growth or acquisitions by unquoted companies and takes a stake of between 10 and 33⅓ per cent of the capital in any company in which it invests. Individual investments are usually of more than £100,000 in companies with a sound track record or proven management. Introductions for new investment through this scheme are usually through the bank's branch network but applications from non-customers are also considered. The bank's business advisory service is involved in the evaluation of potential investments.

Company Story

Banks may still fail to invest even when an entrepreneur, who is an experienced manager with a long track record at a senior level, comes forward with a well-thought-out and presented business plan. That is where the venture and development companies step in. David Rennie had that experience when he went looking for finance to start his own company renting electronic test equipment; he eventually found his money from those other sources and after his first year of operation the returns were sufficient to make the banks feel a little sick at missing out.

'I went the rounds of all the major clearing banks, talking not just to branch managers but going up to the level of assistant general manager but it produced nothing. And if this happens with my background and a good business plan I wondered what happened to the others.'

David Rennie and his partner, Bob Mundy, were two of the best known personalities in this area of industry and Mr Rennie was a prime mover in establishing and developing the concept of short-term test equipment rental in the 1960s. He was, as managing director of the parent company, instrumental in setting up a company called Livingston Hire which became one of the largest in this specialist field and also spawned another rental company. Bob Mundy was sales director of Livingston. The market in which these companies and Mr Rennie's Microlease operate was expected to be worth about £10 million a year by 1984. Microlease reached break-even point ahead of schedule in its first year, had a takeover offer after only six weeks of trading, and by its second year was heading for a turnover of £500,000 and pre-tax profits of £100,000.

This would not have been possible if the financial backing to start had not been found in the right form; in fact it came through the Small Business Capital Fund. One of Development Capital's directors, Bob Gollman, went on to the board of Microlease as a non-executive director. The financial backing amounted to £90,000, which was partly in the form of an equity stake in Microlease and the remainder in a loan of £70,000 over five years at an interest rate of 13 per cent.

'I was perfectly happy with the idea of equity participation; I'd rather be in a position of having a smaller share of a big pot than a big share of a small pot. And Small Business Capital and Development Capital were in no way pressing for an excessive share anyway, in fact they insisted that I took a larger share of equity than I anticipated I would have,' says Mr Rennie. He found there was a difference in attitude from his discussions with many other financial institutions. 'It was not just accountants we were talking to, it was people who had an understanding of what business is about; people who were, for example, engineers, aware of the meaning of tolerances and why a rigid, purely financial approach will not lead to the creation of new business enterprises.'

Microlease's business is the short-term rental of sophisticated electronic test equipment, some with a capital cost of many thousands of pounds. In fact capital spending in the first year amounted to £450,000, double what was planned. 'To begin with we were a little worried at the size of the lines of credit Mr Rennie was talking about but we quickly saw that there were going to be no problems on that score,' says Mr Gollman. Capital spending continued at a high rate for the second year with £500,000 being planned. 'In a way we are a kind of electronic grocery shop in that we make our assessment of what kind of equipment the customers are likely to need, what demand there will be for that particular piece of expensive equipment and then stock up our shelves,' says Mr Mundy. 'Decisions on equipment are crucial, especially in assessing the potential demand. We want always to be able to meet the needs of the customer but at the same time we don't want high cost equipment only being used for one month in the year and spending the other eleven months on the shelf.'

Rented test equipment is used throughout the electronics industry by both large and small firms. It can be used either as a back-up when a manufacturer's own equipment fails and an immediate replacement is needed for a short period or when a new product is being developed and equipment is required only for the length of the research programme. This is one reason why a firm like Microlease can have growth potential even at a time of recession: short-term rental is an obvious way of avoiding having money tied up in expensive capital equipment at a time when liquidity is tight.

Appropriately for a company engaged in a high technology sector of industry, Mr Rennie makes full use of the benefits which technology can provide in helping him to run his own business. 'Control of overheads is of the utmost importance in running a business and using equipment such as word processors and computers helps you to do that.' One of the first pieces of equipment he invested in was a relatively sophisticated word processor, which enabled the administration work to be handled by himself and a secretary. The processor, used for invoicing, sales ledger, and equipment records, cost £7,500. 'The whole of my business is contained on a few floppy discs, of which I keep one set in the office and the other in my briefcase. We don't need large numbers of clerks or typists to do these jobs, with all the problems of labour turnover and pay these can bring.'

Keeping track of expensive equipment is also part of that control of overheads as it is obviously uneconomic for it to be left at a customer's premises after the end of the rental period simply because someone forgot it was there. A £35,000 computer was installed in 1980 to act as a kind of policeman to prevent this happening. But new technology was not taken on blindly. Soon after the company was formed Mr Rennie was being pressed to lease a copying machine; on examining his needs he found they could be equally well served by a £125 copier from a local shop. He did eventually move on to a more sophisticated copier, but not before time. Microlease produced profits of £700,000 in 1985 and has been successfully launched on the Unlisted Securities Market.

Management Buy-outs

One of the most interesting business developments during recent years has been the acquisition of companies by their management teams; until 1979 management buy-outs were relatively rare in Britain although well-known in America but with many executives now willing to take the step towards independence the trend is likely to continue. There are some venture and development capital firms such as Candover Investments which have been specifically set up with the aim of financing management buy-outs as well as other projects, while well-established institutions such as 3i are heavily involved. 3i has in fact been a leading light in the field and the growth of management buy-outs generally can be gauged from the fact that in 1977–1978 the corporation completed only five deals; in 1979–1980 this had risen to 49, followed by 69 in the next year. At present nearly two deals a week are being completed.

A management buy-out takes place when the managers of a business are able to buy the company from its previous owners and run it themselves. In the majority of cases this will normally entail the financial institution putting up the majority of the money but acquiring a smaller equity stake than the managers. Usually the manager's funds amount to about 20 per cent of the capital and 80 per cent of the equity. The institution supplies the 80 per cent balance of the capital and takes the remaining 20 per cent of the equity. These ratios depend on the size of the company. As the amounts needed to buy independence increase, the percentage of the equity that remains in the managers' hands will probably fall unless they are able to increase their proportion of the funds. Financial institutions such as 3i do not want control and where the costs become very high it is usual for the deal to be arranged through a syndicate, ensuring that no single outside shareholder has more than the managers.

The management buy-out offers both the rewards and risks which come with ownership. The failures that have occurred in management buy-outs have so far been few but they do happen and management should be aware of the risks being taken. For example, head office charges may be an irritating expenditure but they do provide service which will now have to be supplied in-house including dealing with the bank, maintaining stock levels for manufacturing, and other statistics which may have been on tap through the group's centralised computer.

There are three main reasons why buy-outs occur. First a large organisation may decide to close down or sell one of its divisions; in many cases this happens when there has been a takeover and part of the acquisition contains elements unwanted by the new owner. Several management teams in good and viable companies have achieved independence because their activities were considered peripheral to the mainstream of the group or no longer fitted into its strategic plans. Previously these companies would have been sold to a competitor with a chance that their activities would be 'rationalised' or run down. A division that is not profitable or is failing to show a sufficient rate of return may encourage a receptive response from a potential seller as may the need for further investment or an urgent need for cash in the parent company.

The second major reason is peculiar to the private company where the present shareholders, for tax or other reasons, may wish to redeem their capital. It is also not unusual for the founders and their families to decide that the time has come to retire or sell out; in these cases the most suitable buyers for owner and employees may prove to be the existing management.

A third reason during the recession has been the rise in bankruptcies and from this apparently unlikely source has come a number of subsidiary companies which have proved viable on their own. The companies are not necessarily loss-making, as in many cases it is the parent company which is in receivership or the owner who has become bankrupt.

Provided there is a willing buyer and seller, the two main ingredients for a buy-out are a good management team and finance. The executives will have to demonstrate that they are capable of running the company on their own and are successful, assessing the prospects and making sound forecasts, and show that withdrawal of group services will not cause any problems.

Management buy-outs usually start with an abnormally high gearing owing to the need for a large element of loan capital which is likely to have high servicing costs. The business must therefore be able to show that it can not only sustain these payments but in time reduce the gearing to more acceptable levels. Each buy-out is different so there are no financial packages available; if a proposition is viable, for example, but is labouring under heavy financial strain because of the high initial gearing it is possible to overcome the situation. But it is better to construct the financial package knowing the constraints rather than risk the future of the business because of over-optimistic forecasts at the start. The success of buy-outs also depends on sensible prices being paid for the companies involved, as there can be too high a price for independence. Sound independent advice is needed to balance enthusiasm: advice from accountants, commerical lawyers, and organisations such as the Business Development Centre at Cranfield Institute of Technology, known as Interwork. The financial institutions, such as 3i, are themselves sources of advice as well as finance.

The range of options for finance is wide now as, in addition to 3i, most of the venture and development capital companies will be interested, as will be the banks through their appropriate subsidiaries, the investment trusts, and pension funds.

Company Story

Businessmen and lawyers do not often sit easily together but John Polmear is fulsome in his praise of the commercial lawyer who provided the right advice at the right time to enable him to realise his long-held ambition of buying the firm, of which he was chairman, from its parent. An earlier attempt to buy the company from its then Canadian owners had failed because, in spite of strenuous efforts, Mr Polmear was unable to raise sufficient finance. The asking price in 1975 had been £270,000 but he could not bridge a gap of £50,000.

In the end he negotiated the sale of the Decorettes Group to Newman Tonks, a Birmingham-based group whose business was manufacturing hardware for the engineering and building industries, a far cry from the wide range of transfers produced by Decorettes. Their transfers range from the sophisticated vinyls used for the E II R logos on Royal Mail vans or the livery on Birds Eye food trucks to the traditional water slides of cartoon characters used by children. The aim of Newman Tonks was diversification into the do-it-yourself market – Decorettes also has interests in the metallic tiles and self-assembly furniture field – and the takeover of Mr Polmear's company was a major move in that direction. But the expansion expected there did not materialise and Newman Tonks began instead to grow in its traditional areas by takeovers which gradually reduced Decorettes from a situation where it was providing as much as 10 per cent of the assets, turnover, and profits of the group to a contribution of 5 per cent.

Although Decorettes retained a high degree of autonomy and relationships with the parent group were good, the diminished role was not to the liking of

Mr Polmear and the management team he had built up over a period of years and there was also an ever-present danger of various functions being taken up to group level. That brought round again the idea of a management buy-out if the Newman Tonks board could be persuaded to sell and the necessary finance raised. By chance, around that time Mr Polmear read in the *Birmingham Evening Mail* the story of a management buy-out of a firm in Leamington, for which finance was obtained from the then National Enterprise Board.

'I got in touch with the people concerned at that company and asked what advice they could give. I was told that an absolute essential was a good commercial lawyer and they gave me the name of a Birmingham lawyer who had helped them. That proved to be very valuable indeed. In fact I believe it was a key factor in the success of our bid and I certainly think that the lack of that advice when I made my first attempt to buy Decorettes was a major reason for failure then. If anyone else wanting to buy out their firm asked for my advice the first thing I would tell them now is to get a good commercial lawyer.'

The lawyer gave them advice on how to make their presentation and Mr Polmear and finance director Ken Smith spent many hours preparing their case in documentary form, eventually producing a bound dossier an inch thick. Instead of approaching the NEB as they first intended the lawyer suggested they should contact 3i for finance. The favourable reaction came very quickly from 3i: 'One of the factors we found particularly impressive was the strength and depth of the management team as well as the quality of the presentation we received,' says 3i.

One of the reasons why Mr Polmear and Mr Smith were able to spend so much time preparing the case without any detrimental effect on the firm's performance was that strong team, with ages ranging from mid-thirties to mid-fifties, giving the succession pattern which potential investors like to see. Most of the management had had experience of large companies too, enabling them to apply the benefits of planning and control systems, for example, the kind of experience which adds to the confidence of an investing institution. During his association of more than 20 years with Decorettes, which is based at Lichfield, Staffordshire, Mr Polmear nursed the company from a loss-making position to a healthy, steady profit maker, though it was never a spectacular financial performer. 'It is surprising what a difference independence can make to a firm's performance, though,' says 3i. Newman Tonks were persuaded that it was in their interests to sell to the management team and the negotiations which followed were tough though friendly, eventually ending in agreement. 3i came up with £500,000 of the purchase price of around £700,000 in the form of a 25 per cent equity share and the rest in loans. Mr Polmear and Mr Smith hold control of the company, with another 25 per cent of the equity divided between the other four directors.

Both trades unions and the workforce of around 200 were informed of the buy-out scheme as soon as it was practicable and such comments as there were supported the idea. For the management team it gave a prospect of stability as well as independence, a control over their own future in a company in which they already had a strong personal identification. The prospect of making a fortune was not really a major element in the decision to go ahead. Decorettes consists of two main divisions, Decorettes Marketing Services, which handles retail marketing activities, and Eagle Transfers, which is the production base, housed in a modern 50,000 square feet factory in Lichfield.

Useful Addresses

British Venture Capital Association,
1 Surrey Street,
London WC2R 2PS
Tel 01-836 5702

Business Investment Digest,
Institute of Directors,
116 Pall Mall,
London SW1Y 5ED
Tel 01-839 1233

Interwork,
Cranfield Institute of Technology,
CPEC Building,
Cranfield,
Bedfordshire MK43 0AL
Tel 0234 750111 ext 598

London Enterprise Agency,
4 Snow Hill,
London EC1A 2BS
Tel 01-236 3000

Venture and Development Capital Organisations

Abingworth Ltd,
26 St James Street,
London SW1A 1HA
Tel 01-839 6745

Advent Ltd,
25 Buckingham Gate,
London SW1E 6LD
Tel 01-630 9811

Alan Patricof Associates,
24 Upper Brook Street,
London W1Y 1PD
Tel 01-493 3633

Allied Irish Investment Bank,
Pinners Hall,
8-9 Austin Friars,
London EC2N 2AE
Tel 01-920 9155

Barclays Development Capital,
Pickfords Wharf,
Clink Street,
London SE1 9DG
Tel 01-407 2389

Brown Shipley Developments,
Founders Court,
Lothbury,
London EC2R 7HE
Tel 01-606 9833

Business Mortgages Trust Ventures,
35 Bruton Street,
London W1X 7DD
Tel 01-493 3841

Candover Investments,
Cedric House,
8-9 East Harding Street,
London EC4A 3AS
Tel 01-583 5090

Capital Partners International,
Kingsmead House,
250 King's Road,
London SW3 5UE
Tel 01-351 4899

Castle Finance,
PO Box 53,
Surrey Street,
Norwich NR1 3TE
Tel 0603 683751

Charterhouse Development Capital,
7 Ludgate Broadway,
London EC4V 6DX
Tel: 01-248 4000

CIN Industrial Investments,
PO Box 33,
London SW1X 7AD
Tel 01-245 6911

Citicorp Venture Capital,
PO Box 199,
Cottons Centre,
Hay's Lane,
London SE1 2QT
Tel 01-234 2769

Clydesdale Bank Equity Ltd,
30 St Vincent Place,
Glasgow G1 2HL
Tel 041-248 7070

Corinthian Securities,
20 Welbeck Street,
London W1M 7PG
Tel 01-486 2234

County Bank,
11 Old Broad Street,
London EC2N 1BB
Tel 01-638 6000

Dartington & Company,
Shinners Bridge,
Dartington,
Totnes,
Devon TQ9 6JE
Tel 0803 862271

Dawnay, Day & Company,
Garrard House,
31 Gresham Street,
London EC2V 7DT
Tel 01-600 7533

Development Capital,
44 Baker Street,
London W1M 1DH
Tel 01-935 2731

East of Scotland Industrial Investments,
42 Charlotte Square,
Edinburgh EH2 4HQ
Tel 031-226 4421

Electra Investment Trust,
65 Kingsway,
London WC2B 6QT
Tel 01-831 6464

English & Caledonian Investment,
Cayzer House,
2-4 St Mary Axe,
London EC3A 8BP
Tel 01-626 1212

Exeter Trust,
Sanderson House,
Blackboy Road,
Exeter,
Devon EX4 6SE
Tel 0392 50635

F and C Ventures,
1 Laurence Pountney Hill,
London EC4R 0BA
Tel 01-623 4680

Grainger and Company,
18 Woodside Terrace,
Glasgow G3 7NY
Tel 041-332 8751

Granville & Company,
8 Lovat Lane,
London EC3R 8BP
Tel 01-621 1212

Gresham Trust,
Barrington House,
Gresham Street,
London EC2V 7HE
Tel 01-606 6474

Guidehouse,
Vestry House,
Greyfriars Passage,
Newgate Street,
London EC1A 7BA
Tel 01-606 6321

Intex Executives (UK),
53-64 Chancery Lane,
London WC2A 1QU
Tel 01-831 6925

Investors in Industry (3i),
91 Waterloo Road,
London SE1 8XP
Tel 01-928 7822
(and area offices)

The London Venture Capital Market Ltd,
21 Upper Brook Street,
London W1Y 1PD
Tel 01-629 5983

London Wall Industrial Consultants,
Smithdown Investments,
15 South Molton Street,
London W1Y 1DE
Tel 01-629 9891

Melville Street Investments (Edinburgh),
4 Melville Street,
Edinburgh EH3 7NZ
Tel 031-453 1919

Meritor Investments,
36 Poultry,
London EC2R 8AJ
Tel 01-606 2179

Midland Bank Industrial Finance,
Midland Bank Industrial Investments,
Midland Bank Venture Capital,
27-32 Poultry,
London EC2P 2BX
Tel 01-638 8861

Minster Trust,
Minster House,
Arthur Street,
London EC4R 9BH
Tel 01-623 1050

Moracrest Investments,
36 Poultry,
London EC2R 8AJ
Tel 01-628 8409

Noble Grossart Investments,
48 Queen Street,
Edinburgh EH2 3NR
Tel 031-226 7011

Norwich General Trust,
12 Surrey Street,
Norwich,
Norfolk NR1 3NJ
Tel 0603 22200

PA Developments,
Bowater House East,
68 Knightsbridge,
London SW1X 7LE
Tel 01-589 7050

Rainford Venture Capital,
Rainford Hall,
Crank Road,
St Helens,
Merseyside WA11 7RP
Tel 0744 37227

Royal Bank Development,
PO Box 31,
42 St Andrew Square,
Edinburgh EH2 2YE
Tel 031-556 8555

Venture Founders,
50-51 Conduit Street,
London W1R 9FB
Tel 01-434 9781

Companies which have a particular interest in financing high technology projects are listed on p 189.

CHAPTER 11

Financing Technology and Innovation

Caution has been a watchword for a year or two now among venture capitalists, and bankers, when considering providing money for projects involving high technology, a wariness arising from a number of failures among technology-based companies recently, together with a growing belief that there is more money to be made from companies that are applying technology to develop their businesses rather than those who are actually at the leading edge of producing new technological breakthroughs. But in spite of their concern about financing the technology sector there are still substantial funds available for companies with the right products and markets for starting-up and expansion.

In order to get their hands on that money, however, promoters of high technology businesses have to recognise the 'vital importance' of a well-prepared business plan, says Martin Scicluna of chartered accountants Touche Ross in that firm's guide to high technology finance. 'Bankers and venture capitalists now put technology based businesses under the closest scrutiny before sanctioning funds and many companies fail to make the grade now. They simply don't have an understanding of the financiers' criteria,' he says. That last comment would probably produce a hollow laugh from Integrated Micro Products (IMP), a successful small company in Consett, Co Durham – on the old British Steel Corporation site, incidentally – which is engaged in leading-edge technology with highly sophisticated multi-station Unix computers. The survival of companies like this naturally depends on heavy investment in research and development, but when IMP was doing the rounds of financial institutions to raise funds for the next stage of its development one bank approached said it might be prepared to provide the funds – but only if IMP cut back its spending in some areas and specifically in research and development, a suggestion akin to a doctor agreeing to give a blood transfusion provided the patient cut his throat.

The reply of companies in the high technology field might therefore be that it is the providers of funds who fail to understand the criteria of industry. IMP did in fact obtain its funding, partly from its own bankers and partly from two venture capital companies, Advent and Equity Capital for Industry.

Quite apart from those points there are also those who believe that it is a serious mistake to imagine that it is the high technology firms who will be the main generators of jobs in the future and that more jobs will come from the more mundane areas of industry which make use of technology to improve their competitiveness. On the other hand, there is a very definite need for the high technology companies pushing at the frontiers of knowledge, developing processes which can achieve just that result.

Another factor to be considered is the frequently quoted lack of suitable high technology projects in Britain which are worth investing in, usually a reason given by financiers when explaining why they are investing in overseas companies rather than in British businesses. The two sides to the equation, the financiers and the technology promoters, will obviously be unlikely to agree with one another and there are certainly elements in the cases of both which are right.

As with many other matters, fairness often depends on which side of the fence it is viewed. Whatever the answer it is true that financiers are still investing in high technology areas which take the time to present their cases effectively.

It is not absolutely necessary to go to a financial institution which specialises in high technology projects to obtain finance for carrying through such proposals, as many of the venture and development capital companies described in the last chapter and the banks themselves are prepared to offer funds for the right kind of proposal. Whether all those companies and banks have the necessary facilities for evaluating a high technology package is another matter: they may have them superficially but not in depth; they may not have them at all; they may just rely on their judgement of the man and back him without necessarily understanding the project fully; or if they do not understand the proposal they may just turn the proposer down. There can therefore be a number of advantages in approaching a specialist finance house for a high technology project and even an innovatory project, if it is in a specialised area, though there is probably a greater degree of overlap there with other providers of venture and development capital.

There is now a considerable range of venture capital companies which have a special knowledge of the technology field, ranging from the long-established Investors in Industry (3i) to younger companies such as Baronsmead, though the latter are tending to move away from the 'leading edge' area of technology. 3i seeks to invest in companies with long-term growth potential and each application is individually assessed as to product market and profit projections, with particular emphasis on the personal qualities and background of the managers of the venture. Once a favourable assessment has been made, a financial package is designed to meet the needs of the business. Experience has shown that a minority stake combined with a medium-term loan is often the most suitable scheme, but other arrangements depend on the circumstances. Interest on any loan is charged at commercial rates and charged on the outstanding balance only; repayments of the principal are spread over an agreed period and only start when the budget projections show that the venture has the ability to repay. Finance may be invested in total at the outset or in stages; the progress of each investment is monitored and appropriate guidance offered, but the day-to-day running of the venture remains the responsibility of the management team. In financing high risk projects a commensurately high rate of return is anticipated, generally from a dividend based on profits or sales receipts and by realising a capital gain if and when the entrepreneurs buy its shareholding or they jointly decide to sell the company. 3i is often prepared to leave its funds in a company for an indefinite period and inject further funds as appropriate, provided its investment is clearly increasing in value. Occasionally a company has been prepared to invest in a project at a very early stage. For example, the Prudential through its venture capital operation, Prudential Venture Managers, which incorporated the high technology fund, Prutec, waited for four years for a project to reach the stage of commercial manufacture. Prutec originally invested £250,000 in the design of a pyrolysis mass spectrometer – an instrument for analysing various substances, particularly in the medical, food and pharmaceutical industries – and saw it through all the hoops from concept to being a viable product in the market place. Another technology oriented company in which Prudential – along with Morgan Grenfell and PA Consulting Services – has a stake is Managed Technology Investors, a company which tends to operate very much a hands-on policy with its clients and has invested in such esoteric projects as a company which manufactures and markets fish vaccines, which have considerable applications in the increasingly important fish farming industry.

Finance is also available from other, less obvious sources, such as the Greater London Enterprise which has set up a research and development fund for innovative products from new and existing companies. In Lancashire the Business and Innovation Centre established by Lancashire Enterprises, a very effective local authority backed enterprise board, has set up BIC Investments, which can provide seed capital finance of up to £25,000 for businesses with growth prospects. There are also other regional initiatives such as that in which high technology companies based in North-west science parks can apply for venture capital funding through Hambros Advanced Technology Trust in conjunction with the UK Science Park Association. The trust has earmarked £1 million to encourage growth because a survey by chartered accountants, Peat Marwick McLintock showed a low take-up rate of venture capital by such companies and highlighted the related problem of attracting relatively small amounts of capital to these young and start-up enterprises.

Company Story

A Scottish company has been launched to develop and manufacture a body scanner to help in the fight against cancer. Physicist Professor John Mallard of Aberdeen University and businessman Robert Davis set up the company, M and D Technology, to exploit fully research being carried out in the university's department of bio-medical physics and bio-engineering. They were backed by financial support from Prutec, the Scottish Development Agency, Scottish Northern Investment Trust, Aberdeen Trust, and Auris Ltd, the university's holding company, with a joint £1.4 million investment package. It aims to carry forward into commercial production nuclear magnetic resonance whole body imaging technology, which has been under development at Aberdeen University for nine years. The university is acknowledged as a leading international research authority in development and clinical testing of NMR whole body imaging techniques and has been supported for several years by the Medical Research Council. Professor Mallard directed the research and is part-time scientific director of M and D Technology.

His university research team researched intensively the NMR imager's application to medical diagnostics, particularly in the identification of tissue diseases, the primary example being cancer. Their prototype achieved exciting clinical results and demonstrated an exceptional ability to localise and identify lesions in more than 500 patient trials. Professor Mallard says the imager has shown itself to be reliable and safe for the patient and already medically valuable. 'It complements and, to a certain degree, competes with other body scanning technologies, such as ultrasonic and X-ray, but our imager has no moving parts and emits no ionising radiation. I believe that NMR imaging will be the big scientific equipment revolution in medicine of the 1980s but there has only been time so far to scratch the surface of all the exciting things to be done.'

M and D Technology has a longer-term objective of commercial implementation of other medical instrumentation research carried out at Aberdeen University.

M and D Technology has an issued share capital of £50,000. The major shareholder is Prutec with 35 per cent of the shares, while Auris has 15 per cent, the SDA, Scottish Northern Investment Trust (SNIT) and Aberdeen Trust have another 15 per cent, and the remaining 35 per cent is owned by Professor Mallard and Mr Davis. Prutec funded most of the deal with a £950,000 cash injection; the SDA invested £200,000 in cumulative preference shares, SNIT £150,000 and Aberdeen Trust £50,000.

British Technology Group (BTG)

The role of the British Technology Group has changed considerably in recent years and it is now a self-financing organisation which is involved in licensing new scientific and engineering products to industry; it also finances the development of new technology. It promotes the development and commercial use of new technology developed through research in the public sector, such as at universities and polytechnics, and provides finance for the development of inventions before they are licensed to industry. It can also offer finance to businesses which want to use their own technology to develop new products and processes. Up to 50 per cent of the funds needed for developing and launching a new product can be provided through the industrial project finance scheme. BTG recovers its investment through a percentage levy on sales of the product or process.

Help from Clearing Banks

The clearing banks are not entirely ignorant in the field of high technology either, contrary to popular opinion, though it may well be possible to find individual managers who are. Lloyds, for example, is one which has gone well beyond the stage of simply having a technical adviser in residence who might be expected to assess a wide range of technological development. It developed a technology appraisal scheme run in conjunction with Cranfield Institute of Technology, a scheme free to customers seeking finance for development or innovative use of new or high technology. Cranfield carries out the technical assessment and then both it and the bank examine the commercial implications. On a local basis Lloyds joined with Birmingham City Council in an investment company housed on the Aston Science Park and called Birmingham Technology, which provides funds in the range of £50,000 to £500,000 for both start-up and development projects in high technology firms. Most investment companies interested in the high technology field are looking for minimum investments of £200,000 to £250,000.

Barclays is also interested in the high technology area, maintaining a high technology team at its Head Office and sponsoring the Techmart exhibition. It also produces a very useful series of booklets aimed at the high technology entrepreneur and containing advice on grants, starting a high technology company, management accounting, project planning and control, and protecting intellectual property. National Westminster Bank also provides a wide range of specialist financing and advisory support for the high technology market, including the facility for the bank to obtain the views of outside technical advisers. A very useful source of information on high technology finance is the *Innovators Handbook*, produced as a result of extensive research over a period of years by the management department of Bath University.

Useful Addresses

British Technology Group,
101 Newington Causeway,
London SE1 6BU
Tel 01-403 6666

The Manager,
High Technology Team,
Corporate Division,
Barclays Bank,
54 Lombard Street,
London EC3P 3AM
Tel 01-626 1567

Birmingham Technology Ltd,
Love Lane,
Aston Triangle,
Birmingham B7 4BJ
Tel 021-359 0981

UK Science Park Association,
44 Four Oaks Road,
Sutton Coldfield,
West Midlands B74 2TL
Tel 021-308 8815

Prudential Venture Managers,
142 Holborn Bars,
London EC1N 2NH
Tel 01-404 5611

Investors in Industry (3i),
91 Waterloo Road,
London SE1 8XP
Tel 01-928 7822

Worldtech Ventures Ltd,
70 Vauxhall Bridge Road,
London SW1V 2RP
Tel 01-630 6161

CHAPTER 12

Going to the Stock Markets

For the majority of smaller companies the prospect of a full quotation of their shares on the Stock Exchange will forever remain a pleasant dream or a nightmare, depending on the point of view – and the number which develop into the glamour stocks of the future, making fortunes for the speculators and sometimes the owners, will remain small. But there are also companies which fall somewhere between those needing and wanting to remain purely private, independent businesses and those which become the fully quoted and listed public companies. There are now two places which give them many of the advantages of a publicly quoted company on the Stock Exchange in raising finance and widening the market for their shares and yet avoid many of the disadvantages, not to mention the cost and complexity of obtaining a full public listing. These are the Unlisted Securities Market (USM) and the Third Market, the latter of which has largely eclipsed the previously expanding over-the-counter market (OTC). Both can be either an end in themselves or a stepping stone to greater things, eventually a full listing on the Stock Exchange.

The Unlisted Securities Market

The Unlisted Securities Market (USM) came into being for a number of reasons: increased awareness of the need to encourage smaller, more entrepreneurial firms to give them access to capital markets with less cost and formality than a full Stock Exchange listing, and because the Stock Exchange itself was concerned at the diminishing number of firms willing to go for a full quotation, as well as a rapid expansion of dealings under its own Rule 163/2. Rule 163/2 has been in existence for more than 30 years allowing Stock Exchange members to carry out specific dealings in unlisted shares with prior approval through the normal mechanism of the market but without the company itself having to comply with any formalities beforehand.

In 1978 because of its disappointment with the number of companies going public, the Stock Exchange issued a booklet publicising Rule 163/2 which attracted a much greater response than it had bargained for. The rule had traditionally been used for infrequent dealings in the shares of organisations such as football clubs and small breweries and had very much a regional character, and local stockbrokers using their knowledge of the local business scene would match buyers and sellers of shares in the area. Publicity for the rule evoked such a response that the Stock Exchange again became concerned that a facility for irregular dealings was growing into a substantial but unregulated market for which the Stock Exchange would be blamed by the general public if things went wrong.

The Unlisted Securities Market was therefore launched in November 1980, with 11 companies making up the market, a figure which grew in the first year to 76 and included well-known names like Merrydown Wine, Reliant Motors, and Intasun Leisure, the tour operators; at the end of the first year the market capitalisation of the companies was £650 million and some £67 million was raised by them on the market. Among the other kinds of business represented were computer and high technology related businesses, builders and property developers, resources companies and retailers. Shares of 30 of the 76 which came to the market in the first year had previously been traded under Rule 163/2. More than 500 companies are now quoted on the USM capitalised at over £4 billion, creating some 500 millionaires.

There are a number of advantages for a company having its shares traded on the Unlisted Securities Market: it enables owners or other shareholders to raise cash when the company enters the market and at any time later; it enables a firm to raise equity capital, one of the cheapest forms of finance, when it joins the market and through rights issues or placings in the future; if one firm wants to take over another it can offer shares in payment instead of cash or a mixture of the two, reducing the cost of acquisition; or it can introduce incentives for employees by developing share option schemes. These advantages were previously limited to the large companies that could afford the cost of a full listing – which could be £200,000 upwards – or whose shareholders were prepared to offer 25 per cent of the company's shares to the public. Only 10 per cent of the shares need to be made available on the USM and the cost involved is very much reduced. Other reasons for joining the USM include increased flexibility in raising funds, particularly as lenders such as banks are likely to have more confidence in a company which has a public quotation, apart from the prestige which can accrue to the business and not just to the owners personally, helping in the recruitment of better quality staff and even better trade terms with suppliers. There are also tax concessions in connection with capital transfer tax.

Among the disadvantages are that the Stock Exchange will insist on rapid disclosure of any information which could be price sensitive, such as dividend and profit announcements, takeovers or sales of assets. The prestige which accrues also brings with it the problem of being prominent in the public view, though nothing like the same extent as a fully listed company. There is more likely to be pressure on the company to declare dividends, and worthwhile ones at that, as the market for the shares grows and the company might find it more difficult to declare or pass dividends as it deems fit. Any increase in the market for a company's shares will also increase the risk of being on the wrong end of a takeover bid.

There are three methods by which a company can be introduced to the USM. The first – and although this might have been expected to be the most common only 32 out of the 76 in the first year joined this way – is the *placing of shares*; this means that sponsors place the shares to be sold with appropriate private or institutional investors.

The second is the *offer for sale*, of which there were just nine in the first year; where the value of shares sold exceeds £3 million, or if the total market capitalisation of the company is expected to exceed £15 million, the Stock Exchange will expect the shares to be offered for sale to the general public, which will involve underwriting costs – the underwriters take up that proportion, if any, of the shares that the public fails to buy – and is generally more expensive than a straightforward placing.

The third method is what is known as an *introduction* – and this formed the majority in the first year with 35 out of the 76 – and usually occurs when a company already has some spread of public shareholders, perhaps 100, and does not want to sell any more new shares. Entry may then be allowed by the simple and relatively cheap introduction. There are few formalities for an introduction: a card giving particulars limited basically to a table of financial statistics covering a period of five years or the company's whole life if this is the shorter, and general information about the company's business. A small box advertisement has to be placed in a leading daily newspaper.

In the case of placings and offers for sale a full prospectus in accordance with the Companies Act must be published, giving comprehensive details of the history of the company and its business, the trading record and prospects, and of the management. A report from an independent accountant on the profits and assets of the firm will have to be provided and must cover any profit forecasts made in connection with the sale of the shares. It does not include, however, one of the costly requirements which have to be met for a full listing which is that the prospectus has to be advertised in the national press.

In order to be considered for entry to the USM a company has to have been trading for at least three years, or to be looking for funds to put into production a new project which has been fully researched. The cost of entry is usually between 5 and 10 per cent of the amount of finance raised. There is no rigid limit on the size of companies entering the market, but as a general rule they are smaller than those which would be seeking a full listing; most of those which have so far joined the USM have had market capitalisation of £1 million to £5 million and profits before tax of £250,000 upwards. Firms with a capitalisation of less than £5 million would not normally be seeking a full listing.

When the USM was established the Stock Exchange envisaged that companies which entered the market would move to full listing when they had reached an appropriate status, with the transition being a straightforward process, but none of the companies in the market has yet made this move.

Entry into the Unlisted Securities Market is an option open to the more substantial smaller company with a good profit record and prospects, allowing the owner to realise some of his or her own accumulated wealth and widening the opportunities for a company to raise finance for its development. It is a step only taken after the fullest possible consideration and preparation with the company's advisers over a period of time and represents the culmination of many hurdles overcome – not to mention the creation of a few more.

The Third Market

The Third Market was launched in January 1987 and was described by the then Chairman of the Stock Exchange as a new market designed to provide an accessible market place for young, growing companies which need to raise capital and to ensure that they do not face unaffordable costs when doing so. 'It will,' he said, 'provide a disciplined market place with a suitable standard of investor protection for many of the shares which are at present traded outside the Stock Exchange,' a reference to the problems encountered by some of the dealers, which made up the over-the-counter market. The Third Market is very much within the control of the Stock Exchange. Some OTC companies have in fact transferred to the Third Market but the move has not been as fast as had been expected and a large proportion of those companies are attempting to get on to the Third Market for reasons such as poor management, inadequate business plans, and materially qualified accounts.

Three types of company can in general be expected to join the Market, though it should be noted that some business activities are excluded, including property, investment, commodity holding or dealing. The three are: businesses with continuing commercial activity and at least a year's audited accounts showing worthwhile flows of revenue; new businesses with fully researched projects and a chance of significant revenue within the reasonably near future, such as 12 months; or as already noted, firms with securities already traded outside the Market.

The advantages are in general the same as for the USM, with the addition that Business Expansion Schemes – as with the OTC – are not excluded and that the lesser requirements of the Third Market make it accessible to a larger number of enterprises. It has the advantage over the OTC of centralised settlement, a formalised and regulated market, two or more market-makers in each, and market-makers underwritten by the Stock Exchange's compensation fund. The main burdens are more administrative and secretarial matters, restrictions on directors' freedom to buy and sell the company's shares, and greater public scrutiny. A minimum trading record of one year is normally, though not necessarily, required, there is no minimum amount of equity to be made available to the public, no minimum size criteria, a minimum number of three directors, a very small advertising requirement, and a prospectus required only where shares are offered to the public.

A company has to be sponsored by a member firm of the Stock Exchange; this is a key step because, unlike the USM, a sponsor takes full responsibility for assessing the firm's suitability, compliance with entry conditions, guiding the later conduct of the business, and maintaining an effective market. The company will have to provide the broker with details of its objectives and background, one year's accounts with an unqualified auditors' report or thorough research to show it can reach a significant turnover in one year, and details of any other relevant matters. Costs depend on whether new money is being raised but in all cases the Stock Exchange waives initial and annual fees. If money is being raised, a prospectus will be needed. It may be that costs are not substantially less than a USM quote, though if no new capital is being sought costs will probably be insignificant. One of the most active brokers in the Third Market is Credit Suisse Buckmaster and Moore.

Further information can be obtained from the Stock Exchange or from such firms as Credit Suisse B & M, whose address is:

Credit Suisse Buckmaster & Moore,
The Stock Exchange,
London EC2P 2JT
Tel 01-588 2868

Over-the-Counter Market

An alternative to a Stock Exchange quotation on either the listed or unlisted markets is the over-the-counter market operated since 1972 by the investment bankers, Granville & Company, who also operate the Lovat Enterprise Fund which provides venture capital for small and medium-sized companies, and the rival OTC market.

The advantages for a company in having its shares bought and sold on the over-the-counter market - a system which accounts for the bulk of share trading in the United States - are similar to those described as applying to the Unlisted Securities Market operated by the Stock Exchange. Further advantages lie in the fact that the initial costs of obtaining a quotation on the over-the-counter (OTC) market are very much less than those for admission to a comparable market. Once the shares of a company are available on the OTC market trading costs are estimated to be on average about one-third of those on the Stock Exchange. Granville's also say that an OTC quotation helps to sustain stable share prices as a result of its sponsorship of OTC stocks in the financial community, including regular reports on each company's performance and prospects and the maintenance of a strategic market in the shares as opposed to a more speculative market.

When a company wants to go public on the OTC market, Granville's first make a preliminary investigation of the company and its needs. They carry out a detailed analysis of the company, examine the reasons for considering flotation, study alternative courses of action open to the company to make sure that public flotation will best meet the needs of the company and give appropriate advice. Granville's try to establish from the start the basis of a continuing relationship with the company, its management, and its prospects. They research thoroughly the industry in which the company carries on business and try to identify those problems which need to be resolved before flotation can take place. That exercise in itself can be of considerable benefit to the client company.

Once a decision is taken to go ahead the procedures for an initial public offering of the company's shares or other securities on the OTC market are begun. These are mainly concerned with preparing certain documents to give high quality institutional investors the basis on which they can make a long-term investment decision. The main documents are the investment report or prospectus, warranties and indemnities, and a general undertaking.

The investment report centres on an assessment of the client's future earning power and is to a considerable extent a development of the analysis of the company and its industry carried out at the preliminary stage. It usually contains a profit forecast and certain historical figures taken from the company's audited accounts. Normally, the company's own auditors are also asked to review the profit forecast and confirm that no adjustment would be required to the historical figures if the investment report were to comply with the fourth schedule of the Companies Act 1948. The investment report is used by Granville's to interest prospective investors in the shares.

This report is supported by warranties from the company's directors in respect of the accuracy of the information given in it. Tax indemnities are also given by shareholders in favour of the company covering certain potential liabilities of the company for capital transfer tax, shortfall and other taxation. All OTC companies also sign the OTC general undertaking, mainly to ensure that they give out relevant and timely information, financial or otherwise, to all shareholders and to Granville's as market makers.

Trading procedures for securities quoted on the OTC market are kept as simple as possible. When trading starts in the shares of a particular company an initial block of shares, generally 10 to 15 per cent of the ordinary share capital, is made available to investors on the basis of the information contained in the investment report. Investors usually subscribe in the ratio of 80 per cent institutions to 20 per cent individuals. The institutions come from the 80 insurance companies, pension funds and investment trusts which are investors in over-the-counter securities; the 3,000 individual private investors are mainly employees, customers or suppliers of the companies whose shares are traded over the counter.

Buying and selling orders are usually received by Granville's over the telephone and then, acting as agents rather than principals, they match the buyers and sellers. There is a standard procedure for settlement; sellers return signed stock transfer forms and appropriate share certificates as soon as possible, and settlement takes place on alternate Mondays. Share certificates are issued to buyers after cash in settlement of the purchase has been received.

The fees charged by Granville's are assessed in accordance with the nature and size of the company's operations and the spread of its interests in different industries. All fees are budgeted and agreed in advance before work starts. Preliminary investigation and preparation fees are by arrangement; commissions for the initial public offering are 2.5 per cent, plus VAT, of the gross amount of the equity securities sold, and 2 per cent, plus VAT, of the gross amount of debt or preference securities sold.

Granville's normally also invest in a warrant to subscribe for unissued shares equivalent to about 5 per cent of the issued ordinary share capital of each client company. This can be exercised within 10 years of its date of issue, and the price will be approximately the value of the company's shares at the time the warrant is acquired. The warrant itself is bought by Granville's at a fair market value, assessed by an independent firm of chartered accountants.

Other licensed dealers involved in the over-the-counter market buy shares for their own book, rather like a jobber on the Stock Exchange, but sell them directly to the general public rather than matching bargains between buyer and seller as Granville's do.

A major advantage of the OTC market generally is that individuals who invest in a company under the Business Expansion Scheme qualify for tax relief at the top personal rates if that company is traded on the over-the-counter market, a relief which does not apply to investments in USM companies.

Further information can be obtained from:

Granville & Co Ltd,
8 Lovat Lane,
London EC3R 8BP
Tel 01-621 1212

Lovat Enterprise Fund,
27-28 Lovat Lane,
London EC3R 8EB
Tel 01-621 1212

Useful Addresses

The Stock Exchange,
Quotation Department,
PO Box 119,
London EC2P 2BT
Tel 01-588 2355

Regional Divisions

The Stock Exchange,
10 High Street,
Belfast BT1 2BP
Tel 0232 21094

The Stock Exchange,
Margaret Street,
Birmingham B3 3JL
Tel 021-236 9181

The Stock Exchange,
28 Anglesea Street,
Dublin 2
Tel 0001 778808

The Stock Exchange,
69 St George's Place,
Glasgow G2 1BU
Tel 041-221 7060

The Stock Exchange,
4 Norfolk Street,
Manchester M2 1DS
Tel 061-833 0931

Further Reading

Managing Your Company's Finances (1982) R L Hargreaves and R H Smith. Heinemann.

Occupation: Self-Employed (1982) Rosemary Pettit. Wildwood House.

The following publications are published regularly, and are frequently updated:

Aids for Industry. North-west England, North-west Industrial Development Association, Manchester.

The Genghis Khan Guide to Business. Brian Warnes. Osmosis Publications, 8 Holyrood Street, London SE1 2EL.

Investors in Industry booklets on: 'Profit and Cash Flow Forecasting'; 'Borrowing Money For Capital Projects'.

Money for Business. Bank of England and City Communications Centre. Distributed by Bulletin Group, Economics Division, Bank of England.

Money for Exports. Bank of England, Bulletin Group, Economics Division, London EC2R 8AH. Tel 01-601 4030.

Official Sources of Finance and Aid for Industry in the UK. National Westminster Bank.

Running Your Own Co-operative. John Pearce. Kogan Page Ltd.

The Small Business Guide. Colin Barrow. BBC Publications.

Sources of Assistance to Small Firms in the North of England. Durham University Business School, Small Business Centre.

Sources of Finance for Small Firms. London Enterprise Agency.

Successful Expansion for the Small Business. M J Morris. Kogan Page Ltd.

Tax Facts and Tables. W J Horner. Mistsave Ltd, 20 Victoria Avenue, Cheadle, Stockport, Cheshire.

Tolley's Survival Kit for Small Businesses. Touche Ross & Co, published by Tolley Publishing Co.

Index

Abbreviations: *add* = address
tel nos = telephone numbers

Index

Index of Advertisers